WALTER PRESCOTT WEBB
His Life and Impact

Walter Prescott Webb 1888–1963. *Courtesy of the Archives Division, Texas State Library*

Walter Prescott Webb

His Life and Impact

Necah Stewart Furman

THE UNIVERSITY OF NEW MEXICO PRESS

Albuquerque

TO JOHN
ERIC, SHAWN, AND KIALA

CONTENTS

LIST OF ILLUSTRATIONS

FOREWORD

As Walter Prescott Webb moved toward his seventieth year, his colleagues in the department of history at the University of Texas knew that the demands of time were inescapable; that a replacement for Webb would have to be found. Oddly, the university taught no formal courses in western history. Webb, considered a western historian, taught whatever Walter Webb was interested in at that moment, which was primarily Webb and his ideas. Bailey Carroll taught Texas history. No one taught anything about western exploration, mountain men and fur trappers, conflict of civilizations along the borderlands, development of western railroads, reduction of the western Indians, or any of the other elements that usually make up a western history course.

The departmental recruiters for Webb's replacement, looking for someone to fill the western history slot, settled on John E. Sunder, a handsome young bachelor out of Washington University in St. Louis, whose particular interest is the western fur trade. Unlike most academics, Sunder has exceptionally genteel manners, meets people well, and is likeable.

At that time, Webb, though aware that we were searching for his successor, was paying very little attention to the department and was taking no hand in the recruitment. When Sunder visited the campus, some of us led him on the necessary tour of facilities and university brass, and then took him in to meet Webb. We visited for a few minutes, but as we started to leave, Webb pointed to me, and said: "Can you stay behind for a minute or so?"

As soon as the others were out of earshot, Webb asked, almost dolefully, "Is that my replacement?" "He's our choice," I replied. Obviously this was the first time that Webb had really faced the fact that he wouldn't teach into eternity. He sat quietly for a while, studying the clutter on his desk, and then looked at me with a half-grin as he said: "Well, at least he's prettier than I am!"

Just as the adjective "charismatic" became a cliché with the advent of President John F. Kennedy, so did another old word, "complex," attain cliché status during the terms of Presidents Lyndon B. Johnson and Richard M. Nixon. Unfortunately the word fits Webb. Curious as well as complex, he was a man who disdained power and yet may well have been the most powerful man of his period on the campus. As Necah Furman points out, he ran with the Austin establishment while never relinquishing the affection and devotion of the town's more liberal element. Although he intended to sit out controversy, he was always sought out by the instigators and usually wound up as the spokesman for one side or the other. He combined enormous patience with a sense of quick indignation. He spoke carefully yet could explode verbally with words that would have startled a mule skinner. Around women, he was Victorian and shy.

Once when Roy Bedichek was sounding off, Webb stopped him in the midst of a score of friends and said: "Bedi, I won't have that kind of talk in my company!" We were all mute with astonishment. Finally Bedichek said with diminished aggressiveness, "But Webb, I've heard you use all those words."

"Yes," admitted Webb, "but I didn't realize they sounded so dirty until I heard them from you."

The problem with most biographers and critics is that they have looked at Webb as an academic, which he was not. He was an intellectual, with great gaps in his knowledge, but he was no academic. The things that generally excite academics concerned him little, and he never engaged in the kind of coffee klatsches that most of them seek for security. When they talked shop, he was uncomfortable, probably because he did not know what they were talking about.

On one occasion he went to coffee with a group from the department, including a younger member whose bright intellect was clouded by an inner drive to prove he was smarter than anyone else present. This assistant professor got the lead in the conversation and was criticizing everyone and everything. Webb put him down rather heavily. Later Webb sought me out.

"I did something this morning that I've never done before. I used my age and position to put down a junior colleague. That is the kind of bad manners I have never practiced."

He sat silent for a long moment, as he so often did. Then he turned to me in all seriousness, and asked: "Now, how am I going to tell that little son-of-a-bitch I'm sorry and let him know I still think he's an SOB?" I never knew the outcome of that dilemma.

As he grew older, he enjoyed the lionizing that went with his growing prestige. Yet around women, Webb often became flustered and inarticulate. He would watch J. Frank Dobie, who solicited adoration, and then snort, "I don't see how Dobie stands it!"

Once when we were in Mason, Texas, for the world premiere of Fred Gipson's *Old Yeller,* some of the ladies hung mistletoe over his head and made a rush for him. His bald head flushed saffron color, and he fled the room like a track star. He was close to rude, but when women were forward, he shrank. Later, as he came to know Terrell Maverick better, he told me about going to the opera in San Antonio with her. "I never saw anything like it—she kissed her way all across that auditorium lobby!" He decided that being the object of affection must be fun and learned to relax and enjoy it.

What all this has to do with history is debatable. The only point in bringing it up is that Webb was a man first, a writer second, a historian third, and an academic last and incidentally. He would have liked to have been a great novelist, but decided not to write fiction because he couldn't handle plots. Since history gave him an inbuilt plot, he wrote from that base. His career can be summed up in his reaction to Fred Shannon's biting attack on *The Great Plains.* Shannon said the book was representative of poor historical methodology. Retorted Webb: "I never looked on it as history—I thought it was art."

In these days of reports and justifications and computerized procedures, Webb would have floundered. He was used to doing things in his own way. Milton R. Gutsch, chairman of the department of history for a quarter of a century, and the university left everyone alone; let each man, in Thoreau's bromide, march to his own drummer, and took for granted that they were good or they wouldn't be there. As Webb often said: "I came along at precisely the right time. Later they never would have hired me, they would never have kept me if they had hired me, and they would never have promoted me if they'd kept me."

He liked to say that he had never sat on a doctoral examination that he could have passed, and some of the critical younger members of the department often argued about whether or not Webb had any standards. There is no answer to that. But he did have compassion, and he did appreciate imagination. He published his first book when he was forty-three, and through Eugene C. Barker's manipulations, he received his Ph.D. some time after that. Today's department of history would not have tolerated such a late start, and so would have missed out on an original mind. But the department in which he flowered left him alone, figured that he had to do things his way, and basked in his honors when they did begin to come in. Moreover, today's department would look on him as old hat, if indeed they had ever heard of him. But he would have shown equal scorn for microhistory, macrohistory, any sort of history that didn't seek to be literature first. He would have considered compulsive publication insulting. To him, it was more important to read Eugene Manlove Rhodes' latest short story in the *Saturday Evening Post* than to grind out another book review to count for his annual report to the dean. At the time he was operating, I suspect that he would have been out of phase in most departments. Certainly he would be now. He hit the right place at the right time.

If Webb were alive to see this biography, he would undoubtedly approve of the content and feel that the author had captured his essence. One can hear him now, saying of his biographer in his wry, flat voice: "Well, at least she's prettier than I am."

Joe B. Frantz
Austin, Texas
November 1975

ACKNOWLEDGMENTS

In the process of gathering material on Webb, numerous debts have been incurred. I must acknowledge my gratitude to those individuals at the University of Texas at Arlington who set me forth on an interesting quest, particularly the late Dr. E. C. Barksdale, Chairman of the Department of History, who suggested that I undertake a master's thesis on the genesis, background, and history of the Walter Prescott Webb Memorial Lectures and in so doing sparked my interest in the man the lectures memorialize. Others at Arlington who provided guidance and inspiration—most of whom knew Webb personally—include Robert Amsler, Leon Borden Blair, Homer Lee Kerr, Sandra L. Myres, C. D. Richards, Blaine T. Williams, George Wolfskill, and Robert Williamson, who was especially helpful in furthering my advanced research.

W. Eugene Hollon of the University of Toledo is to be commended for the trust in a graduate student which he exhibited with the generous loan of his own personal Webb Collection sent through the mails. The assistance of Gene Wise of the American Studies Department of Case Western Reserve University of Cleveland, Ohio, especially his suggestion of a methodological approach for inquiry, is appreciated. Other well-known individuals in the field who took the time and effort to answer questions concerning their association with, or knowledge of Walter Prescott Webb, include John Francis Bannon, Ray Allen Billington, James Lea Cate, John W. Caughey, Avery O. Craven, Odie B. Faulk, Joe B. Frantz, Paul Horgan, William T. Hutchinson, Walter Johnson, Hubert Mewhinney, Jim B. Pearson, Rupert N. Richardson, C. L. Sonnichsen, Rex Strickland, and Wilbert H. Timmons.

Friends and relatives of Webb have also been cooperative and gracious in answering correspondence and granting interviews, especially his daughter, Mrs. William Bradford Bugg; his widow, Mrs. Terrell Maverick Webb; his sister, Mrs. Ima Wright; his private secretary, Mrs. Eileen Guarino; associate and former student, Miss Llerena B. Friend; business partner, Mr. Rodney

Kidd; and attorney and former Chancellor of the University of Texas, James P. Hart. Outstanding among Webb's friends and devotees is, of course, Mr. Cecil Bernard Smith, Sr., of Austin, Texas, who has done so much to preserve the memory and promote the ideas of Walter Prescott Webb, and who has been a personal benefactor to me.

Without the generous assistance of Chester V. Kielman, Director of the Barker Texas History Center, Margaret Francine Morris of the Special Collections Division of the University of Texas at Arlington, and especially of Dorman H. Winfrey, Director of the Texas State Library, this study could never have been completed. At the Texas State Library, Millicent Huff, editor of *Texas Libraries* and an excellent photographer, deserves a special vote of gratitude. John Kinney and Gene Carefoot of the Archives Division at the Texas State Library and Robert Tissing of the Barker Texas History Center were patient and helpful during my research visits with them.

At the University of New Mexico, I am greatly indebted to my major supervisor, Richard N. Ellis, for his continued support and confidence in the value of my endeavor, and to Donald C. Cutter, and Joel M. Jones, all of whom have provided me with expert guidance and assistance, while at the same time allowing me the freedom to pursue my interests in my own way. My appreciation also goes to Joy Meldrum for her typing expertise. Financial assistance in the form of a generous research grant from the Webb-Hinds Fund of the University of Texas at Austin and a typing stipend from the Student Research Allocation Committee of the University of New Mexico have helped defray the expense of this project.

INTRODUCTION

Technological society sanctions and places dominant value on that which is not merely creative in the esthetic sense, but also according to the practical. In the analysis of psychologist Jerome S. Bruner, the creative man provides instruments for manipulating the world, "physically as with the creation of the wheel or symbolically as with the creation of e $=$ mc^2."[1] By these standards Walter Prescott Webb, famous western historian, was most creative and successful; and he did his share of manipulating. The ideas and views he expressed were not merely stimulating in the esthetic sense; they also urged men to action. For an intellectual and a scholar he was of rare genre—an academician who did not fit the mold—paradoxical and pragmatic, he was called an "unfashionable kind of historian."[2] As instruments, Webb used new ideas and historical concepts, intellectual curiosity, and an exploratory nature. He was imbued with a sincere concern for the individual, his state, and the nation. His influence and impact reached far beyond academe, to the halls of Congress and on to London and Paris. He treated a broad spectrum of topics—local, regional, national, and international, and sought to popularize history, as he interpreted it. His ideas, concepts, and actions touched the lives of individuals and institutions.

As a multifaceted man for all seasons, he could lay claim with equal validity to the titles of famed historian, challenging teacher, environmentalist, civic leader, successful dealer in real estate, owner of boys' ranches, or poker player, among others. He stood apart from the rank and file academician, not only because of his many accomplishments, but also because of the intangibles of personality and character that earned for him a devoted following among friends, former students, and associates. Described as a man of penetrating insight, caustic comment, and brilliant originality, he was at the same time shy, introspective, and sensitive. Yet he was imbued with a certain strength of character and conviction that enabled him to express his views boldly.

Considering his humble beginnings as a poor farm boy, the story of his rise to fame is as inspiring as it is remarkable. What is equally remarkable is the fact that more than a decade after the death of this man, who won nearly all the honors his profession could bestow, there is still no full-fledged biography of his life. There are, to be sure, many brief compilations by those who knew him best, but no attempt has been made to weave together the complete fabric. Whereas the best biographies are often those, according to Catherine Drinker Bowen, that have been written after all others, there must always be a starting point—that initial attempt from which the definitive composite will evolve. This then is that initial effort.

The story of Walter Prescott Webb must be portrayed against the background of patterns permeating the society of his age and locale, for he was very much a product both of his region and of a transition period within American life. From his vantage point at the edge of the frontier, he was an active observer and participant as one age evolved into another, as two civilizations met and were transformed. In writing his partial autobiography, which he titled appropriately, "The Texan's Story," he explained what he felt to be the value of this record:

> Perhaps the story may have some validity as an historical document covering a phase of Texas and American life in the transition period between the open frontier into which I was born and the closed planned world into which I have been carried, not too willing, by the passive process of living.[3]

This partial autobiography, deposited in the *Webb Collection* at the Barker Texas History Center in Austin, along with the invaluable *C. B. Smith Collection of Webb Papers* at the Texas State Library comprise the essential sources from which to piece together the formative years of Webb's life. The *Jenkins Garrett Collection* at the University of Texas at Arlington also provides a plethora of supplementary material. Interviews and correspondence from friends, relatives, and former associates have provided additional information, particularly relating to his later years and career.

The works of Walter Webb are in themselves a revealing commentary on his development as a historian as well as on the evolution of a society blessed with an open frontier to that of "the closed planned world" devoid of free land. Born in 1888, by the time he wrote his last major work, he was sixty-four years old. He had seen the days of the bicycle built for two wheeling along under clear blue skies transformed into a Strangelovean world where Texas cowboys rode missiles through polluted heavens. Publication of his most thought-provoking book, *The Great Frontier*, in 1952, marked the peak of his development as a historian and the logical progression of a remarkable mind. He started his literary adventures on the local scene with *The Texas Rangers*, proceeded to regional history with *The Great Plains*, on to a national study in *Divided We Stand*, ultimately expanding his perspective and reputation to the international realm with *The Great Frontier*. Because his works spanned such a period of time, one can see reflected in them the changing patterns of historical thought, which in turn reveal the status of American society. His emphasis on environment and the impact of industrialization is apparent throughout.

Therefore, this attempt to determine the factors instrumental in the development of Walter Webb must necessarily take into account his place in time and space. Any attempt to trace the genesis of his original ideas or to determine his impact upon the field of American history must bear in mind that his life was inextricably linked to Texas, to the West, and to a kaleidoscopic era in American history. Webb lived in transaction with his environment and because of that provided a refracted image of his own cultural milieu. As a participant in such a period, he carried with him a living knowledge of the Old, while observing with intelligent understanding, the changes being wrought by the New. He was first and foremost a Texan, embodying much of the best within that state, although he eventually transcended his provincial bounds within the intellectual sphere. This story then attempts to trace his development from Stephens County farm boy to historian of global acclaim. If in the telling, I can provide insight into this transitional era in American life, Webb's stated purpose will have been served. At the same time, I hope to touch upon the human characteristics of a man whose memory is still greatly loved and respected, and who retains a place in the hearts and minds of those who knew him—a man who was indeed a tall Texan who cast a long shadow.

1

PROLOGUE:
"THE SEARCH FOR WILLIAM E. HINDS"

He fitted the arrow to the bow
Set the mark and insisted
That the aim be true
His greatness of heart is known
Best to me.

W. P. Webb, *The Texas Rangers*

In the rolling hill country of Austin, Texas, an elderly man sat down and composed an article that would soon be published in the July 1961, issue of *Harper's Magazine*. Memories of a full life played in the background of the man's mind as he began writing what was, in effect, a feature-length and extraordinary want ad. His story began:

> For more than fifty years now—since May 1904—I have been searching for a man I never saw. Though he died forty-five years ago, the search grows more intensive as I approach inevitably the time when I can no longer pursue it. The reason I continue this search is that I owe this man a great debt. It would mean a lot to me if I could report to him how a long-shot investment he made in Texas finally turned out.[1]

The author of the ad was Walter Prescott Webb. He was himself the long-shot investment, and he had turned out well indeed.

As one of America's foremost historians, Webb could recall with pride his progress from poor, hardworking farm boy to Distinguished Professor of History at the University of Texas, and President of both the American Historical Association and the Organization of American Historians (formerly the Mississippi Valley Historical Association). Beyond the domestic realm Webb

4

had accepted invitations to be Harkness Lecturer at London University, Harmsworth Professor of History at Cambridge, and in 1950 had lectured as featured speaker at the International Congress of Historians in Paris.

In 1961, however, at age seventy-three, Webb was searching for information on the man who had provided him the avenue to fame and success. The object of the *Harper's* story was William Ellery Hinds, a New York importer of novelty goods. Webb sought to repay Hinds by releasing his story to the public at large. He hoped that their lives might somehow be enriched by the same spirit that had brightened his own life as a Texas farm boy. Being a pragmatic person, Webb also hoped that the inspiring story he was publicly revealing would result in the establishment of a scholarship fund to provide assistance for mature and needy students. In the original draft, the story was overly sentimental. Suggestions from *Harper's* editor, John Fischer, that "a little editorial pruning" would help, made Webb stomp around indignantly for a while, but he finally agreed. The result was still emotion laden and imbued with Webb's deep feelings of responsibility for a debt not fully paid.[2]

The response to Webb's story was tremendous and went exactly as he had planned. After hearing of his approach in launching the project, a friend observed, "His slant, pitch and appeal, in my opinion, was deliberately premeditated and chartered as carefully as an early solo bandit planned a New Mexico bank holdup." The finished product confirmed Webb's sense of mission and his objective of focusing attention on, and "selling" opportunities for individual advancement. His other goal of discovering more about his benefactor only partially succeeded, for the information received was scanty. He learned that Hinds had been born in Brooklyn or Staten Island in 1850 and had died of diabetes in 1912; he left a modest estate and had never married. It remained for Webb to find the real Hinds in the hearts of the American people and within the actions of one individual in particular, C. B. Smith, Sr., of Austin, Texas, former student, business associate, and friend. Smith, who respected Webb greatly and believed in what he was attempting, made the necessary promotional arrangements: he circulated copies of the Hinds story to some 2,000 persons, contributed his own check for $500, then compiled many of the responses in a leather-bound edition for presentation to Webb at a meeting of the Austin Town and Gown organization. Webb, extremely touched by the magnitude of Smith's efforts, concluded a letter of gratitude to him saying:

> The University has given me a great deal, not only what passes for an education, but an opportunity to do the sort of work I most wanted to do. I am glad that I am in position to do something in return. My own life, though rather hard in the early years, has grown richer as I have gone along, and here lately it has become very rich indeed.[3]

The first check received for the Hinds' fund came from a contributor in Connecticut who said that he was a "damn Yankee," and requested that it be spelled in two words. Webb reminded him that William E. Hinds was also a Yankee and that he "rated him pretty high." He then matched the amount sent by the northern donor, and turned the money over to the university for the establishment of a memorial fund to provide interest-free loans to students.[4]

After publication in *Harper's*, "The Search for William E. Hinds" was reprinted in *Reader's Digest* as a human interest story and continued to elicit public response. Webb admitted in later years that he valued the Hinds article as much as anything he had ever written "because it moved so many people to do something worthwhile." Replies and donations from people all over the United States revealed the impact of this dynamic communication, which apparently symbolized to them, as it did to Webb, the attainment of an American dream. It reiterated the mythical ideal that America is indeed a land of opportunity for those willing to strive for it. In the opinion of a Texas state senator, "These instances of human achievement like Webb's are what makes our land a great country."[5] In Webb, the myth had been made manifest.

Then, as now, the Hinds story appealed to the nostalgic yearning for the "good old days" that runs as an undercurrent in the minds of many Americans. It was a symbol of stabilization in troubled times, an anchor to an agrarian past. As Webb himself explained, "in this day of cynicism, this throwback to something very human and inspirational may strike a responsive chord that has not had much exercise now for a long time." To Chancellor Harry Ransom, the human values perpetuated by the Hinds story would also serve the best purposes of the university.[6] Objective achieved, the Webb-

Hinds Fund at the University of Texas stands as a living memorial to his benefactor and as a source of opportunity for many.

As Webb wrote the Hinds story, his mind returned to the years of his youth and the factors responsible for making him the man he became. The full emergence of this outspoken, perceptive, and sometimes controversial historian stems not only from the fateful influence of his benefactor, but also from the hardships he encountered, from his childhood environment, and from the heritage and character bred in him.

2

LOOKING BACK:
THE FORMATIVE YEARS

*It wasn't Indians that were important, nor adventures, nor even getting
out here: It was a whole bunch of people made into one big crawling
beast. . . . The westering was as big as God, and the slow steps that
made the movement piled up until the continent was crossed.*

John Steinbeck, *The Red Pony*

Walter Prescott Webb once admitted that he had no intellectual
interest in the "Late Unpleasantness Between the States," which
may appear unusual considering that he was a Southerner, although
a Southerner of western persuasion. In fact, he asserted that he
found the Civil War an "unpalatable" subject for inquiry—namely,
because he was too close to it through heritage and family
association to be able to view it objectively and unemotionally as
he felt a historian should.[1] He had heard firsthand the unvarnished
stories of the "lingering agony" that was Reconstruction. He had
seen the scars it had left on his own family and section. And it
would be many years before he addressed himself professionally to
even a related topic.

The imprint of this tragic period on the minds of second-
generation Southerners like Webb was branded even deeper in
burning reality on those who had experienced the era. With
General Robert E. Lee's surrender of the Army of Northern
Virginia at Appomattox Court House on April 9, 1865, the prodigal
southern sector was welcomed back into the Union, but not
without suffering and penance. Despair and desolation remained
like a pall hovering over the blackened Grecian columns, burnt-out
gins, and anemic cotton patches. The burden of defeat lay heavy on
an impoverished land.

Webb's ancestors, who had filtered down from Virginia and

South Carolina to Mississippi during the prewar years, weathered the squalor and disorder of a land torn asunder by civil strife. On October 19, 1881, with the eternal optimism of youth, Casner P. Webb and Mary Elizabeth Kyle were married in the small town of Aberdeen, Mississippi. With Reconstruction only four years in the not so distant past, time and prosperity had yet to build the pink clouds of nostalgia that would stereotype the turn-of-the-century era as "the good old days." The deflationary pressures of the 1873 depression had hit farmers especially hard, and the Webb clan was no exception. As so many before them, the young couple looked westward for new opportunity, and in 1883, with their young daughter, moved to Caledonia in Rusk County, Texas.[2] Walter Webb's family was caught in the magnetic pull of the westward movement. Like a small cog in a human machine of migrants, they moved in stops and starts toward a new land.

Not only was Texas a "new land," but a new class of people was populating it. Casner and Mary Kyle, like other destitute products of the Civil War, exemplified the new breed. They were enticed by free land and liberal laws like the various state homestead acts. Similar to the federal law of 1862, one provision exempted 200 acres of land from foreclosure for debt. The state had an effective promotional campaign as well. Southern newspapers printed articles touting the availability of land for the taking, claiming that all "a man needed was 'good character, industrious habits, and one or two boys.'" Texas needed these boys, also, to strengthen the Indian-blighted frontier line, to man the idle cotton plantations in the east, and eventually to extend the parameters of the far western edge of settlement.[3]

The Webbs were part of this last tide of immigration into Texas, the stream of which followed two paths—one, leading to the piney woods where tenant farmers took over the old plantation territory, and the other, flowing further westward toward the 100th meridian, pushing the cattle kingdom ahead of them. Casner and Mary Kyle took the logical route, first to the East where the stately columned homes of the gentry decorated the wooded landscape in deserted splendor, and eventually moving further westward to the arid edge of the frontier. In East Texas they found others like themselves, anxious to dispense with the langour and aristocratic aura of the fallen "planter class," and eager to get on with the business of living. Although the label itself survived in other states, in Texas, even the name "planter" disappeared. These new Texans, "Bourbons" as they were sometimes called, were economically oriented and followed the railheads westward, building cotton gins and warehouses in preference to stately mansions. This new class left the trappings of gentility and their Negroes in the South. Flamboyant and often devoid of "good taste," these were the characters that people the pages of Faulkner's novels. It was this same breed that took King Cotton further inland to the Dallas-Sherman County line. To East Texans of southern descent, this was the West, and it was here that they carried with them intact their "Negro-baiting," "Yankee-hating" social inheritance. From the piney woods to the plains, southern culture diffused.[4]

In this respect, the Webbs played their part, retelling tales in the southern tradition, and a young boy listened, never fully to escape their imprint. In another aspect, however, Casner Webb was a man with a difference: he was educated, at least to the degree that he could teach school. Thus, during this period he chose to lead the semi-itinerant life of a part-time farmer and schoolteacher, setting up shop wherever and whenever the local citizens and seasonal harvests allowed. He earned a reputation as a strict disciplinarian, an important prerequisite in those days when it was fashionable to run off the teacher. According to Webb, his father "had the misfortune to be one of those . . . who never learned to run," and in fact, had "a good deal of hell in him."[5]

The first Texas schools, such as those Casner Webb presided over, were unimpressive in structure, consisting of one long room with a table or rostrum across the front for the teacher and a large drum-like stove, upon which chalk dust settled and burned crimson when hot. The benches were handmade plank, and double doors at the rear opened onto a dusty playground. Rand McNally geographies and McGuffey Readers were the "common intellectual fare."[6] In such a setting Webb watched his father mete out lessons in learning and social responsibility. On more than one occasion his methodology included brute force, although Casner Webb made it a point never to leave marks of physical abuse. Situations frequently arose when he was forced to put a student out of commission. One such instance involved a ruffian by the name of Will Norris. The boy drew a knife in anger, and Casner had to tackle him barehanded. As they wrestled to the floor, Webb's father grabbed the boy's throat and choked him until he turned blue in the face and finally relaxed. His task was not made any easier when the boy's sisters joined the fray, bludgeoning their teacher with a fire shovel and a stick of firewood. In court, the knots on Webb's head made it appear that he had received the worst end of the bargain while there were no visible signs of violence on the recalcitrant pupil. And wisely, perhaps, Casner Webb admitted nothing.[7]

From Caledonia, the Webbs embarked on the second phase of their westward trek, stopping in the piney woods of Panola County in East Texas where Walter Prescott Webb entered the American scene on April 3, 1888. For a time the family lived in an airy two- or three-room house surrounded by cotton fields. Webb recalled walking down the rows, crushing cutworms with his bare feet. An Englishman named Mayo boarded with them. In the evenings the mysterious man sat on the doorstep smoking his pipe, weaving tales of London among the wreaths of smoke and exciting a young boy's imagination. Another memory concerned Negroes stealing corn, and the feel of danger as his father got down his revolver and went to the fields to scare them off, while his mother protested. The boy sensed what he called his father's "high and fractious spirit" and his mother's anxiety, and determined that they were a "domestic team unmatched in temper and disposition."[8]

As a youth, Webb was a stubborn and sensitive child who developed into a shy, introspective man, unable to forget the humiliating experiences of childhood. As an adult, he cited as his first recollection of youth, feelings of anger and exasperation. For some reason, perhaps a stitch in his side or orneriness, he had decided to pull a sit-down strike in the middle of the road. Thereupon his older sister forcibly pulled him by his ankles dragging his head in the sand, which flew into his eyes and mouth. Webb never forgot the sense of utter helplessness of that journey, though he claimed to have experienced similar feelings many times in later years. On another occasion, as the family prepared to go buggy riding, Webb was placed in the box at the rear, where he could only see backwards and hear nothing of the conversation. Thus ostracized, he found some tools and in revenge threw these overboard, revealing what he called "a trait for barking my shins on inevitable situations." To Webb, the joys of childhood existed largely in the minds of adults. As a grown man, he claimed to be able to rationalize himself out of most dilemmas and to escape mental misery "through reason and philosophy"; however, Webb confessed that as a youngster, he could do neither.[9]

In 1892 the family made their last major move westward, settling in the Stephens-Eastland County area. This was merely the first of many relocations within that region, however, as Casner presided over rural schools for one- and two-years stints. It was a significant move for the Webbs, one that carried them from the humid woodlands of old America into a new arid environment. In East Texas from whence they came the terrain and cotton-culture economy made it merely an extension of the Old South, but the dry plains of West Texas created an obvious geographic dichotomy. In retrospect, Webb stated, "There is no confusion in my mind as to what happened in the two contrasting regions." In the Hinds story he claimed that it was here, on the edge of the frontier, at the age of four, that he began his research for *The Great Plains.*[10]

Webb's father had preceded Mary and the children, now three in number. The trip was a trying experience and the young mother was somewhat distraught with managing her brood and baggage, too. Pinpoints of light heralded their late night arrival at the Waco station and cabmen with swinging lanterns called out directions to the various hotels. The family went to live temporarily with a relative in Eastland County. Uncle Jasper, according to Webb, had a long white beard, a yardful of goats, and a reputation as an eccentric. After acquiring a position at a place called Acker, Casner Webb moved his family to a house on a hill set amid blackjacks and scrub oaks.[11]

The Webbs eventually became the parents of seven children, but every other child was to die at a young age and every other child happened to be a boy. It is understandable that Walter, as the only surviving male, became the focal point of his parents' pride and hope. After Mittie Alma, the eldest daughter, who had been born in Aberdeen, Mississippi, in 1882, a boy named Houston arrived. He died in 1886 at twenty months. Walter came two years later, followed by Kyle, who died at the age of two. A sister, Ella Ruth, was born July 11, 1893, while the family lived in Wayland. Another boy named Bruce was born at Breckenridge in 1896, but died in infancy at three weeks. Ima Jewel, of the black eyes and bouncing curls, arrived at Ranger on December 25, 1898. She remained the baby of the family and became Walter's favorite.[12]

During these early years, high infant mortality although tragic, was not uncommon, a fact that did little to assuage the family sorrow. Webb remembered that on one such occasion he had awakened in the night to a great commotion. A screech owl had entered the house, and his father was trying to scare it out. According to superstitition, the owl was an ill omen and his mother was frantic, for she took the sign seriously. The next night, Walter again awoke to noise, confusion, and the sound of crying: "Death had entered . . . and claimed the youngest member."[13]

In other respects, pioneer conditions still existed in Stephens County. Indian raids, violence, cattle rustling—all characteristics of a frontier society—were hardly history and in milder forms still marked the close of the century. As a youngster, Webb listened intently as old people sat and reminisced, not of centuries past, but of real-life struggles for survival. By 1870, bison hunters had decimated the Indian food supply, violating the Treaty of Medicine Lodge, and frantically, the Indians launched retaliatory war. During the period from 1866 to 1876, local ranchers in Stephens County had been forced to organize for protection against raiding parties. Military force helped contain hostilities and by 1880, settlers started pouring into the area. Even in the 1890s, during Webb's childhood, violence was not entirely a thing of the past. Young men still liked to sport revolvers, and disputes between feuding factions were a definite reality. En route to town one day, Walter and his father encountered the Heatley clan, armed and primed to rectify an injustice perpetrated by a rival group.[14]

Other factors in the cultural milieu began to mold the boy's thinking, particularly his acquaintance with the western environment. He lived through the drought and panic of 1893 and witnessed the heavy hand of Nature. In later years, he recalled growing to manhood in a land where he "saw cattle starve and freeze, and came near seeing people do the same thing." He recorded many of these impressions in *The Great Plains*, vivid descriptions of rapid climatic changes—the blue northers preceded by black clouds and sand, causing incredibly rapid drops in temperature (from fifty to twenty-five degrees), and the hot winds and hail storms that could wipe out a year's toil in a matter of minutes. In Stephens County where he lived, as in other areas of the plains region, the people adopted the windmill to harness the wind's energy and make up for water deficiency. Yet the wind remained a malevolent force, frightening, drying, and destructive.[15]

One incident in particular indelibly imprinted on the young boy's mind the power of such phenomenon and greatly influenced his thinking in later life. The event occurred in the nearby town of Cisco sometime between sunset and dark. Black clouds began to build, accompanied by an angry wind and lightening. Anxiety prevailed and soon homes were exploding while women attempted to save their families "by paraying [sic] and getting under the bed." News of this disaster created in the region a great fear of tornadoes. Webb wrote: "Every cloud took on a sinister aspect and was a signal for all and sundry to 'go to the cellar.'" The cellars themselves were dismal holes in the ground, reeking of dampness, shrivelling potatoes, dry onions, and fear. To a youngster (and elders, too), "The experience was horrible—this waiting to be blown away." In time, Webb determined that these mad dashes for the cellar, as he termed it, "induced a fear which the risk did not justify."[16]

On the lighter side, Webb also recorded in *The Great Plains* the folk expression of the impact of wind on pioneer life, an attempt typical of a society trying to lessen the burdens of reality. " 'Does the wind blow this way here all the time?' asked the ranch visitor in the West. 'No, Mister,' answered the cowboy; 'it'll maybe blow this way for a week or ten days, and then it'll take a change and blow like hell for a while.'"[17] As a successful historian, Webb admitted that he found it impossible to study a culture apart from its physical geography. This approach was especially relevant in his work on the American West where his early life and later scholarly investigations showed the environment to be "an overwhelming force" causing men and institutions to "bend to its imperious influence."[18]

During Webb's early years, most West Texans were still on horseback. Wagons, too, were a common mode of transportation. Walter remembered going with his father on a freight haul to Cisco where they spent the night under the stars in the wagon yard after renting camping space for fifteen or twenty-five cents. The smell of wood smoke and brewing coffee heightened his senses and he listened with big ears as men discussed "hard times and the price of cotton." Later he went to look at his first dead man found under the

Texas and Pacific bridge.[19] The "T & P," like railroads by other names, served as a lifeline to the frontier. In some cases, railroads were responsible for the building of towns, providing inlets and outlets for supplies and produce. On the other hand, like schizoid mechanical monsters, they contributed to the demise of those villages they bypassed, molding the lives of women and men. The Webb family would also feel its iron touch.

Casner Webb's next teaching assignment took the family to the village of Wayland, which rested at the foot of Stealeasy Mountain and boasted an artesian well. Here Walter became involved in typical boyish ventures, playing with matches, stealing a ten-penney nail from Spicer's General Store, and suffering the pangs of retribution when his mother forced him to return it. The owner, a benevolent German with a wavy beard, distributed mail and sold kerosene oil, nails, calico, cheese, and other sundries. To a youngster, Spicer's store was "a wonderful place." It was here, while standing beside a hot stove, that the boy received a nickel from a drummer for having such a big head. Everyone commented on his oversized head, Webb noted, "but this was the first time it had ever paid a profit."[20]

Young Webb was not remembered as a particularly handsome child. Years later, E. C. Barksdale, Webb's close friend, returned with him to Ranger, where they stopped to visit with an old-time resident. The elderly lady looked at Webb in surprise and in a sort of nasal twang commented, "Well, if it ain't little pop-eyed Walter Webb."[21] He was a very bright child, however, and was considered to be precocious by his first teacher, Mrs. C. P. Jones. A neighbor of the Webbs, Mrs. Jones realized that the five-year-old boy had an unusual mind and asked her school board that he be allowed to visit her primary class. Walter was delighted and listened carefully, especially to the geography lesson. "Miss Lessie," as the teacher was then called, asked one of her pupils where he lived and requested that he point it out on the map. The boy answered, "Texas," and then proceeded to place the pointer on South America. Walter raised his hand and said, "He comes a long way to school," then got up and showed the older students the correct location.[22]

On Fridays the class recited impromptu speeches, and Walter always had something to contribute. His teacher felt that one verse in particular was worthy of recording, especially for a five year old:

Meet me sister, meet me
And let us run a race
Last year you used to beat me
In every little chase.

When one of the big boys failed to come up with a "Memory
Gem," saying: "For a fact, I lost my speech in a Buffalo track";
Walter responded, "Miss Lessie, he had better find it."[23]

In Wayland, the Webbs were also neighbors to the Hodges
family. Valston Hodges was a Baptist preacher and justice of the
peace, a man Webb described as "high-spirited, fractious, and for a
preacher, profane." In fact, the whole family, according to Webb's
recollection, "was blessed with a violent temper," but the father of
the brood and Casner got along splendidly. One memorable
evening Walter and his father made the trek to Spicer's store to
purchase kerosene oil to fill the lamps. For one reason or another a
disagreement developed between Casner and a couple of the men.
Words were exchanged, and Webb drew a revolver (borrowed from
Valston Hodges). Scared half to death, Walter jumped between
them and created such a scene that he felt he possibly prevented a
shooting. It seems that Webb and his friend, Hodges, had certain
traits in common.[24]

This individualistic strength of character and the respect Casner
Webb engendered made a lasting impression on his son. Webb
inherited his stubborn streak and his power of conviction; neither
did he turn away from a good fight, as university regents and
administrators would later testify. Webb also credited his father for
pushing him "out into the world," always exhibiting confidence in
his ability. It appeared that Walter's actions warranted his father's
confidence, for he very early showed himself to be a responsible
boy with good common sense. On one occasion, his father had sent
him to town with ten dollars to make a purchase. Walter was riding
a young pony called "Barney," a "weedy, stringy, and brainless"
piece of horseflesh that Casner had acquired as a colt for the trade
of a razor. At the crossroads the boy met a fellow mounted on a
"round-rumped blue mare" with a beautiful head and ears. Walter
could not resist the opportunity and forwardly suggested a trade.
Deceived by the boy's youth and the prospect of making some extra
cash, the man listened. They haggled until dark, but Walter ended
up with the blue mare—the same mare that he would later be
forced to sell to pay for his books at the Ranger school. He was

almost happy as he changed saddles and rode homeward, experiencing the pleasure of being astride a good animal that made riding a delight. However, the small amount of money he was carrying created some sobering thoughts.[25]

With apprehension, Walter dismounted at the gate. Deciding not to prolong the agony, he called his father out into the moonlight and confessed:

"Papa," he said, "I traded Barney off for this pony." Casner gave one look and exclaimed almost gleefully; "You did!"

"Yes," Walter said, encouraged by this reaction, "but I had to give boot, three dollars."

"That's all right," his father answered, "I wouldn't trade back for ten." He obviously shared his son's low opinion of Barney, and when the man reappeared the next day to "rue back," as Webb called it, his father sent him on his way, and the boy kept the blue mare.[26]

Although Webb seemed to dwell on his father's influence and strength of character in his autobiographical reminiscences, his mother too, in her way, broadened his vision. She encouraged him to read and provided him with that all important dime with which he purchased a subscription to *The Sunny South*, the magazine that opened the portals of opportunity through correspondence with his benefactor, William E. Hinds. In other respects Webb was learning things for himself. As he explained, he was going "farther afield in tentative experiments with living, and the fact that I did not burn off the range, set fire to the house, and drown in the tank was due to the shortness of the grass, the thickness of the chimney, and the shallowness of the water."[27]

Water, or the lack of it, was a definite problem to these farming people and was a commodity much appreciated. Walter soon became aware of this fact when his father decided to devote more time to cultivating his land. Unfortunately the year he made this decision was the year of the drought. The Webbs had moved again, this time to the Carroll place on the south side of the Breckenridge-Albany road. They broke the ground with a plow pulled by a mule, whose rear end Walter soon learned not to tamper with. Springtime came, but there was hardly enough moisture in the ground for the seeds to sprout. The cotton made it up, but only to six inches in height. The pigs were a problem, too. Since there was nothing to feed them, Casner turned them out to forage mesquite beans and acorns, whereupon they also became a problem for a German neighbor. This man had chosen a fertile little creek valley to farm and was consequently one of the few people to have a decent garden. When the Webbs' pigs decided to pay their respects the German penned them up to protect his vegetables and rushed over in a stew to see Casner:

"Mr. Vebb, them vite pigs of yours come mit in my garden, root 'em all up everting. I put 'em up, in de pen, and you come get 'em and pay me von dollar for each," he demanded.

"Why bless you, Fritz," said Walter's father, "you just keep the pigs. You are welcome to them. I wouldn't give you a dollar for the whole outfit. They are yours." Casner was serious. He knew the German couldn't feed the pigs any more than he could and that he did not want them either. Later on, the neighbor returned:

"Vebb, you come get them damned pigs. I don't vant 'em."[28]

During this year of drought, people came from miles around to Craighead Pool to haul away barrels of water in their wagons. Under such conditions, farm life was extremely difficult. In Webb's memory of those days, poverty was associated even with the food they ate. "Thicken gravy," a concoction made of bacon grease, flour, and water, seemed particularly revolting to the young boy, who, in later life, came to relate it to "the bastard food of the poor." Cornbread was somewhat better, Webb decided, and really delicious with cold sweet milk. This combination remained one of his favorite meals, much to the disgust of his daughter, Mildred, who like all the Webb clan, had strong food prejudices. Mrs. Terrell Webb recalled that although these were difficult years, her husband spoke affectionately of his parents, though less affectionately about chopping and picking cotton.[29]

Walter Webb grew up in a time and place that registered unconscious impressions of a transition era. He felt the poverty, the harshness of his environment, and began to realize that "the West was a powerful magnet," luring men ever onward to greener pastures. He saw the hired hand, Dave, kiss his mother good-bye and ride west on a mouse-colored mule. And he saw the Hodges' powerful son, Tom, stride off in tall boots. "Tom," his mother said, "Remember, what I told you." Webb later knew that here he had witnessed the final words of what he called, "the first act in an American drama." Several years later, Dave returned, wearing good clothes and the calm manner of the professional gambler. Not all the young men went through the formal ritual of leaving—the family gatherings, the sad good-byes—a few left secretly in the night. Through his teaching in various counties, Casner had become acquainted with many of these boys, some of whom stopped at the Webb home en route, making it a sort of way station West.[30] By the time he had reached young manhood, he had seen the westering spirit become a thing of the past.

At nine years of age Webb witnessed something which caused him to begin to think and to doubt. It was an unusual friend who helped the process along. "Bounce," a sturdy black and white mixed-breed, was "the" dog in Webb's young life. When he died, the whole family wept. Webb remembered, "We did not bury him, as city people do, but took him down to the draw and left his body under a live oak tree, . . . [where] I went often to witness the process of decay." In the springtime, the grasses came up green and tall where Bounce lay, but the silent ache in the boy's heart remained, and his young mind began to doubt the orthodoxy he had heard preached in summer revivals. If good people went to heaven, why had Bounce been barred? In retrospect, Webb decided that there was "something in the harshness and compulsions of life in West Texas, even in Stephens County, that caused doubts in the minds of small boys."[31]

From the same locale, only ten miles from where Bounce died, another young boy grew to manhood. Harry Yandell Benedict, destined to become the first Texan to serve as president of the University of Texas at Austin, also felt the impact of his surroundings. He saw the grass eaten off the range, and waterholes dried to mud traps where cattle bogged, bawling and suffering for days until death relieved their misery. Benedict later told Webb that he could not bear "the unmerited suffering of these animals" and orthodox religiosity was no comfort for the obvious injustice.[32]

In later years, the University of Texas Board of Regents queried Benedict concerning his views. According to the story, regent Lutcher Stark demanded to know if Benedict believed in God. "'Do you mean an anthropomorphic God?' asked Benedict." With that, "The regent went for the dictionary and the trial was never resumed." "Fortunately," Webb concluded, "neither my dog nor Benny's cows can be tried for teaching us to think for ourselves."[33] Thus Webb's thinking processes were formulated by the emotional experiences of youth, although his home environment combined with his own questioning intellect were also influential factors. The religious attitudes of his parents exposed him to two divergent viewpoints, but there is no evidence that the beliefs of one or the other were forced upon him. Mary Kyle attended Protestant services, Baptist or Methodist, perhaps both, and read the Bible to her family.[34] Walter's reaction to this is unknown, but on one occasion at least, during tornado weather, he recalled being so scared that he begged her to read "the good book." For once, he said, she was too frightened to oblige. Casner Webb, on the other hand, read the Bible so as to be better able to refute its precepts. As a skeptic, he had little tolerance for the pious mouthings of religious hypocrites and is said to have told one benighted soul, "Hell is so full of your kind that their legs are sticking out the windows." The Webbs occasionally attended religious revivals, those typically noisy and emotional phenomena that met the needs for socialization as well as spiritualization within frontier society.[35] In perspective, Casner Webb's skepticism and his son's early doubting were not anomalous to the religious temper of their era in the broader sphere.

By the 1870s, the fundamentalist religion—characterized by oldtime revivalists spouting "hell-fire" and brimstone and based upon literal interpretations of the Bible—felt the impact of Darwinism and "higher criticism." This latter development, which emanated from Europe and involved critical scriptural analysis, meshed fairly closely with Casner Webb's particular brand of religiosity. Neither did the Webbs adhere to the social gospel of Walter Rauschenbusch, but this was not atypical for rural areas.[36]

Functional Protestantism *was* typical, however, and logically so. Church meetings held in the open under shady groves provided a source of companionship for isolated farming families, an opportunity for the women to gossip and dandle babies, and for the men to discuss crops, politics, and common problems. These functions, sometimes lasting for days and interspersed with barbecues, basket suppers, and bazaars, set the moral tone and mores for a frontier society. In the plains region the Old Testament orthodoxy had a particular relevance for the majority, especially the uneducated. These pioneers could see parallels with their arid environs and the biblical land of Canaan. In many respects they suffered as did the children of the Israelites, beset with heathen enemies, scourged by voracious grasshoppers and parching drought. Like the Israelites, they had chosen this soil, and with the help of nature and God, they fought with tenacity, intolerant determination, and Hebrew strength to maintain their toehold. Even their hymns invoked the imagery of plentiful water and rain:

> Shall we gather at the river
> The beautiful, beautiful river;
> Shall we gather at the river,
> That flows by the throne of God.[37]

To people near the farm line of the 98th meridian, these words had special meaning, but there were always those like Casner Webb, who looked at the world in a different light.

His son, Walter, never became an affiliate of a religious denomination, although he respected the rights of others to worship as they pleased. Perhaps best described as a mystic (for reasons later explained more fully), he did practice Christian living through good works, for he had learned firsthand the benefits of such a philosophy through William E. Hinds, whose actions he considered the epitome of "applied Christianity."[38] During the course of their correspondence, Hinds mailed a verse to his protégé embodying this philosophy:

> We live in deeds, not years;
> In thoughts, not breaths;
> In feelings not in figures on a dial.
> We should count time by heart throbs;
> He most lives, who thinks most,
> Feels the noblest, acts the best.[39]

If Webb had a religious creed, it was simply to live so as to leave the world a better place, a creed inculcated through friendly persuasion and example during formative years.

These early years were also characterized by mobility as the family's relocations exposed Webb to new faces and small villages within the span of several counties. The Webbs spent the next two years near Eliasville located on the Clear Fork of the Brazos River. It seemed that Casner Webb taught nearly every school in the area—South Prairie, Peach Creek, Veale, Oakley, and Merriman. Walter's own school attendance was irregular during this time, but he learned to read and to write, which broadened his vision and fired his imagination. He never forgot the excitement of owning his first book, purchased by saving premiums from Arbuckle's Four X coffee. After collecting a certain number of signatures, one was entitled to order a prize, and Walter chose *Jack the Giant Killer*. The book that arrived at the Lacasa post office was his very first piece of mail, "the beginning of a long series of thrills and shocks" that came to him by this route. Full of expectation, Walter read it as he rode "Old Charlie" homeward. The post office remained an intriguing place to him, even as a grown man, and with good reason. As he explained, "Most good things have come to me through the mail." These small boxes, with glass windows to tantalize, afforded anticipation and speculation, good news or bad, a publisher's check, or what Webb termed "some other demonstration of the magic of living."[40]

Farm living was certainly not magical in the positive sense of the word, except that it sometimes appeared miraculous that these early families survived. The year 1898 was such a year for the Webbs. On Christmas Day his third sister, Ima, was born, "the only dark-haired member of the family" and the only one to resemble his mother. These were difficult times. Walter's mother had her hands full with the new baby, and Casner nearly died that winter of influenza. The weather was bitterly cold, to the extent that the bucket of water left in front of the fireplace froze solid and buckled in the middle from expansion. Kerosene oil turned thick and grey, "like bacon grease in August weather." The family made one last migration before they settled, an event which to Walter marked "the beginning of a new chapter." This move took the Webbs very close to Ranger in Eastland County. The children attended Bullock School just past the Eastland boundary, and Casner taught at Merriman. These numerous relocations registered with the growing boy, and like Tom Sawyer, he found himself "looking for some visible change" as they crossed county boundary lines. The Webbs now had entered the Cross Timbers section, an anomalous extension of blackjack and post oak jutting from the Red River into central Texas.[41]

With its red clay base and dwarf timber, the Cross Timbers disrupted the smooth fertility of the surrounding black prairie land like a wart on an otherwise unscathed hand. The first settlers had quickly claimed the blackland on either side, realizing that it was better suited to cotton and machine cultivation, but the last wave of emigrants had no choice and found themselves faced with the prospects of clearing stumps and coaxing a living from the sandy loam. Yet the terrain had its redeeming grace; although it was not as fertile as the prairie, it did hold moisture and would produce crops long after the harsh sun had parched the blackland dry. Eventually the area would become famous for its sweet potatoes, peanuts, and watermelons.[42]

At the turn of the century, however, the deep shade from the scrubby trees retarded the growth of good grass and even the cattle and horses had a leaner look. As Webb characterized it, the sociological aspects of the Cross Timbers "are as remarkable as its physical character, as if part of East Texas got isolated and moved over into the West." People from the blackland disdainfully looked down on the area and its inhabitants, referring to it as "the shinnery," or "the sticks," and considering themselves "slightly superior." Webb believed that the negative stigma attached to the region actually provided motivation for its young people to get up and away. "No boy with any ambition," he claimed, "wanted to live in the Cross Timbers and so many of them were determined to get away that they burned the midnight oil, sacrificed their youth, and paid any price necessary for the escape." He felt the story of his own emancipation to be typical of the success stories of others from the same locale.[43]

The Webb children attended the Bullock School only one year, and it was here that Walter earned the nickname, "Doc." Their teacher, Charles Pettit, who later became a wealthy oil man in Dallas, had asked his students to write down what they wanted to be when they grew up. Walter was naive enough to be honest. Instead of claiming that he wanted to be a good poker player or cowboy, he admitted that he wanted to be a doctor. To Webb, "this nickname was torture," but couldn't compare to the monikers tacked on to some of the others.[44]

Highlighting these years of intermittent schooling was a session at Oakley School, taught by Miss Lena Langford. Miss Langford, according to Webb's description, weighed approximately ninety-six pounds "soaking wet," and wore her golden hair braided like a coronet around her head. One day Walter and a student named Jim Goswick had a rock fight. Since the fray wasn't serious, Miss Langford punished the boys and the episode was supposedly forgotten. Some time later, however, two of the older students had a bloody "knock-down, drag-out" that attracted the attention of the whole school. When they decided that they were "too big" to be whipped, and Miss Langford too frail to do anything about it, the boys were reported and fined. When the culprits revealed that Walter and Jim had been involved in an earlier fracas, the officers charged them also. Webb remembered, "My father was very angry with me for starting a criminal career thus [sic] early, . . ." but secretly enjoyed the situation. Casner decided that he was not about to pay a fine. Consequently, he and Mr. Goswick hired Earl Connor of Eastland to defend the boys for a ten-dollar fee.[45]

On a bright and sunny day that in no way matched the moods of their young defendants, the fathers set out with their "erring offspring" in a farm wagon for Wayland, some ten or twelve miles away. Casner Webb's old-time friend, Hodges, still presided as justice of the peace, holding court in the front room of his home for lack of more official quarters. When they arrived, Walter saw that there was quite a turnout. Buggies and saddle horses crowded the yard. In spite of the circumstances, Walter enjoyed seeing his childhood friends, some of whom had grown up "with surprisingly pleasant results," he noted. The constable called the court to order and Walter went on trial first. His lawyer, Earl Connor, sporting a black mustache and looking very debonair in a dark suit, requested that the jury be dismissed, and this was granted. Then after the prosecution presented their witness, Miss Lena took the stand. Webb recalled that she looked very prim and dignified as she stood on a "goods box" surrounded by spectators. After answering the questions posed, she stated with quiet conviction that she felt that she had already handled the situation quite adequately. With that, Connor rose and concluded his extremely brief case. "Your honor, the defense rests," he said, and the "comic farce," as Webb labelled it, was over. Both cases were dismissed.[46]

The trauma of the episode and the excitement of returning to scenes of his childhood motivated Walter to spend the following Sunday writing an account of his return, which he entitled "Back Home." He made no reference to the actual occasion for it, however. He sent this article to the *Breckenridge Democrat* and the editor, Harbert Davenport, who later became one of Texas' better land lawyers, agreed to print it—the first piece Webb ever published. Meanwhile, the growing boy was assuming more and more responsibility at home since his father was away teaching during the week. Also, an event had occurred that altered their lives.[47]

After teaching at Merriman, Casner Webb took a summer job on the Texas and Pacific railroad where he suffered a serious injury that crippled him for life. He had been overseeing a gang of construction workers loading rock on flatcars when one of the rocks fell, crushing his foot. Walter harnessed the team and rushed his father to the doctor, who set the foot in a cast. The broken bones failed to heal properly necessitating the amputation of four toes. Casner was forced to rely on a cane the remainder of his life and as a result of the accident, sued the T & P Railroad for damages. His attorney, Ben M. Terrell of Fort Worth, won the suit, and the settlement granted turned hard luck into opportunity. He realized that the days of the fighting school teacher were nearing an end; Walter was old enough to be a big help with the chores; and he now had the financial means to secure a permanent home.[48]

In 1902, when his son was about thirteen years old, Casner took possession of 160 acres of Stephens County farmland under the Texas preemption law, which held that ten years of occupancy, improvements, and paid taxes validated the claim. This quarter section of the Cross Timbers had originally belonged to Phil S. Lehman of New York, who in Webb's estimation, "had wisely gone off and forgotten all about it." In ten days time, they had put up a pine-boxed house. Webb's father was still teaching, so the responsibility of running the homestead rested on the young boy. Water had to be hauled from Ranger nine miles away; there were fields to be cleared and crops to be tended. For two years Webb was not able to attend school at all. His only escape from the bleakness and drudgery of farm life lay in the vicarious world of books.[49]

Since there was a tradition of reading within the Webb family, Walter's parents encouraged his literary interests to the extent that meager finances would allow. Reading had been a passion with him from the age of ten, and he had combed home and countryside for material. Among the publications he devoured were *The American Boy, The Youth's Companion, The Saturday Blade, The Chicago Ledger,* and *The Tip-Top Weekly,* purchased from a peddler. From *The Tip-Top Weekly,* he perceived something of college life at Yale through the exploits of Frank Merriwell. Even at this young age, he began to think about going to college, although the prospect seemed extremely remote. Webb's love of and exposure to books was a mixed blessing. It gave him new knowledge and new ideas that he hungered for, but it made him want more—more than circumstances would permit. As Webb himself said, "This reading opened such a wonderful world that I developed an aversion to the one that lay around me." To a young boy with a quick and inquisitive mind, a boy who liked best to read, the years from thirteen to seventeen seemed "an eternity."[50]

One day Casner Webb casually remarked to his son that he should become an editor. Webb later said that he didn't even know what "an editor" was. Still the remark whetted his curiosity and exerted considerable influence on his life. Soon thereafter, young Webb visited the newspaper office in nearby Ranger. He peered over the editor's shoulder until finally the exasperated man suggested that he leave. But Walter had noticed a veritable treasure-house of magazines and papers stacked in a corner and gathered up enough courage to ask if he could take a few. Probably to get rid of him, the editor consented. One of these magazines was *The Sunny South*, edited by Joel Chandler Harris, and the boy liked it so well that his mother allowed him to subscribe to it. In desperation, Webb wrote a letter to Mary E. Bryant, editor of the gossip column, asking for information on how a poor farm boy could get an education and become a writer. With this bit of self-assertiveness, the boy set in motion the wheels of fortune. His letter was printed in the May 14th issue of 1904, and in response came a reply from William E. Hinds of New York.[51]

Webb never forgot the excitement of receiving that piece of mail. It had arrived late one afternoon while the sun was beating down fiercely on the boy and his father as they plowed a young corn crop. They were leaning on their Georgia stocks, resting and letting the horses "blow" when Walter's sister came running to the field and presented him with a letter written on quality stock in a bold black script and sealed with red wax. Hinds' letter, initially missent, and addressed merely to "Prescott, Ranger, Texas, % Lame Teacher," advised the boy to maintain his aspirations and keep his sights on lofty goals, saying, "as you know, there is no such word as *fail*, in the *lexicon* of *youth*." The fact that the letter reached the boy at all was in itself fateful. Fortunately, the bearded postmaster, Mr. John E. Griffin, had determined that it belonged to young Walter Webb. The impact of the letter was significant. As

Webb explained, "It wrought a transformation and crowned an ambitious boy with a sense of obligation and opportunity." Hinds followed his words of encouragement with a windfall of books and magazines, including such well-known titles as Lyman Abbott's *The Outlook,* a magazine pertaining to Washington affairs called *The National, The American Boy,* Oscar S. Marsden's *Success,* and others. He suggested that the boy send him narratives and descriptions he had composed to help him learn to write. Their correspondence continued and each Christmas Walter would also receive a tie, the likes of which Stephen County had never seen.[52]

Casner Webb, although not a demonstrative man and somewhat sharp of mind and tongue, appreciated his son's desire for an education and realized the value of it. Like others of his time and generation, he shared the nation's rising interest in educational advancement, not only because it was for him a part-time profession, but also because he saw it as a necessity for his children's welfare. By the 1890s, as historian Frederick Jackson Turner had proclaimed, the American frontier was disappearing. Even in rural areas, people began turning to frontiers of the mind, a trend sharply reflected in the statistics of educational expansion. Within the period from 1898 to 1914, for example, enrollment in elementary schools grew from sixteen million to more than twenty million and more than doubled in the high schools, a trend that was particularly obvious in the South.[53] The success stories of those produced in the Stephens-Erath county area—Harry Yandell Benedict, Edward Everett Davis, Robert Heffner—bore witness to the validity of this belief, even in the West Texas shinnery. As a young boy, Webb recalled hearing talk around the family dinner table of the accomplishments of H. Y. Benedict in particular, and also of Robert Heffner, who became a respected member of the state supreme court of Oklahoma. He felt that they must have subconsciously motivated him to seek out a similar path to success through education.[54]

Thus, in 1905, in order to provide his son and daughters with the opportunity he felt they should have, Casner offered to move the family to Ranger, provided that Walter could earn a second-grade teaching certificate in one year's time. Fortuitously, the farm had prospered under his father's expertise. Casner approached the subject scientifically, studying dryland farming techniques and experimenting with the growing of fruit trees. The rapid rise in urban population, some forty percent between the years 1900 and 1910, provided new demands for domestic produce, and Casner found ready markets for his fruit. After a particularly good year, when the farm had been blessed with plentiful rain and a good harvest, the Webbs made their move to Ranger. Walter accepted the challenge to produce a teacher's certificate within the allotted time frame, and worked and studied diligently. He also made sacrifices, selling his blue mare to buy school books, sweeping the schoolroom floors to earn his tuition, and running the suction pipe at the Ranger cotton gin on weekends and after school.[55]

His principal at the Ranger School, J. E. Temple Peters, must have been a man of exceptional caliber, especially for such an early period in education and in a rural area. Although small in stature, he managed to control his charges without resorting to the more common and forceful tactics. Described by Webb as a really "civilized person," he had the ability to instill the desire to be civilized in the young people around him as well. In addition to preparing his students to take the teacher certification exams, he also taught them social graces, an effort that his pragmatic patrons did not especially appreciate. Along with the course work, Peters explained the correct procedures for shining shoes, tipping waiters, and sending candy to dates. He also encouraged his pupils to "wear clean linen," "tailor-made clothes," and "to stay at good hotels," if they could afford it. To a farming community more accustomed to dirt than daintiness and dandies, Peters' ideas were regarded as "high-falooting" and slightly heretical.[56]

In spite of social standards, he was not perfect and occasionally made the grammatical error of saying "ain't." Walter suspected that he used it to create a bit of diversion, particularly after one young lady called his attention to the fact. Peters graciously told her that she could correct him if he slipped. This same young lady indulged in a bit of impertinence not long after and Peters lost his temper and berated her soundly. When he paused for breath, the girl replied sweetly, "Mr. Peters, you daid [sic] ain't." He eventually married her.[57]

By the time Webb started this year of intensive training he had attended school intermittently for eight years. He discovered that certain deficiencies in mathematics and grammar were the hardest to overcome. By the day of the examination, Walter was ill with tonsillitis and running a fever of 103°. Peters, who had spent many hours coaching his students, also conducted the certification exams at the county seat. By taking aspirin, which seemed to fire his brain and sharpen his faculties, Webb was able to finish the test. When he walked up the aisle to turn in his exam, he staggered from weakness and exhaustion, but recalled that he never once thought of quitting. The opportunity was too great to destroy.[58]

After the term ended, the Webbs returned to the farm, where Walter waited anxiously for the board's decision. Again good news came by mail; an official looking envelope arrived containing only a second-grade certificate. To Webb, "it was a certificate of emancipation," a parchment that outranked all others that he would ever earn. The same year that Webb started teaching, his father resigned to devote all his time to farming. Walter Webb was now eighteen years old and he was free to pursue the profession he had chosen. He was anxious to try his wings and as he said, "impose my ignorance on those who were only a little less so." With the encouragement and assistance of family and friends, an exceptional teacher, and a benefactor from afar, he had launched a career, modest though it might be.[59]

To his early patrons an education meant reading, writing, and arithmetic, and not much more. Parents that had none of these abilities helped build the schoolhouses, hauled firewood, and sometimes paid the teacher in produce or poultry. This concern, however simple in nature, was the sign of progress and public acceptance of the educational process. Even within the shinnery of Stephens County, Texas, parents like the Webbs began to equate education with opportunity, and with a great trust released their offspring to the teacher with the admonition "to learn 'em" and "whoop 'em" if they needed it. In 1905, the Texas system still operated on a rather haphazard basis with schools often organized by popular demand for brief periods of time. It was in a school of this nature that Webb started his career.[60]

Casner's respected reputation as a teacher helped his son in acquiring a position, and Walter found himself assigned to a small school some thirty miles away in a hilly area of Eastland County. This first school, called, with some exaggeration, Mountain School, lay close to the home of an uncle, Bailey Barton, whom Webb described as having a "billy-goat beard" and kind heart, and who was also a trustee. Casner and Walter drove over in the buggy to the Bartons, where the young teacher was to board for the six-week summer session. He paid $7 a month for board, and from his salary of $43.50 per month, saved money.[61]

The weather set the stage for a dismal first day. On a rainy July morning with the rising sun shadowed by heavy clouds, Webb started off to walk two miles from the Bartons through wet grass and weeds to reach his school. He dreaded meeting the parents that he felt sure would be there on the first day, but the weather kept them away. This was false assurance, however, that things were going to run smoothly. In the schoolhouse, the bedraggled teacher noted that the water bucket had to be filled, and commandeered a couple of the boys to accompany him to the well that lay on the other side of the barbed wire fence. To reach the well, they had to cross a stile, which unfortunately shielded under its steps a large nest of yellow jackets. As the boys preceded their teacher across the stile, they irritated the wasps so that they were primed to dart out and sting Webb under one eye, which soon began to swell. To make matters worse, on the way back they met a group of newly arrived students. One barefooted pupil surveyed the crowd closely, mistook Webb for one of the boys, and commented for all to hear; "Guess our little teacher ain't coming this mornin.' "[62]

That first year, the "little teacher" taught three schools, the second being the Barnett School, which held a four-and-a-half month session. He finished the year at Center Point. Not all of his experiences during this initiation period were so disappointing. Following the advice of his New York friend and correspondent, William E. Hinds, he had been developing his writing ability by composing descriptive narratives, then, as he said, "throwing them in the school stove." One day he decided to test his effectiveness on an audience. After writing a description of what he had observed on the way to school, he cornered a young part-Indian boy of seven or eight to listen to him. Little Henry Woods' response was gratifying: "Fessor," he said with sincerity, "that shore is pretty." The composition had moved its listener, and the writer, for the first time, felt the satisfaction derived from such an experience.[63]

Webb always enjoyed a moving story and even in the autumn years of his life recalled the thrill of reading a red-backed third-level reader that contained a "marvelous" story about Abou the Arab. The story told how Abou and his horse were captured by the enemy during a war; how Abou had been bound hand and foot; then miraculously rescued by his faithful horse, who delivered his master safely, then promptly fell dead from exertion in front of the campfire. Webb said that as a youngster, he read the story over and over again and cried every time as if it were the first. He liked books that evoked emotion, and hoped that he, too, could develop this gift. He had deep feelings about writing even as a boy: "I loved words," he would later say, "their music, their meaning, their magic, the rythm [sic] they take when put together in a certain order, and their impact on the human mind and on human lives."[64]

Words, and the books containing them, had certainly made an impact on the life and mind of young Walter Webb, and he sought to pass this on to others, but he realized that he needed more education to do so. After setting some sort of a record by teaching three schools in one year, he saved enough money to return to Ranger for the 1907–08 school term, again under J. E. Temple Peters, who had become Webb's good friend, and who was now assisted by Nels Rosenquest, a new teacher from the University of Texas. This turned out to be a very good year for the young man, something like a vacation from the hard work of farm life. He studied—particularly mathematics—for he had decided that, "if I could keep up in mathematics I could skip all the other subjects." This is exactly what he did, but he also played. For the first time, he enjoyed the companionship and spirit of youth as he developed friendships with young men and women his own age. Among his friends were Homer Danley, a "big, loose-jointed boy" and the best baseball pitcher in the gang, and his deskmate, a boy by the name of Dowdy. Appropriately, the two were nicknamed "Bull Danley" and "Cow Dowdy." Dick Bruce played third base and Evan Barnes first, with Walter manning second somewhat inadequately.[65]

Never much of an athlete, Webb's inclinations were toward the literary. At his urging the gang broke into the schoolhouse one night to hold a debate. The result of this harmless bit of vandalism was the organization of the Ranger Debating Society. Although Webb was the founder, he claimed that he did not win a single debate within the society. Peters proved to be the most talented and the most popular debater in the whole group. Originally established as a secret society, limited only to "the men," the girls' curiosity and persuasiveness won out, and as Webb recalled, "with secret delight, we let them in." The high point of the organization's history occurred when the Ranger team was challenged to debate another school and Webb and a boy called "T-Bone" Long were

chosen to represent them. The Ranger debaters returned victor-
ious; but the real crowning event of the year for Webb came in the
spring when he went to Eastland and passed his examination for a
first-grade teaching certificate. Soon thereafter he was elected to
teach at Merriman, one of the best schools in the county and the
same school where his father had once presided.[66]

At Merriman, much to his father's disgust, he held out for the
tremendous salary of $75 a month. He was unaware that his school,
situated on a knoll approximately 3,000 feet from a Baptist Church
and cemetery, rested upon a deposit of oil worth millions of dollars.
The young man relished the rise in prestige that accompanied his
role as a small-town teacher. As he said, "I was wearing good
clothes and moving in the highest circles of local society." He had
indeed "gone to the top in several respects." He enjoyed teaching,
having the time to read, and he particularly enjoyed making the
acquaintance of a pretty dark-haired girl named Esther Bailey.
There are no documents to determine the extent of their relationship, but Webb's sister, Ima Wright, recalled that he had quite a
crush on her. He also found himself the object of still another young
lady's attention—a school teacher by the name of Susie Milam.
Susie and her friend, Lizzie Manchin, had boarded with the Webb
family on two different occasions. He was never romantically
interested in Susie, a tall, rather homely girl with prominent teeth,
although she would have preferred it otherwise. Since Webb's
friend, Paul Crowley, courted Lizzie, Susie and Walter occasionally accompanied them on outings.[67]

They continued their friendship and correspondence while she
attended the Normal school for girls at what became Mary Hardin-
Baylor in Belton, and he attended the University of Texas. In 1912,
however, after meeting his bride to be, Webb asked Paul to explain
the situation to "his Western girl" and help him sever relations.
Paul agreed to pass the word through Lizzie that Webb had "a
little girl up there that he is dead in love with."[68] In spite of female
involvements, the young teacher's biggest worry seemed to be the
fact that teaching occupied so few hours. He considered this "an
affair of conscience"—as a farm boy he was accustomed to working
a twelve-hour day. To Webb, "there seemed to be something
immoral about quitting at four o'clock."[69]

As Webb took this step from farm boy to schoolteacher, from
populist poverty to Smalltown, U.S.A., he brought with him the

trappings of his environment. Although he would earn fame as a cosmopolitan historian, he remained, in many respects, a turn-of-the-century "gossamer goose," symbolic of a generation of farm boys who participated in the American exodus to an expanding urban society. Webb's personal experience in mobility possibly provided the inherent understanding that he later revealed in *The Great Frontier*, wherein he expanded the agrarian perspective exhibited by Frederick Jackson Turner. Turner did not stress the fact that the lure of the frontier could be replaced by other forms of abundance, even before the bounty of soil fertility exhausted itself in the late 1800s. Webb, on the other hand, realized that industrial growth began to offer opportunities far greater than that of the isolated farming community. The amenities of mechanization, movies, cars, and radios, eventually pulled American people to urban centers. Webb himself had felt the tug, and later vividly explained this phenomenon and its result in *The Great Frontier* by quoting the grandfather from John Steinbeck's *The Red Pony:* "No, no place to go, Jody. Every place is taken. But that's not the worst—no not the worst. Westering has died out of the people. Westering isn't a hunger anymore. It's all done."[70]

For Webb, too, Westering was becoming a thing of the past. He might have remained a small-town schoolteacher had it not been for another fateful letter from his benefactor—a letter that set him back on a course with destiny. Webb remembered the day well, January 9, 1909. It was in the dead of winter and the cold winds were blowing so gustily that "pebbles from the playing fields rattled like buckshot against the side of the school building." He walked to the mailbox and found a bulky letter from William E. Hinds, asking him of his plans for the future. "Perhaps I can help you . . ." Hinds wrote, "after all the best thing in life is to help someone if we can. One would count it a great thing (to remember) if they had helped someone, that had afterwards become famous or great." He also inquired about his teaching, his students, and as an afterthought asked Webb if he had considered going to college. Toward the end of the month, Hinds wrote again requesting more information in reference to his college plans, specifics regarding expense, and urging him to practice his writing. The implications of Hinds' letters set the young man's mind to reeling. Only the sons of doctors and lawyers or other prosperous people went to college. This must be destiny, he thought. He began to place his life in perspective, and realized that what he was doing was merely a means to an end.[71]

Hinds' letter in the winter of 1909 marked the beginning of a financial arrangement that provided the avenue by which Webb obtained a college education. He was to use his savings to enroll and get started at the University of Texas. When he exhausted his funds, his benefactor would provide monthly financial assistance to a limit of $500, whereupon the boy would drop out of school and earn money to repay the debt, then reenter under the same arrangement. With the prospect of a college education in sight, Webb conserved his money that last semester at Merriman, practiced his writing, and with difficulty, as he said, restrained himself "from making a bid for the girl I had a very hard time forgetting." When he looked back on his life in later years, he saw himself during this period as a gyroscope that wobbles, spins, and deviates, but always returns to a course established by heredity and environment; and, he could have added, the steady direction of a friend.[72]

3

THE MAKING OF A HISTORIAN:
THE UNIVERSITY OF TEXAS AT AUSTIN

*If Texas like Pompei, should be buried under a blanket of ashes, and
all the written records of its civilization should be lost, the scholars who
unearthed the remains two thousand years later would . . . in time
come to the conclusion that Texas culture revolved around something
called a school. They would reach this conclusion because they would
find a school building in every community from the smallest to the
largest.*

W. P. Webb, "Cultural Resources of Texas"

By the time Webb began his college years the emphasis on
education in Texas had long been an historic tradition. The lack of
such opportunity had been considered important enough to serve as
one of the prime grievances listed by early Texas colonists for
proclaiming independence from Mexico. Between the years 1836
and 1916, according to former University of Texas Chancellor
Harry Huntt Ransom, "Texas was wealthier in educational imagination than during contemporary times." This was the period of
the big push for educational development in the state, but these
early visionaries had little more to support them than determination. Then came opportunity in the form of black gold when lands
set aside for school endowments were found to rest atop major oil
fields. Thus physical resources of the state provided means for
cultivation of "resources of the mind." When students reached
college age, many of the more fortunate journeyed off to the citadel
of higher learning in that state, the University of Texas at Austin.[1]

Through the beneficence of his friend in New York, Webb was
able to join this select group and in the fall of 1909, with $200 he
had saved, he boarded the train for the sleepy capital of Austin,
Texas. The train pulled into the station at five o'clock on a clear
September morning. The city lights were dimming with the

dawn and an elderly Negro peddled papers at the depot. Another, called Pindar, hauled away the trunks of incoming passengers. With some impatience the young man waited at the station until the town began to stir. He ate breakfast, then took the streetcar north to Twenty-second Street. At this stop he got off and walked west to the Cliff Caldwell home, where he would be boarding along with other Stephens County boys, among them Nels Rosenquest who had returned to the University from his teaching slot at Ranger, and Webb's friend, Paul Crowley. Their landlord, C. M. Caldwell, originally from Breckenridge, was completing his law degree. He and Breck Walker would eventually develop the large oil field in the area of his old hometown.[2]

Like other students from the heart of Texas they had come to attend their state's major institution of higher education. In 1909 the University of Texas was still provincial in orientation. Founded in 1883, for years the first male students wore Stetsons and carried revolvers to class. When Webb arrived, it had been civilized to some extent. He plunged into academic life only scantily equipped: three credits in English, four in history, one half a credit in civics, and three and a half credits in algebra and plane geometry. Because of his age and background, the registrar had agreed to his admission on individual approval. It was here that this lack of early schooling and the many grades skipped began to tell.[3]

During these university years, Webb continued his correspondence with Hinds, who received samples of his protégé's work and progress reports. To the man's credit, he never criticized him for either, always sending words of encouragement and a check when needed. Hinds' own letters, full of news of the New York scene—an invitation to dine at the White House, or a fantastic electric illumination show—provided a vicarious glimpse of a world beyond the provincial bounds of Texas. Even before Webb's departure for Austin, Hinds had encouraged the young man to send him essays for comment and criticism. A postcard mailed in April 1909, and received while Webb was teaching in Merriman acknowledged receipt of a composition entitled "Nature," saying, "Yours, with 'Nature' received; think it very good, but will make some notes in the margin; as you wish—Will return it soon." This fortuitous relationship continued until Hinds' death in 1912. Webb always regretted that he had never met the man personally and on one occasion after making some extra money, suggested to Hinds that he pay him a visit. However, his benefactor advised him to save his money for the next school term.[4]

In spite of the mediocre grades that Webb earned during his college years, Hinds undoubtedly recognized his protégé's promise, for Webb's undergraduate papers illustrate clearly the stage of his mental development, his personal attitudes, and the promise of greatness. Many of the English themes, written between 1909 and 1911, are autobiographical in nature. One, entitled "The Chain" is a preliminary attempt at recounting the Hinds' story. Another, "My Object in Studying English Three" elucidated Webb's desire to be a writer. In this course, he hoped not only to learn letter writing, but claimed to be taking it "for the enjoyment which composition work affords me." During his freshman and sophomore years when he still aspired to become a writer, he admitted that he "went in heavy for English with results that were not entirely satisfactory either to me or to the Department." To Webb, "The relationship between a split infinitive and a hanging participle was a mystery. I did learn that either one, taken by itself, was disastrous." His English instructors, such as Clyde Hill of Dallas, made him "painfully conscious" of the existence of such grammatical technicalities. Mr. Hill read Webb's first theme in front of the class "as an example of good writing and bad punctuation." In rebellion, the young man soon came to believe that if you knew how to write, the punctuation didn't matter. With this rather flip attitude, he exhausted his instructor's patience by writing a theme on choosing a profession, in which he characterized the "doctor a quack," "the teacher a fraud," and "the lawyer a shark." The instructor berated him for his lack of sincerity, saying, "It is a pity you do not try always to be sincere when discussing a serious subject. . . . Your work has some promise. What you need to fulfill this is sincerity, a rigid excision of all tendency to puns, and a strong desire to express the truth, brilliant or homely."[5]

Webb took this criticism to heart, and in later years propounded the same philosophy but never could reconcile the idea that punctuation was more important than content. Other English professors were not so kind, nor did they all offer criticism of a constructive nature. A paper entitled "An Adventure," written for English 1.11 early in 1909, bore the terse notation "Hardly Satisfactory."[6]

Responses such as this must have been disappointing in light of

Webb's professed desires to become the member of the staff "of a high class magazine," or a "traveling newspaper correspondent."[7] His professors obviously wanted him to write in the exaggerated romantic style which deemed that the more flowery the phrase, the more beautiful the writing. Above all, the phrase must be punctuated correctly. When Webb tried to adhere to this style, the results—at least when viewed from a contemporary perspective —were less than satisfactory. An essay entitled "The Old Home-stead," for example, became a highly sentimentalized version of farm life in Stephens County. In order to write a romantic description of what was in actuality a drab and dirty existence replete with squealing pigs, Webb invoked a mist of southern words that clouded the backbreaking chores and added Grecian columns to the rude plank house that he had helped his father build. The delightful sound of "the jangle of cowbells" and the joy of chasing "red calves over the dewey grass" was so incongruous with reality that he probably wrote with tongue in cheek, having become irritated with the whole romantic literary concept. In spite of the embellishments, the descriptions of his family are revealing. He depicted the family gathered for dinner with his mother at the head of the table and his father sitting opposite him, with "features a little stern. He is not quite satisfied with crop conditions this year, but he never is." Then Webb waxed more eloquent as he described his little sister as "The dark-eyed, dark-haired, fair-cheeked girl of six autumns, who sits at my side, [and who] is the sunshine, idol, and ruler of the home."[8]

Exercises showing the greatest talent and most favorable reception were those written on subjects about which he had firsthand knowledge. Brief compositions on topics such as "The First Rabbit Hunt," "The Rattlesnake," "The Growth of a Cotton Boll," and "A Boy's Education," earned the instructor's marginal comment of "Well done." Considering the D's made in English courses, these were apparently in the minority. He had written "The Old Homestead" essay as a freshman. By the time he was a sophomore, his patience with teaching methodology in this department was growing thin.[9]

In a paper entitled "The Freshman's Attitude Towards English 1," he openly charged his professors with inundating students in grammatical technicalities to the extent that they drowned "all spontaneity." This clear-cut and blunt presentation endeavored to enlighten the instructor as to the sad state of affairs within the department as Webb saw it. He classified the students into groups: those who had no talent for the subject; those who had not had adequate preparation in the high schools, even though they liked the work; and the careless student who desired only a pass. It is clear in which category Webb placed himself. He then attributed the poor attitudes of the students to the professor's penchant for what he termed, "splitting hairs as it were, instead of teaching what the Freshman considers better and more essential things," eventually creating a view of English as something "almost hideous." In sum, there was "too little consideration to the subject matter," and "too much attention to technique." Ironically, his professor noted that this paper was obviously sincere, but that it contained a surprising number of grammatical errors—as if to illustrate Webb's point.[10]

His attitudes did not change with age. In 1915, while teaching in Cuero, he heard through his fiancée, Jane Oliphant, that Stark Young, the promising young agrarian, was leaving the department for greener pastures. Webb's response was characteristic: "Stark Young is to be congratulated; the University is to be pitied; the dead English department—the Calloway School—is once more supreme and free." In his autobiography, written in middle age, he expressed the same sentiment saying: "Words and the stuff you make of them antedate grammar, and all the rules taught so religiously in college."[11]

Webb exhibited this same independence of mind regarding classical poetry, claiming that he felt that other forms of verse were also worthy of study. He was obviously not too impressed with the great bards, and his professor was not overly impressed with Webb's paper, commenting: "The interest of this theme almost justifies the length—when seventy-five other themes are to be read." After studying English for three years, Webb became convinced that he could not write.[12] Papers written for other courses proved this to be an incorrect assumption, however. "Record of Stephens County in the University of Texas" is a good example as it was written with knowledge and personal interest. In this paper his talent for writing with directness and clarity of expression is not shackled by linguistics or romantic formalism. Other papers included essays on educational psychology, for Webb at this point was thinking of preparation for continuance of his teaching career in the public schools.[13]

During his first two years at the university, Webb lacked the driving force necessary for real success. He had no absorbing purpose and as he explained, "rather drifted than steered." He seemed unable to follow the structured programs issued by his professors. Instead he read at random, pursuing a rather haphazard course of learning and hoping that something would happen to create order and purpose in his life. This was to be a characteristic trait for Webb—this inability to discipline himself according to a stipulated pattern; rather he tended to go off on tangents of his own creation. As he later admitted, it was a trait that brought him "rich prizes and deep humiliations."[14]

By his sophomore year he had found a professor who became instrumental in shaping his historical thinking, a flamboyant and controversial individual by the name of Lindley Miller Keasbey. In 1910, when Webb first became acquainted with Keasbey, he had just been made chairman of the newly created department of institutional history. Webb considered him a great teacher and remembered him as:

> "a striking figure with a tawny complexion and tawny hair set on a fine head. Every feature of his face was expressive, and especially his eyes which sparkled and changed with every thought he expressed." His class of two or three hundred students fell quiet when he entered, dressed to a spiffy extravagance, and "for exactly thirty-five minutes he would expound his philosophy of history, economics, and life, showing how our institutions originated and evolved, and doing it in such a logical manner that one could almost repeat the lecture days after. He was supposed to hold the class an hour, but never did so to the despair of the administrative offices who wanted regularity. There was nothing regular or conventional about the man, and he refused to yield to petty rules made for petty faculty members."[15]

More than likely, the man's personality as well as his ideas appealed to Webb, who was somewhat unorthodox himself. Keasbey, the son of a cultured and wealthy family in New Jersey and an honor graduate of Harvard and Columbia, seemed destined to butt heads with administrators who did not share his socialistic views derived from postdoctoral work in Germany. As a personal friend of Woodrow Wilson, he had been asked to Bryn Mawr as Wilson's replacement. Then in 1905, Keasbey took a professorship in political science at the University of Texas.[16]

Prior to Webb's acquaintance with Keasbey and as early as 1908, the man's views were creating dissension. Reports reached the regents that Keasbey dispensed with the practical economics of money and banking for idealistic topics reeking of socialism. At this point, he was granted a reprieve, possibly because he was so popular. "All the students admire him," President David Houston admitted, and "He gets a great deal of work out of them, stimulating them to much reading." Moves were also underway to separate the departments of sociology, social science, and economics, and when a new man, Alvin Johnson, arrived to take over as head of the department of political science, disgruntled administrators found a means of solving 'he problem temporarily by creating an anomalous department called institutional history and placing Keasbey in charge of it. Here for the first time, Keasbey could cross disciplines at will and teach his special amalgam of sociology, history, economics, geography, and anthropology.[17]

Even at this point, Keasbey's career was in decline. He had been dismissed at Bryn Mawr for his political beliefs, and would suffer the same fate at the University of Texas. During the prewar years he and Woodrow Wilson had consulted on many matters. According to Keasbey's wife, they had been friends for twenty years and both agreed that the United States should not become involved in the European war. After Wilson was elected president, he changed his views, but Keasbey remained firmly pacifist. Many of the friends he had been associating with were called to Washington to take responsible positions with the Wilson Administration: David Houston, formerly president of the university, left to become Wilson's Secretary of Agriculture, and later Secretary of the Treasury, while another friend and former university president, Sidney Mezes, became an advisor at Versailles. Others, too, received appointments. Thomas Watt Gregory became Attorney General, and Colonel E. M. House as friend and advisor influenced the president's thinking. "It hurt me," Mrs. Keasbey admitted, "to see all of my personal friends going on to Washington and my husband ignored and left behind."[18]

In 1917 Keasbey became actively involved in the peace movement and left Austin to associate with such known socialists as Norman Thomas. When news of his actions filtered back to the capital, the words "traitor" and "treason" were bandied about. This time there was no hiding place and Keasbey was dismissed. Apparently he never taught again, but in ill health retired to Arizona where he raised dogs. Dr. Mezes and his wife joined them there after his service with Wilson.[19]

After Webb published *The Great Plains* in 1931, he wrote to Keasbey expressing his appreciation for his teachings. In reply, Keasbey commended Webb on a good book, but stated that he had overestimated his contribution to him. Keasbey revealed, too, that he now believed the methodology he had espoused during Webb's days as a student to be inadequate, and perhaps subconsciously he insulted the approach that Webb used in *The Great Plains*. As he explained to his former student, he had answered only the easiest questions, "to wit: When, Where, and How. The harder questions are Why and Wherefore; the hardest questions are Whence and Whither. . . . The further way towards Whence and Whither starts from Relativity and the Quantum Theory and extends into the Fourth Dimension." In this same letter Keasbey concluded with a more direct slam, saying:

> Anyone with any sense can see at once that the environment is essentially passive and could not possibly act as anything further than an efficient cause of something already formed or in the process of forming. In our haste we are so apt (historians especially) of taking *post hoc* for *propter hoc*. That was my error, which I passed on to so many students.[20]

Despite the obvious divergence in viewpoints that had developed as Keasbey grew older, when he first arrived at the University of Texas, his intellect and ideas were tremendously exciting, particularly for Walter Prescott Webb, who saw a special relevance in them. From Keasbey, Webb claimed he began to understand the changes wrought as people adjusted themselves to their environment, a concept of geographic environmentalism perhaps gleaned from the Italian economist, Achille Loria, whose works Keasbey translated. Webb had credited Keasbey with giving him an understanding of "the relationship between an environment and the civilization resting upon it." From this man, Webb learned a methodology or approach, a "rational theme" and a "logical sequence of thought." As he explained in his presidential address before the American Historical Association in 1958, "It was Keasbey who taught me, and many others, to begin with the geology or geography, and build upon this foundation the super-structure of the flora, fauna, and anthropology, arriving at last at the modern civilization growing out of this foundation."[21] This is, of course, the format that he used so effectively in *The Great Plains,* but it is also obvious in papers written as an undergraduate for Keasbey and others.

These ideas of geographic orientation made sense to a young man whose existence had depended upon his environment and the whims of nature; however, Webb recalled that his first "real awakening" to the importance of physical geography had occurred much earlier. It had in fact resulted from his introduction to a text by W. E. Davis entitled *Physical Geography,* a red clothbound book that he used in his first teaching assignment at a country school. This book, according to Webb, "was something that made sense from the first, something I had seen when hunting horses in the early morning."[22] Thus Keasbey's approach supported the tack that Webb's mind was already taking. His professor's ideas were not antithetical, but were instead supportive to his own inherent beliefs, experiences, and developing mentality. Webb's mature mind would prove to be an interesting combination of the pragmatic and the conceptual, the latter being obvious less frequently, but with brilliance when it occurred.

Webb also appreciated what he called the "logic" of geographic determinism and attributed critics' charges of rank materialism and Marxian implications to frustration for not having at their disposal an equally orderly explanation for the drama of an unfolding culture based solidly on the ground. In 1960, speaking to the Association of American Geographers in Dallas, he acknowledged the kinship of Keasbey's (and his) approach to Darwinism. He traced the genesis of the geographic approach to the Englishman, James Button, who published his *Theory of the Earth* in 1795. Button was the man, Webb said, "who first perceived that the physical forces that formed the layers of the earth are the same forces operating today on the surface." He noted further that Button's ideas predicated those of Darwin by seventy-five years. Therefore Webb saw the "key" or method that Keasbey had provided him as having been generated by, or at least closely related to, the evolutionary theories that came to be labeled as Darwinism.[23]

Some of his undergraduate essays exemplify this influence, as in a 1914 exercise for Institutional History 107. In Darwinian overtones Webb summarized: "In conclusion we have man the product of heredity and variability operating through adaptation and selection in connection with environment to bring about the improved structure of man." In a similar vein, he expressed what he termed "The Theory of Imagination" as it pertained to the development of creative synthesis; "On one side," he stated, "is environment, giving sensation, perception, and imagery, the objective materials of creative imagination. On the other side is heredity, self, emotion, giving the projective force. . . . ." These factors combined, according to Webb's analysis, determined the nature of individual creations. Citing an example, Webb said, "Columbus perhaps conceived the idea of a new route to India in a moment, but his unconscious preparation had been in progress all his life, at Genoa by the sea, and later in his capacity as a mapmaker."[24]

The parallelism is obvious. In an uncanny manner, Webb might have been explaining his own development as a historian. Although he conceived of the Great Plains concept in a flash of insight, his unconscious preparation through the influences of heredity and environment had been in progress all his life; first on the arid edge of the frontier and later in his capacity as student, teacher, and historian.

It is understandable that some of the most promising of Webb's undergraduate papers are either those written for Keasbey or those that in some way reflect his influence. It was Keasbey who had provided Webb with the means to utilize that which he had experienced or was in the process of assimilating. An essay for political science entitled "Geographic Features as A Factor in the United States of America," illustrated the Keasbey approach and expressed Webb's ideas about causative effects of environment that strongly predicated the Great Plains concept to come. In this paper he indicated the influence of physical features on European states, then applied the principles discovered there to the United States of America. Webb introduced his ideas saying, "The process of crystallization about geographic unities is not so well marked in

America, as in Europe and is not yet complete. But geographic features have played a wonderful part in its history from long before the discovery of the continent to the present time." In the remaining pages of this paper Webb traced some of these influences, relying heavily on Ellen Churchill Semple's *American History and Its Geographic Conditions*. In summation, he stated:

> Having traced the development of the United States from the Atlantic to the Pacific, and having seen it complete its geographic unity, we may note some interesting geographic features. First, the expansion was along lines of latitude, east to west, and not along lines of longitude north and south. Climate, acted as a barrier in both directions.[25]

Earlier in the paper he had illustrated how the acquisition of Texas had completed the geographic unity of the United States, but concluded by making the grandiose suggestion that the northern part of Mexico should be acquired to fulfill the geographic unity more perfectly! (As unusual as it may sound today, this idea was being bandied about the United States Senate at the same time.) It is noteworthy that this early paper gave a glimpse of Webb's tendency to telescope or cover the panoramic view at the expense of factual support. He was chided for this by his professor and suffered the same criticism later, as a well-known historian.[26] This, too, was the result of Keasbey's penchant for the global view; he introduced his protégé to the broad canvas and a method of painting the past with bold strokes.

A paper entitled "The Collegiate-Communal System Versus the Republican-Patriarchal System in the History of Medieval Europe" perhaps best illustrated the general thesis and pattern of investigation that Webb used in *The Great Plains*—namely that environment determined the characteristics of civilizations. As examples, in this essay he used two environments separated by an imaginary line which ran through the Alps connecting the Pyrenees and the Balkans. The territory to the north he labelled "Collegiate-Communal" and the area to the south, "Republican-Patriarchal." He depicted arrogance and wastefulness as characteristics of the northern sector and conservative humbleness as characteristic of the south. His next step was to investigate the differences or contrasts between the two systems and apply them to historical fact, in much the same manner as he would contrast the humid environment of the American woodlands to the aridity of the plains fifteen years later.[27]

Another paper written for political science, yet reflecting his mentor's interest in the geographic and economic bases for the development of institutions, was an essay entitled "Some Influences Determining the Political Theory of the American Revolution." To start with, Webb clarified his views by stating that he considered geographic and religious forces of enough importance to occupy separate headings, and proceeded to summarize the impact of physical geography on institutions saying: "The geographical *environment* of America *made for individualism* and freedom of action. The vast *natural resources made the people economically independent.*"[28] This was evidently a significant grain of insight since he was to use it in expanded form as an integral facet of the Great Frontier concept. Therein he expressed his contention that America was blessed with traits such as individualism as a result of frontier abundance; then with the demise of the frontier in the form of free land, he showed how these traits suffered and the individual became the pawn of corporativeness. "The individual will tend to lose his identity in a growing corporate life," Webb predicted in *The Great Frontier*, and earlier in the book "Corporateness is now the primary fact and the dominant force in modern life, and whatever men are to have of individualism they must come at by making terms with a corporate world and not a frontier one."[29]

A common denominator of nearly all of Webb's early papers is that they demonstrate a fertile mind in the process of maturation, a mind already imbued with seeds of concepts and ideas that were to make a strong impact on the field of American history. That an undergraduate had reached such an advanced stage along the path to mental maturity may appear unusual, but Webb was not a typical undergraduate. He had a late start academically, being twenty-one when he started work on his Bachelor of Arts degree; he had read extensively; and he had been a teacher. These factors, in spite of limited formal schooling, combined to give him more maturity and most probably, more preconceived ideas than younger students.

One such idea, expressed in an essay for Institutional History, entitled "The Future of the American Negro," presented a completely depressing view of the condition and plight of this race in the United States. According to Webb's interpretation, the Negro's value as a citizen "is a minus quality"; furthermore, "As a political creature, then, the negro [sic] seems to be a failure." Webb continued: "He cannot hope to equal the white man, and should not strive for those fields of activity in which he suffers so serious a handicap, the negro [sic] must find his place and realize that he is a distinct, separate, and inferior caste, and that he will be dominated by the white until he is in turn able to dominate—which will never be."[30]

Judged by today's standards, these phrases ring of racial prejudice, yet his opinion was not so derogatory as dismal. He simply believed that Blacks did not have the opportunity to elevate themselves in white society. In the 1900s this view was shared by many. Webb was not only reflecting his family heritage, which upheld traditions of the old South, but also exhibited the general disenchantment and social temper of a nation recovering from the ravages of Reconstruction and adjusting to the influx of immigration and the rise of industrialism.

By the 1890s, even reformers began to have more empathy for the southern situation. The genteel classes felt dispossessed by the economic industrialist whose new wealth gave him the power that old families once had wielded. The middle classes, too, exhibited disillusionment. They found their positions threatened by inexpensive immigrant labor and witnessed the formation of new coalitions under political bosses who began to destroy their power structure. Henry James, observing the various nationalities strolling on the Boston Common, commented bitterly, "the people before me were gross aliens to a man, and they were in serene and triumphant possession." With the spread of such attitudes, racial stereotyping began to include immigrant groups as well as Negroes. Thus by the turn of the century, according to Kenneth M. Stampp, "xenophobia had become almost a national disease."[31] Social Darwinism was in vogue, nationalism was on the rise, and attempts were made to heal sectional strife. And finally, sociologists and anthropologists had developed what they believed to be convincing evidence that Negroes were inferior to Whites intellectually. In 1916, not long after Webb wrote his paper on the future of the American Negro, anthropologist Madison Grant published *The Passing of the Great Race.* Grant, exemplifying the dominant theory of many social scientists at that time, proclaimed, "there appeared in the last century a wave of sentimentalism which at that time took up the cause of the negro, and in so doing apparently destroyed, to a large extent, pride and consciousness of race in the North. . . ." Furthermore, according to Grant's analysis, immigration and the Civil War destroyed what he termed "a distinct" and "splendid type" of North American by eliminating "the best breeding stock on both sides."[32] This then was the national temper at the time Webb was an undergraduate and considering the future of the American Negro.

In Texas, as in other parts of the South, time would, in many respects, stand still, and Webb was very much a product of his cultural milieu. As late as the 1960s, for example, it was not uncommon to see signs reading "Nigger, don't let the sun set on your head in X-ville," or to see a billboard in Greenville, Texas, reading "Blackest Land and Whitest People." The depression era called attention to the deprived status of the poor white, as well as the American Negro, and Hitler's xenophobia during World War II caused America to look at herself with a more critical eye. Changes in the social climate, such as these, helped to accelerate the civil rights movement, resulting in the legislation of the 1950s and 1960s. The University of Texas, however, remained as one of the last bastions of racism, and did not integrate until ordered to do so in 1950. This initial attempt, even then, was unsuccessful.[33]

Long before this time, Webb's personal attitudes had reflected a transition, and characteristically he tried to do something about it. To the consternation of an assistant, for example, he proposed the integration of the Texas State Historical Association when it was not politically feasible. Furthermore, he went into the state of Mississippi and told the citizens of Oxford that "the state was plain stupid if it permitted its historic adherence to racial segregation to bar its material progress." He felt that the racial problem could be solved quite simply by allowing the Blacks to grow rich along with everyone else. His associate, Joe B. Frantz, recalled that "he almost got run out of the state for his solution."[34]

As Webb's close friend, E. C. Barksdale, explained, "Webb and [J. Frank] Dobie were products of their bringing-up." If Webb had a really strong prejudice, it was more than likely pointed in another direction; namely, that "subconsciously he still had the Alamo-Texas Ranger chauvinistic myth deeply engraved."[35]

In the southern states racial attitudes were intensified and, in Texas, included the Mexican and Indian people. An English composition written by Webb and titled "Cheeko" portrayed the main character as a brown-faced little boy of Mexican-Indian descent, hampered by heritage and breeding, a characterization similar to those Webb would express twenty years later in *The Great Plains* and *The Texas Rangers*. He wondered what the future would hold for Cheeko: "With the blood of the Indian and of the Mexican in his veins, and the environment of the American Caucasian, he is a mongrel indeed. From one ancestor he inherits cunning, from the other treachery, and from his environment he will acquire knowledge which will enable him to use both cunning and treachery in the most crafty and effective way."[36] Phrases with a similar ring in *The Great Plains* and *The Texas Rangers*—"there is a cruel streak in the Mexican nature, or so the history of Texas would lead one to believe"; and the blood of the Pueblo Indian, "when compared with that of the Plains Indians, was as ditch water"—evoked charges that Webb used racial explanations of American history.[37] In later years, Webb regretted that he would not have time to revise the book for that reason. Prior to his death he began working on subjects related to the Rangers once again.[38]

In sum, his undergraduate papers reflect a mind more mature than most, one marked by strong conviction; one that had been shaped not only by the process of living, but also by a brilliant teacher, Keasbey, as well as through association with others such as Eugene C. Barker, Frederick Duncalf, and Charles Ramsdell. From the available documentation of these early years, the portrait of Webb that emerges is that of a young man of strong mind and independent thought, searching for academic support for his own observations and experiences, and finding in Keasbey's direction the key to create cohesion and meaning out of the vagaries floating half-formed in his mind. The conclusion one reaches after reading these early papers is that they predicated to such an amazing extent the concepts for which he would later become famous. They stand as evidence that Webb's mind was not particularly malleable, that he had already formed, or was in the process of formulating, specific ideas relating to his future profession as historian and teacher. His sad experience with the English department, which doused his hopes for a literary career per se, was in reality fortuitous. Because of it, he turned to institutional history for relevance in learning, and in so doing, found a tool that stood him in good stead. Still imbued with a latent desire to write, but equipped now with ideas of his own and a key to the interpretation of the evolution of cultures and the land from whence he came, he was better prepared to take his rightful place in the world. Never, of course, would he shed his provincial bounds totally, and eventually he wisely quit trying. It is doubtful, too, that he was ever able to rid himself of all the prejudices so much a part of his heritage, but his outlook would broaden; he would champion equality and the rights of the individual; and the parameters of his scholarly perspective would eventually transcend his regional orientation to become global in scope.

4

MOTIVATION AND INSPIRATION:
JANE AND THE ORIGINAL IDEA

*By sheer force woman can make man do nothing, but by her influence
she may inspire him to heaven or drag him to hell. I understand
perfectly all the things man does for the woman he loves. . . .*

W. P. Webb to Jane Oliphant
September 28, 1914

*I . . . was off on the first lap of the great adventure, to write the history
of the oldest institution of its kind in the world. The story led west, to
the frontier, to vicarious adventure of the body, and to real adventure
of the mind. Though I was not aware of it then, I had found my field.*

W. P. Webb, "History As High Adventure"

By dwelling on academics, the illusion may have been created
that Webb's life was all work and no play. While this is not the case,
his social activities were restricted by the limitations of his pocket-
book. During his sophomore year, he engaged in some of the usual
college tomfoolery but never to the extent that most students did,
not only because of his financial situation, but because he, in fact,
avoided it. Webb was older than most college freshmen and felt
that he never had the time to waste on social events. He did have a
deep-felt obligation to get a college degree and make a success of
himself. He also had family responsibilities to meet as he provided
for a portion of his sister Ima's schooling expenses. Although
Webb interrupted his schooling periodically to replenish his
finances and repay debts, he was able to spend his freshman and
sophomore years in continuous residence.[1]

In spite of a bout with typhoid fever in the summer of 1910, he
recovered in time to return to the university and participate in an
infamous class fight during which a freshman shot and killed a
sophomore, resulting in passage of the law prohibiting hazing. He

51

also took part in the less tragic but considerably more humorous event that occurred at the Hancock Opera House where Griffiths' Hypnotic Show was appearing. A group of about 200 students, Webb included, decided to test the authenticity of the show and therefore purchased a half dozen eggs which they fired at the hypnotized stooges on stage, who as Webb recalled, "falapped [sic] to their feet with the motion of a landed fish." This melee closed the show, but the event received some unfavorable publicity from a local editor whose son had the misfortune to be one of the stooges.[2]

At the end of his sophomore year, Webb owed his benefactor about $500. According to their arrangement, Webb cast about for a job in order to repay him and with the assistance of his friend, Paul Crowley, obtained a position at Bush Knob School in Throckmorton County for $90 a month. Nora Price, the aunt of future University of Texas President Homer Price Rainey, became his assistant. Throckmorton County lay to the west of Stephens County and, as Webb noted, "was still in the pioneer stage." The farmers had just moved in; the land was productive; and the majority of the populace still lived on outlying farms and ranches, some of which were being divided. Occasionally, a good crop the first or second year enabled the owner to pay for his land very quickly. Webb observed that ranching people were the "aristocrats" of this rural society, and during a Christmas visit with the E. Davis family on the Hash Knife Ranch, he made many observations that were useful in writing *The Great Plains*. On the long ride across the Davis spread, he "counted the carcasses of thirty-five cattle that had died from cold and starvation through the winter."[3]

After the school term ended, Webb signed a contract to become a salesman of stereoscopic slides in the coal-mining district around Strawn and Thurber. This turned out to be a successful job and took him over a wide sector of West Texas and up into the fertile cotton country surrounding Ada, Oklahoma. Webb boarded in Thurber, a coal-mining town organized by the unions in 1900, and owned and operated lock, stock, and barrel, from churches to saloons, by the Texas and Pacific Railroad. Here he received some of the insight that enabled him to write in *The Great Plains;* "There can be no question that the railroads transformed American life." He noted, too, that "Instead of the roads going to the towns, as they had done in the East, the towns came to the roads."[4] He had a room in the home of a family of Seventh Day Adventists on a typically dusty, unpaved street with the deceptively elegant name of Park Row. To Webb, the sociological aspects of this town of various nationalities and 7,000 people were unique. Webb recalled that "it was the most interesting place I have intimately known, and in many ways the most tragic." Geographically, too, the town was somewhat anomalous. The major portion of it lay in Erath County, where liquor was prohibited by law, but the Snake Saloon—which Webb felt was surely "one of the largest in the world"—was located conveniently just over the line in Palo Pinto County, which was wet. While Webb resided there, the town was in its heyday and vibrant with living. Eventually oil supplanted coal; the miners struck; and hard times took their toll in Thurber.[5]

Some time later while waiting for a train in Denison, Webb met his former landlord. The man walked in and asked for money to tide him over until he could get a job. As a Seventh Day Adventist, he did not believe in working on Saturdays; the miners were on strike; and his children were going hungry. Webb gave him the money and a lecture to boot:

"Geiger," he said, "Your family is starving. You are a miner. The mines work two days a week now, and one day is Saturday. You won't work on Saturday. I believe that a man's first duty is to provide for his family, and I would do it if I had to work Saturday, Sunday, and every other day of the week."

The man swallowed a time or two, and with tears in his eyes, he said: "I can't go against my religious convictions."[6]

Webb had difficulty comprehending this brand of religion, but he did understand the process occurring in Thurber. With the mines no longer profitable, the railroad withdrew financial support, leaving only iron tracks to guide one through the dirt and mesquite trees. A lonely gas pump marked the spot where people had once lived and died.[7]

When the time came for Webb to leave and return for another year at the university, in honor of the occasion, he wrote a poem which he sent to his mother in Ranger. Webb summarized his impressions of his stay in Thurber in the following verses:

I'll wash the dirt from off my feet,
And to Thurber say farewell.
Its dusty streets and smooty sheets,
I'll see no more—ah well.

There's nothing here but booze and beer,
Except an occasional fight.
Life is cheap and talk is dear,
For in this place might is right.

Men spend their nights at the saloon,
The women at the ball,
And in the final reckoning,
Hell will claim them all.

But I've fooled so long already,
It's too late to be a Prof.,
So I'll go back to Austin,
And be a rowdy soph.[8]

Webb was actually returning to start his third year of study, but in his poem felt the need to take a bit of poetic license. By the end of his junior year, he felt that he was still drifting. He had no established goal to work toward, although he had decided tentatively that he would pursue a teaching career. He had toyed with the idea of going to medical school but reasoned that this route would take too many years and too much money. What was lacking in his life to this point was a motivating force to provide the drive necessary to reach success in whatever endeavor he chose.[9]

In the summer of 1913, Webb discovered that source of inspiration in the shape of a very attractive girl who lived next door. He was rooming that year with Dean T. H. Shelby and his wife at 1714 Lavaca Street and noticed one day that a girl with beautiful brown hair was standing in the yard. In accordance with the social formality of the era, he asked Mrs. Shelby to introduce him. "My motive," Webb said, "something to give me purpose, came just before the term ended when I met the girl that I later married. . . . On this occasion I went off the deep end, and in so doing found a new objective." Webb's "new objective" was Jane Elizabeth Oliphant, the daughter of a respected Austin family and a teacher at the State School for the Deaf. Described as being a "brilliant woman," Jane soon captivated Walter Webb. A watermelon party hosted by the Shelbys provided the proper opportunity for their friendship to ripen and by the end of the summer, he knew that he wanted to see more of her. This must have been a very exciting time in the young man's life; the same week that he met his future bride, he was offered positions at three different schools. [10]

Finances had once again required that he teach prior to completing his degree, and in response to a well-written letter enumerating his qualifications, he received offers from two schools on the plains and one in South Texas for the 1913–14 school term. Choosing to escape the wind and the sandstorms, he headed south to Beeville, taking with him tender thoughts of his newfound friend in Austin. The year 1913 marked the beginning of a new chapter in Webb's life; he had met the girl who was to act as his guiding light, and he had acquired a respectable teaching position in a good-sized town. Furthermore, he was twenty-five years old and realized that it was high time he began to carve a place for himself and make something of his life if he ever planned to be in a position to share it with anyone. [11]

Yet he felt some trepidation as he made ready to leave for Beeville. The history assignments did not seem insurmountable, in spite of the fact that he had only two introductory history courses to his credit—one taken under Augustus C. Krey, who later went to the University of Minnesota, and the other taken with Frederic Duncalf, who remained to become a member of the "Old Department." The courses taken under Keasbey were not pure history as such, but transdisciplinary in orientation and more akin to cultural anthropology than any one subject. When Webb learned that in addition to teaching history, he was expected to be the Beeville tennis coach as well, he experienced a bit of uneasiness. In retrospect, Webb claimed, with some exaggeration, that he never got a job that he was really prepared to hold. [12]

Nevertheless, he set out from Austin, spent the night in San Antonio, and arrived in Beeville the next day. By August 12, 1913, he was situated at Mrs. Offutt's Boarding House and enjoying the breezes that blew in off the Gulf and cooled the hot summer temperatures. The level, rather monotonous landscape of the fertile farmlands contrasted with the beautiful hills he was accustomed to in Austin; but he found the city quite interesting—a "town with a personality" he called it—full of windmills, tent shows, revivals, and interesting people. He knew many of the teachers who had been students at the university. Whatever loneliness he might have felt was lessened by his correspondence with Jane, which initiated the beginning of a three-year courtship. [13]

Shortly after his arrival, Webb sent her a postcard properly asking if she would be interested in corresponding. When she failed to acknowledge, he finally broke her reserve with a long newsy letter about his new position, admitting that he considered postcards as merely "that excuse one sends when one has nothing to say." Very early in their relationship, they decided to write at will. As Webb explained, "It will please me very much not to count letters with you"; he claimed that such correspondence always died by "arithmetical retrogression." Instead, he stated his intent of writing according to "inspiration, revelation, or other means," of things that he felt would be of interest. She, in turn, informed him that neither should he expect her to answer all his letters. Webb's somewhat piqued response indicated that he had established his rules largely for his own benefit. Being somewhat "put out," he wrote back, "You certainly possess the art of being unkind. . . . But I am told that is true of all the few women who combine as you do the two rare qualities of beauty and great intelligence."[14]

Webb kept Jane informed of his duties, which were numerous. He stayed quite busy outlining work for three history classes, monitoring tennis, teaching the boys gym tricks, and taking them on hikes to the country and the "old swimming hole." He proved to be so popular that they crowned him "a king of good fellows." Soon thereafter he noticed a group meeting under the water tank and discovered to his embarrassment that they had also made him their new scout master and deposed the old one at the same time. The situation was resolved when Webb agreed to become his assistant. In spite of a few such awkward situations, he seemed genuinely to enjoy his students, whom he considered "as fine a set of young Americans as the average school affords, barring a few 'bad ones' among the boys, and a few conscious beauties and would be society belles among the young ladies."[15]

He enjoyed the townspeople, too, and a Mr. Burrows, in particular. Burrows, the owner of the hardware store, and a man of sharp wit and business acumen, also took his meals at the boarding house. Webb recalled that the well-known revivalist, Sid Williams, who was in town conducting a big meeting, ate with them one day and expressed his irritation at the fact that a tent show was providing competition for his revival. Burrows remarked that he had attended the show, adding, "I'll try anything once." The preacher then turned to Burrows and hoping to embarrass him, asked if he had also attended his meetings. "Yes—once," Burrows replied. The loud silence that followed was interrupted only by the small sounds of eating.[16]

Webb appreciated the character of small towns and their inhabitants. He was an astute observer and was interested in people from all walks of life, seeming to search out individuals regardless of station, who reflected the basic honesty and wisdom of the unpretentious. In his later works, he painted the verbal pictures of these towns realistically, neither glossing over the rough, nor exaggerating their attributes, but accepting them as one facet of the mosaic of American life. Some years later, he would learn that the conservative calm of Beeville had been shattered by racial and religious strife with the rise of the Ku Klux Klan. Even in 1914 there were hints of the brewing tempest of intolerance. War rumors caused the Anglos to glance with aspersion on the Mexican faction, which comprised the majority of the populace in this South Texas region. At this time, Webb was too much a part of the cultural milieu himself to be objective. He wrote to Jane that there was speculation that the Mexican faction might become trouble-some. He had heard some of the boys planning "to get up a crowd and go out and whip some Mexicans," which he felt to be indicative of the general spirit of the town. And if this occurred, he wanted to be in on it, "for I do not like a Mexican," he admitted.[17]

During the war years and shortly thereafter, this atmosphere of suspicion, fear, and intolerance was a national malady, charac-terized by the revitalization of the Ku Klux Klan in 1915. It thrived particularly well in small towns like Beeville where the adults secretly craved adventure to enliven an otherwise drab existence. The white robe and hood hid well "the village bigot" who fancied himself "a knight of the Invisible Empire," defending not only the White against the Black, the Gentile against the Jew; but in South Texas, particularly, the Protestant against the Catholic.[18]

As the semester in Beeville passed, Webb began work on an article for the folklore society and looked forward to spending his ten-day Christmas vacation in Austin. He planned to work in the library and visit with Jane, and on December 13, sent her a note requesting the pleasure of her company at the Hancock Opera House for the Christmas night engagement. Webb returned from the holidays very much in love with his "dear Jean," as he occasionally called her. "During the day," he wrote, "I am busy and do not have time to think, but in the evenings I never fail to think of you, and want to see you, and listen to you. Jean, I believe I am in love, in fact I know I am, and you are the victim." Jane, or "Jean," responded with proper late Victorian reticence, causing Webb to write in perplexity, "It is still a mystery to me how anyone can prize an affection, which they in no way return."[19]

During their first year of courtship, Jane's response was consistently less effusive than Webb's. Her family felt that she might do better, which may have also tempered her reaction to her suitor's outspoken feelings. When she suggested that they merely "be friends," Webb told her bluntly: "I haven't a single Platonic feeling to offer you, and I cannot deceive myself into saying I have. One's friends are all alike, and numerous; you are totally different and alone; you are Jean."[20]

Webb's Christmas vacation in Austin not only strengthened his love for Jane, but also his desire to work with a purpose. "My trip up there had changed my whole attitude toward reality," he wrote: "I am living now for the possibilities of the future. I have a new contentment with life, and am working better and more seriously and earnestly than ever."[21] Webb's activities included the collecting of folklore and active participation in the Texas Folklore Society. Perhaps it is only logical that Webb's first attempt at writing since his rebuff by the university English department should develop as a result of his research into folklore, which is in itself a link between literature and history. Webb had finished an article on folklore during the fall and at the summer meeting of the society his paper was given "first mention" by the *Daily Texan*. In his love-struck state he attributed all his successes to Jane's influence: "I am glad you enjoyed the papers at the Folklore Meeting," he wrote: "You know someone said that no man does his best unless he is doing it for some woman he loves."[22]

At this point Webb began to chart a course for himself professionally and made plans to attend the teacher's meeting in San Antonio toward the end of the semester. He dreaded certain aspects of the trip, such as the proposed tour of the Experiment Farm, and admitted to Jane, "I am hoping to escape the ordeal. Mr. Dodd [a fellow teacher] suggests that I take the headache, but that, I believe, is not a masculine excuse."[23] The speeches of some of the participants at these affairs were particularly grating to Webb, who was never able to muster much patience when confronted with vacuous verboseness. He considered the platitudes being expounded just about as soothing as "the flapping of a shutter in the north wind about 1:30 in the morning." In later years, he referred to the meetings of the various historical associations in much the same vein, calling them "the annual flesh markets" and looking forward to the time when he would no longer have to endure them.[24]

During the formative years of his career, however, Webb realized the value of the contacts he would make and calculated carefully the steps that would advance him further in his profession. He steadfastly believed throughout his life that men are, to a large extent, masters of their own destinies and souls. He maintained the philosophy that "you become what you want to become, attain what you want, barring providential hindrance, if you want it badly enough."[25] At this point, what Webb wanted was to progress from the public school level to a position in the state normal schools. This was the goal that began to take shape in his mind. Such prospects were not entirely remote, for he had investigated the possibility of teaching English at the state normal school at San Marcos, although this initial effort did not materialize.[26]

Meanwhile Webb was enmeshed in year-end activities at Beeville. His reputation as a tennis coach was growing due to the natural ability of two left-handers, Curtis Walker and Everett Rittenour. Lloyd Gregory, who later became a tennis champion at the University of Texas also played that year. In the spring, the Beeville boys journeyed to Austin where they won every set in the tournament and took the state championship of the newly formed Interscholastic League. As Webb admitted, they had the talent, and he had "the good sense to stay out of the way." The tennis boys returned heroes, and he feared that they might not survive the victory with all the "speechifying," as he called it. The senior class held a reception with the team enthroned on either side of their loving cup; they were awarded a forty-dollar victory collection; and finally, a three-act play was held in their honor depicting in farcical style their activities in the big city of Austin. Their coach was characterized, too, as was Jane, whom the boys had met while there and complimented highly. Webb, however, refused to relay the kind words, saying that she might become vain, "like they will unless this applause stops."[27]

One of the most pleasurable events of this very successful year occurred when Webb learned that he had won a scholarship in institutional history, through the assistance of Lindley Miller Keasbey. Webb had been making arrangements to return to the university, securing the necessary funds from a friend and a relative; therefore, word that he had received an award was good news indeed. He had been teaching history to a class of seniors, when the Superintendent entered the room to make an announcement. As usual, according to Webb, it took him "always to do nothing at all," and while he was talking to the students, Webb happened to glance at a news article listing the recipients of the nine awards given that year. He was pleasantly surprised to find his name included. The scholarship for $100 would be a help, and it was quite an honor as well.[28]

The Beeville superintendent hated to see Webb leave at the end of the year and attempted to entice him to stay, but he realized that the degree was essential if he wanted to attain the goals he had established for himself. Furthermore, he frankly admitted that he would never feel secure without one or two degrees after his name. He was also anxious to return to Austin to be closer to Jane and once again enjoy the evenings spent sitting in the porch swing watching the moths flutter around the street lamps.[29]

Back in Austin, Webb prepared to enter the academic routine. Graduation was in sight and he had his work laid out for him, or so he thought. Once again it seemed that fate decreed otherwise. While he was working in Keasbey's office one day, Edmund Valentine White—a large rawboned man who would later become Dean of Texas Woman's College—walked in and told him that there was a vacancy at the Southwest Texas State Normal School in San Marcos. They needed someone to fill in for an instructor who was ill. Webb knew Cecil Eugene Evans, president of the college; thus White felt that Webb would get the job if he applied. Since his financial arrangements had mostly fallen through, Webb found the prospect of a well paid job, and a job in a normal school at that, very enticing. He asked which courses he would be expected to teach. "Education and mathematics," White replied. Webb's hopes fell, for he knew very little about either subject. His friend encouraged him to try it: "Aw, Webb," he drawled, "go on down there and get the job. The mathematics is just elementary algebra, and the education—there ain't anything to it. You can handle it."[30]

Webb decided it was worth a try, borrowed $15 in cash from Edward Everett Davis, who became dean of the North Texas Agricultural College at Arlington, and boarded the Katy train for San Marcos. Since he was gambling, he decided to give his dice a full roll. After arriving at dusk, he registered at the nicest hotel for dinner, then called a horse-drawn cab that plodded in style up the hill leading to the college. Webb had the carriage wait, and within a quarter of an hour, he was riding back down the hill with a job that paid the incredible salary of $150 a month. That night excitement ruled sleep completely out of the question.[31]

In preparation for his move to San Marcos, Webb requested that his scholarship in institutional history be deferred until after he returned. University officials granted his request although the scholarship would later fall through due to the outbreak of war and curtailment of loan funds. He disliked having to leave Jane and his Austrian friend, Emil Sevario, who had been tutoring him in German; but finances made the decison a matter of pragmatics. Furthermore, he considered it an excellent opportunity to move up in the world and to attain his goal of teaching in a normal school—temporarily, at least. At the time he seemed to feel that there was a good possibility that the appointment would develop into a permanent position. Again he credited Jane's influence for helping his progress this far. "By sheer force," he wrote, "woman can make man do nothing, but by her influence she may inspire him to heaven or drag him to hell. I understand perfectly all the things man does for the woman he loves."[32]

In San Marcos Webb found a nice room with a beautiful view, high on a hill overlooking the town. Here he roomed with Alton William Birdwell of the history department. There are indications that at this time Webb weighed nearly every move he made with a view to the future. The arrangement with Birdwell, for example, he admittedly considered a pragmatic one. He hoped that he would be offered a position in the history department if one developed. Jane, too, began thinking increasingly in terms of their future and wrote him of Harry Yandell Benedict's bid for the presidency of the University of Texas. Webb's response to her was revealing: "You may be sure I am very anxious for Mr. Benedict to be president. I think his appointment might in time mean something to me, though I had not thought of it in that sense very much until I got your letter. If [Oscar Branch] Colquitt should be appointed, I would not have as much chance as the son of a downtown saloon-keeper, so far as he is concerned."[33] It is obvious from this statement that Webb's long-term goals began to crystallize as he calculated a means to join the professional coterie at the state's major university. If Harry Yandell Benedict could escape the Stephens County shinnery to aspire to the presidency, then it was not too farfetched that another of its products could eventually earn an academic berth in the same institution.

Just how he could make this come about was not clear. The immediate job at hand proved to be quite challenging. His duties as teacher of elementary algebra and education were not too difficult, but his job as registrar and bookkeeper was another matter. His problems were compounded by the fact that he "didn't know a debit from a credit," and, too, the college used an elaborate bookkeeping system introduced by R. M. Hambly of Austin. The only solution was to spend a few days in San Antonio and learn it.[34] In addition to his duties, Webb took correspondence courses while in San Marcos, attended the Texas State Teacher's Convention in San Antonio, and practiced his writing, which he sent to Jane for criticism. Being a gracious and not altogether unprejudiced critic, she sent the paper back with many positive comments. Webb's response was somewhat caustic: "I don't want favorable nice comments; I *want* criticism, constructive, and candid—at least the latter." Responding further to her compliments he stated, "Getting into print is the only known proof of ability to write, and I shall make no claims until I have the proof."[35] Although Webb later claimed that he lost the desire to write after his experience with the university's English department, it appeared that he never gave up the prospect entirely.

Webb was obviously struggling to get ahead as best he could and Jane was doing her share, too. Now that she and Walter were talking about marrying the coming summer, she added her determination to his that their plans for the future would materialize. While Webb was still in San Marcos, she continued making plans for his graduation by checking on the necessary requirements he still had to fulfill. Webb's aspirations of staying at the normal school were rudely shattered when he learned that the man he had replaced was returning. This was a disappointing turn of events; nevertheless he felt confident that he would be asked to return when a vacancy occurred. A. W. Birdwell promised him that he would be considered for a position in the history department at the first opportunity. Although Webb was dejected by this development, he started making plans to return to the university to get the B.A. degree by the end of the school term.[36]

Before he left, however, he faced the task of balancing the books, which proved to be a real chore. For some unknown reason, he could not get them to tally. Jane wrote, inquiring if he had finished, to which he replied shortly: "No, I am not through with the books. They are out of balance. I shall have to go to work on them in real earnest tomorrow night. They are never finished, so you need not ask that anymore."[37] Obviously out of sorts, Webb finally learned that President Cecil Eugene Evans had cashed a counter check for $3,600 to pay miscellaneous expenses and had failed to notify the bookkeeping department. With this large headache behind him, he returned to the university with adequate funds to finish his senior year. He applied himself academically, making better grades than ever before, and finishing a year's work in two terms. At the age of twenty-seven, he had finished an undergraduate career that he felt to be "completely lacking in distinction" and had yet to show Hinds a return on his investment.[38]

In May of 1915, the school board of the South Texas town of Cuero elected Webb to serve as principal of their high school. That summer before reporting he went to Ranger to help at what he jokingly referred to as the Webb Agricultural Station. He and Jane were anxious to get married, but their plans had to be postponed due to finances and family problems. Webb was in debt for school expenses and the job in Cuero would only pay $133 per month, but the most imminent problems concerned their families. His youngest sister, Ima, was now sixteen, a bright girl with a cheerful disposition, and Webb was very fond of her. He saw her growing up without the benefit of good schooling and no opportunity to better her position in life. Webb could see that she needed direction, otherwise, he feared that she would grow up and "marry some worthless cuss." Webb decided that he should share at least part of the burden of her schooling expense and, if necessary, take her to Cuero with him to see that she had access to a better school system. The family eventually resolved the problem by making arrangements for her to board at Breckenridge long enough to acquire a teacher's certificate and graduate. The assumption of family responsibility proved to be typical of Webb and one that he would bear throughout his life in one form or another. In Ima's case, too, he illustrated good common sense and foresight. By providing her with a means to help herself, he was also enabling her to share with him the responsibilities of their aging parents which he knew would eventually devolve on him.[39]

Jane, too, had family obligations. Her father, William James Oliphant, suffered from cataracts and had reached the stage where an operation was imperative to preserve his eyesight. Jane had to care for him during this period, particularly while he recovered from surgery. Finances were, of course, the basic reason for postponement of their marriage. They both realized that Webb must go north to work on his master's degree if he were to advance in his chosen profession. Nevertheless, Webb somewhat impetuously attempted to move the wedding date forward: "Would you have us wait until I am encumbered with two or three degrees and disencumbered of all my hair before we marry?" he inquired humorously. "Of course, I know that it would not be wise for us to marry at Christmas, but I do not want you to keep putting off the time."[40] Jane, at this point, appeared to be the steadying influence, but the pressures of family problems and finances began to show on both.

Correspondence between Jane Oliphant and Walter Webb during their courtship indicated a rather worshipful southern attitude on his part, with Jane placed on the proverbial pedestal, although in one instance he showed considerable irritation with her for saying somewhat unrealistically that she liked being poor.[41] Webb had developed very early in life a healthy regard for money, as his successful business ventures in later life would attest.

During his summer at the farm, Webb busied himself with the usual chores—cutting firewood, pruning branches, picking peaches, and even acting as nursemaid to a sick nephew. Webb's middle sister, Ruth, and her two boys were visiting and the oldest had developed a high fever and convulsions. Ruth felt sure he was going to die, and as Webb observed, "acted accordingly"; therefore, he was left to take control, ordering cool compresses to bring down the child's temperature. "Such is the life on the farm," he reported in his letter to Jane, who worried about his health, cautioning him about overtaxing himself with farm work. Webb did not enjoy either the work or her solicitation. "You must not scold me so in your letters," he wrote, "It is bad enough to be marooned out here and blistered from sole to crown."[42] Webb's attitude toward farm life had not changed, and the pressures of attempting to settle family problems and find the means to take a wife were bothersome.

In September Webb assumed his position as principal of Cuero High School. Although he liked and respected his superintendent, A. S. Bush, he was lonely, and unimpressed with the town and its people. He admitted to Jane, "I do not like Cuero and expect to leave if I can go to a larger city."[43] This attitude was perhaps to be expected considering his frame of mind, the fact that the position could not compare to the previous one at San Marcos, and also because the salary of $133 left small margin for the savings that he needed so desperately to accumulate.

In Cuero, Webb introduced Keasbey's approach to teaching in an experiment with his tenth-grade history class. This experience provided him source material for the article entitled "Increasing the Functional Value of History" to be read at a teacher's meeting and published soon after. Based on the problems method of instruction, Webb's paper reflected the influence of John Dewey, whose educational philosophy was receiving widespread acceptance during this period. Webb hoped that his presentation would enhance his professional status and help him make inroads toward his objective of escaping the public schools and obtaining a permanent position at the college level. He set his goals high and plodded steadily toward them, suffering setbacks and disappointments along the way, but obstinately refusing to surrender. At Cuero it became obvious that he had not given up his goal of obtaining a position at the university itself. Now, the war, as well as natural attrition, was creating vacancies. When Jane wrote that Stark Young, who in the thirties would become well-known as one of the Southern Agrarians, had left the English department (a move that Webb considered a wise one), he wrote in return, "The University is certainly losing many of its good men. It will need more, and I hope sometime to be one that is needed."[44]

With this goal in mind and with Jane's encouragement, he carefully laid the groundwork. When the Ex-Student Association newspaper, *The Alcalde*, suggested organizing groups of former students in various towns to foster "Texas Spirit," Webb quietly promoted the idea to the university men at Cuero. They received the suggestion enthusiastically and planned a banquet at a local hotel to launch the project. "I am going to stay in the background myself, owing to the fact that I am a stranger and cannot afford to appear officious," Webb wrote to Jane. However, he added that he felt sure that word of his part in the development of the group would not go unnoticed by the Austin people.[45] In small ways he was striving to gain recognition in university circles and carefully planning his way upward.

Other plans now included a September marriage, but it was difficult for the young couple to be practical and continue to wait the few remaining months. Webb had allowed himself to become very much under Jane's spell. In January of 1916, he wrote, "I do not think it is right for you to have so much influence. . . . Surely you do not want me to lose my whole identity. It seems to be merging into yours completely."[46] Since Beeville, the two had been experimenting with mental telepathy, writing at appointed times and answering questions unasked verbally or by letter, with results that were evidently convincing to Webb. He had reached the emotional state where he felt that Janey's wishes literally became his desires and through her influence, his acts. He claimed to be so in tune with her psychically that he knew when she was sick, prior to her telling him.[47] And now he felt that she was exerting her power over him to move their wedding date forward to June in order to accompany him north to attend summer school: "I am going to give up the fight, because I am unable to resist you," he wrote. "You asked me to think it over in regard to the Chicago trip. It is thought over, and decided so far as I am concerned. We are going to marry in June and stand or fall together on that issue. I have lived without you as long as I can." Although there had been much talk of Chicago and a mention of Columbia, by summer he had decided to attend the University of Wisconsin.[48]

Webb asked Jane not to insist on accompanying him initially because it would be financially impossible for him to manage. Since this was the case, Jane suggested that the sensible thing to do would be to wait. Walter agreed, admitting that her "sensible argument" was in thorough keeping with her usual good judgment. "You are the steadying force in my life, and I have come to realize how fully you may be trusted in the serious things," he admitted. "But in spite of all your sound counsel, my good Angel Jean, I am of the same opinion still. . . . Between a trip to Chicago with 1/3 credit towards a Master's degree, and three months with you, I blindly choose you." However, the ultimate decision rested with Jane, whose common sense prevailed. The wedding date was set for September, after Webb's return from his summer of study.[49]

By springtime Webb's financial situation thoroughly disgusted him. As he candidly revealed to Jane: "I am sick of school work on starvation wages. As long as I am alone I can get along. But for your sake, I want money, money, money, and I am going to have it." With this in mind, he began to investigate business ventures that he could operate on the side, including the establishment of a company to distribute cosmetics and a brokerage concern. Jane did not think highly of his business schemes and urged him to continue with their plans. Somewhat sarcastically, he replied, "I never knew that you were so infatuated with the teaching profession, or that you held the calling in such high repute." Nevertheless, he adhered to her wishes and began to look for a way out of Cuero.[50]

In March he accompanied the school's baseball team to Victoria, the South Texas "city of roses," where he stayed overnight at the Denver Hotel, in order to attend the teacher's association convention the following day. (They had made the trip from Cuero in Fords—going thirty miles in one hour and ten minutes!) Webb knew that Charles S. Meek, the superintendent at Old Main High School in San Antonio, whom he called one of the "big-uns" in Texas public school education, would be there; and he planned to wrangle an interview with him. The careful finagling Webb went through to accomplish this end showed the seriousness of his intent. He did manage his interview with the innovative Mr. Meek, who asked him if he would be willing to come to San Antonio at the same salary. Webb agreed, promising to send credentials, and reported to Jane enthusiastically, "Did you ever see a scheme work more perfectly? . . . I love to work plans like that."[51]

Before taking a wife and a new position in the city of San Antonio, Webb had to take that trip north to attend summer school. On June 28, 1916, he boarded a train and arrived in St. Louis, Missouri, at 10:30 a.m. There he changed lines for Chicago and Madison. As the train pulled out, he noted a new kind of poverty—one to which he was not accustomed—a sweat shop district populated with gaunt women and hungry-looking children.

Coal smoke darkened the windows of the factories and covered everything with a sooty film, including Webb's new hat. The train arrived in Chicago at 7:45 p.m. and reached Madison by midnight.[52]

In Madison, Webb luckily found an upstairs room at 412 North Lake Street, an old brick house only two blocks from the campus, and conveniently located on the streetcar line connecting the state capitol with the university. Lake Mendota was approximately the same distance away. He considered the room a bargain: he paid only $1.50 per week for rent and $.60 to $.75 daily for meals. After a bout with the flu that kept him restricted to the infirmary for a few days, he began his history studies under the tutelage of George Clark Sellery and Lawrence M. Larson. The Texas and Dixie Clubs, organized by a contingent of Southerners at the university, made Webb feel more at home, but the high point of the summer occurred in the library one day where he noticed a girl reading *The History Teacher's Magazine*. He saw that she stopped in flipping through the pages at his article and "waded" through the whole thing. Unable to resist the temptation, Webb passed her a slip of paper saying that he had noted that she was reading "The Problem Method of Presentation" and what did she think of it. The girl replied that she hadn't finished it completely, but considered it "interesting—and practical—if one has the sources." Webb then informed her that he just happened "to be the writer." Further conversation revealed that an instructor for an advanced class in history had assigned the article for outside reading. Inordinately pleased at such recognition of his work, he wrote to Jane; "What do you think of that?"[53] With a touch of prophecy, Jane predicted: "That article is going to help you a lot in the future. I knew it would when it came out in the magazine. The first thing you know you will be offered a place in some university. . . . That instructor's recognition of your work is the most important compliment that has been paid your work."[54]

As the date for their wedding approached, the couple made decisions regarding the affair via correspondence. Jane refused to have even an announcement party given by friends, preferring to have a very dignified ceremony attended only by close relatives. "Like you," she wrote to Webb, "I want everything about our marriage as quiet as we can have it and I will not have any display of any kind."[55] While in Madison Webb purchased her engraved wedding band and sent it by registered mail for fear that he might lose it. In August after the summer session ended, he returned to the Webb farm, then went on to San Antonio to choose an apartment for himself and Jane. He finally decided on rooms at Mrs. Fortner's Boarding House located at 203 San Pedro. Room and board would cost $50 a month, which left very little in excess from his teacher's salary, but he looked forward to a raise at the end of the year.[56]

On Saturday, September 16, 1916, Walter Webb and Jane Oliphant were married at the bride's family home at 1716 Lavaca Street in Austin. They scheduled the simple wedding ceremony at 5:15 p.m. in order to have time to go to the train in a carriage rather than a taxi. After a honeymoon night spent at the St. Anthony Hotel, they moved to their rooms at the boarding house. That first year in San Antonio was happy and exciting for the newlyweds. The threat of a world war and increased military activity added an extra flurry of excitement, and the pageantry and Spanish culture of this historic city intrigued them. They spent leisure hours wandering through the maze of streets and enjoyed a weekly ritual of dining out at "The Original Mexican Restaurant."[57]

During the winter, Ida Hinds, the sister of Webb's benefactor, came to visit. She and Webb had become friends through correspondence after he had received news of Hinds' death. In the process of settling the estate, the family lawyers pressed Webb to pay the balance outstanding on his loans. When his sister discovered this, she graciously assumed his promissory note personally, knowing that her brother would have preferred it this way. Miss Hinds, a former teacher who was something of a suffragette, had been spending her retirement years lecturing and doing child welfare work. She stayed in San Antonio only during the cold season, then journeyed to California. In April of 1918, Webb received a letter containing an undated memorandum from Miss Hinds, which read: "I enclosed your note in directed envelope so if anything happens to me, it will be sent to you. If you receive this, you will know that I have passed away and you are under no further obligation. Consider the matter closed as there is no one else that would be interested." At that time the note showed that he owed a balance of $75, which he did not repay to his benefactor's estate. Yet it was paid, according to Webb, "over and over again to those who needed it." Thus Webb followed Hinds' example—by helping those in need.[58]

Meanwhile Webb was teaching at Old Main High School, and Jane was substituting. With World War I in progress, there was a demand for teachers, qualified or otherwise. Jane even taught a course in agriculture for two weeks, during which time her husband had to tutor her at night, as she did not know one implement from another. She also substituted for Webb when he was called back to Ranger when his eldest sister, Alma, died of a stroke.[59]

The death of Alma in the fall of 1917 preceded a rapid change of events for the Webbs. The Ranger oil boom was in full swing and his father had leased his land for a healthy sum. Now, however, Webb learned that Casner wanted to sell the farm, which he felt was the wrong thing to do. At the same time, Webb began experiencing problems in the professional sphere. He had difficulty adhering to the principles of his superintendent, the innovative Charles S. Meek, whom Webb described as "a man with a lot of advanced if not revolutionary ideas derived from a misunderstanding of John Dewey." Webb could not agree with the educational philosophy which proposed that everyone should be passed regardless of "industry or brains," nor that the only required subject should be English. Neither could he agree that contract terms need not be fulfilled. After failing to receive a promised advance at the end of the first year, he and a science teacher informed the superintendent of what they pretended was "an oversight." According to Webb, "It was a rough interview and Mr. Meek won every round." He did not resign, but took his outraged dignity to the streets of San Antonio seeking new employment. He considered becoming a newspaper reporter but was advised against it. Then after making what his employer later termed "the poorest damned application for a job of anyone he had every known," Webb was hired as bookkeeper for Rees Optical Company. Soon thereafter, with what he described as "malicious pleasure," he turned in his resignation at Old Main High.[60]

Webb had become so depressed and disillusioned with the teaching profession that he sold all his books except two. He worked five months for Mr. Rees who advised him to study optometry, paid him nearly twice as much as his school salary, and taught him some practical economics. At the same time, the Webbs learned that a baby was expected, and that his father was seriously trying to sell his land to speculators. Webb felt the need for direction. For a practical person, he turned to an unusual source—the well-known fortune-teller called Madame Sckerles, reputedly the consultant for many of San Antonio's leading businessmen. Webb decided to give her a try. He called her number and a woman's voice answered. Webb told her that he wanted to make an appointment and she scheduled him for four o'clock a month in advance. "Do you wish my name," he asked. "No, it is not necessary. I'll know you," she replied.[61]

At the appointed time, Webb went to a modest dwelling in south San Antonio and entered a hall where two or three other people were waiting. Soon a frail-looking little woman with gray hair opened a door on the left and glanced around. She then looked directly at Webb: "My appointment is with you," she said. Although others tried to argue, Madame Sckerles ushered Webb back to a stark room where she sat down behind a small table, her customer situated across from her in a straight chair. The woman's prophetic powers were indeed impressive as she related details about his family—information that hardly anyone in the city knew. She revealed that the expected baby would be a girl and it was (Mildred Alice). She told him that his father would sell his land, but that no oil was present. This he did, and speculators drilled only dry holes. As for the future, she told Webb that she saw him around books, much to his dismay, since he had just left the teaching profession in a huff. As he got up to leave, Webb placed a dollar bill on the table. Madame Sckerles deposited the money in a box, then returned a half dollar change, sliding it across the table with her index finger. "That is for the baby," she said.[62]

In all three predictions Madame Sckerles was correct. While Webb was still teaching, he had given a presentation to the Texas State Teacher's Association on the teaching of history in the public schools. Frederic Duncalf, a professor of medieval history from the University of Texas, attended the convention and liked what he heard. Webb had also published an article on the same subject, which "made him an expert," as he later facetiously observed. If it did not make him an expert, it did call attention to Walter Webb, and when Duncalf returned to Austin, he suggested Webb's name as a candidate to teach a course for prospective instructors of history in the public schools. The established professors were not interested in working outside their fields, and therefore voted to offer him the position at $1500 a year. On Armistice Day, 1918, Webb joined the University of Texas faculty, becoming, as he very aptly phrased it, "an example of institutional in-breeding which frightens all universities save the two that practice it most, Harvard and Oxford." As if on cue for a predestined role, or by some strange quirk of fate, Webb entered the same room at the same hour to teach his first class, that he had entered as a freshman nine years previously.[63]

Jane had preceded Webb to Austin in April to await the birth of their daughter, Mildred Alice, who arrived July 30, 1918. After Webb's return, he and Jane and the baby remained with the Oliphants. Jane was occupied taking care of Mildred, who was sickly and required extra attention. Upon the advice of the family doctor, a sleeping porch was added to the house in order that the baby would have full benefit of the fresh air, and a nurse named Frances came to live with the Webbs to assist the new mother. Frances was eventually replaced by a nursemaid, remembered only as "Lena," and nicknamed "Hantee" by the little girl.[64] With a baby daughter and a new job, Webb's life began to take on new dimensions.

By joining the University of Texas history faculty, he became a member of a remarkable group eventually referred to as "the Old Department." Among the distinguished historians included were Charles W. Ramsdell, Thad W. Riker, Milton R. Gutsch, Frederick Duncalf, Frank B. Marsh, Charles W. Hackett, Eugene C. Barker, and Walter Prescott Webb. These men, all of whom joined the faculty between 1899 and 1918, remained at Texas until they died or retired. Barker held the record for longevity, teaching at the university for fifty-two years. Rudolf L. Biesele and Carlos E. Castañeda were also among the older professors, but members of the Old Department themselves recalled that these men had joined the faculty several years after the original group. Professor Herbert Eugene Bolton was also an early member of the history faculty, but left for the University of California in 1909. Medievalist Augustus C. Krey went to the University of Minnesota, but returned to Texas to teach toward the end of his career. Webb was to be one who stayed, and in 1918 embarked on the beginning of a forty-five year association with the University of Texas.[65]

Here he taught a course on the teaching of history, and did some graduate work on the side. University enrollments had almost doubled with the culmination of World War I. The new instructor's duties were heavy as classes were crowded with returning soldiers attempting to piece together the fabric of their lives. Webb recalled that they were a "heady-self-assured" breed who knew what they wanted. He enjoyed his "place" in the university, but knew that he would have to take measures to secure it. He had signed on under agreement that he would work for an advanced degree, and his seniors reiterated the importance of this step. He knew, too, that writing and research were important prerequisites to professional recognition. In this regard, Webb did not consider himself a research-oriented scholar and never condoned the practice of publication in scholarly journals to impress one's peers. Down deep, he was then, and always remained, a writer at heart. He had the desire to produce in such a fashion that the general public, rather than professionals, would want to read his material. He would never write many book reviews, and many of those he did write were for the *Dallas News*, always a favorite with him. His contributions to the "learned" journals rested mainly on his presidential addresses to the two major historical associations of which he became president.[66]

As the fledgling on the University of Texas faculty, Webb was fortunate in that the grand old man of the history department, Eugene C. Barker, maintained a policy of tolerance and patience regarding publication by his faculty. Rather than resorting to pressure, the department used a much more effective methodology. Everyone worked. Quite simply, Barker and others set the example. And the young man who failed to contribute began to feel lonely, and therefore motivated to investigate on his own. As Webb explained, "It is the sort of treatment which in the long run brings out the best qualities."[67]

This approach began to motivate Webb, too, and he looked for a way to capitalize on the opportunity now available to him. He knew that he had the chance to gain recognition and the respect of his superiors. Yet he had no specific area of interest. The department reflected the inclination of its senior members—Eugene C. Barker, Charles Wilson Hackett, and before he left for California, Herbert Eugene Bolton—to the Spanish Southwest. Webb, however, was Anglo-oriented, knew little of this field, and was not particularly interested in cultivating it. He had tentatively decided to write a master's thesis on the Texas Land Office at the suggestion of Chairman E. C. Barker, but could never get excited about such a dry prospect. He still had a yen to write for public consumption in an interesting, as well as informative, manner. Then he happened to take note of the increasing news coverage of events relating to the Texas Rangers.[68]

During the war years, the Ranger forces had been increased in number and in license to take action against anyone, German spy, draft dodger, or Mexican national, who aided or abetted in any way the Central Powers. The force increased to 1,000 and most of the men were stationed on the Texas-Mexican border where revolutionary activities had created a turbulent state of affairs. The enlarged Ranger battalions began committing crimes that made it difficult to differentiate them from those they sought. As a result of the rapid expansion of the force, many men who were incompetent became members, a deficiency complicated by the fact that under Texas governors Oscar B. Colquitt, James E. Ferguson, and William P. Hobby the Rangers became a political tool.[69]

In an attempt to clean up the Rangers, State Representative J. T. Canales of Brownsville introduced a bill to increase the pay for men in the force in order to attract individuals of higher quality. In the House debate that followed, certain unsavory facts were revealed concerning killings, assaults, and tortures, perpetrated by members of the force. In the charges lodged by Canales on January 31, 1919, the majority of the complaints related to maltreatment of Mexicans. The ensuing investigation resulted in the severe reduction of the Ranger force, the ouster of corrupt political figureheads within the organization, and the passage of the law of March 31, 1919, which provided that any citizen could file a complaint against a Ranger and institute legal action, if investigation by the adjutant general deemed it necessary. This was the situation being widely publicized when Webb began to look for a subject. In the Ranger saga, he knew that he had found a topic to interest the public, and he discovered that no comprehensive biography of the force existed. Webb then went to Barker and suggested that he substitute "The Texas Rangers in the Mexican War" as a research topic for his master's thesis. Barker was amenable, and commented dryly, "I would rather you write of the Rangers anyway."[70]

Webb had embarked on the first of his adventures into the historical past, and the trail led westward, as he recalled, "to the frontier, to vicarious adventure of the body, and to real adventure of the mind. Though I was not aware of it then, I had found my field." For the first time, Webb worked with primary documents, the yellowed letters and reports that revealed the excitement of a past era. The Texas State Archives, located in Austin, proved to be a convenient research source, although he would later ride with the Rangers to flavor his writing with the reality of experience. The thesis itself was limited to actions of the Rangers in the Mexican War, but he planned even then to expand the scope of the work into a full-scale biography of the Ranger force.[71]

The advice of friend and poet Albert Trombly served to reinforce the tack that Webb was now taking. "Webb," he said, "you are fundamentally a pioneer, a frontiersman, and there is nothing you can do about it."[72] Essentially he advised Webb to stop pulling against the stream of nature and capitalize on his inherent understanding of the land from whence he came. Webb's quest had never been a search for identity; he knew all too well that he was a Stephens County farm boy, but he was searching for recognition for himself and eventually for his region. For a time, he attempted to accomplish this end by circumventing his heritage, then regained a more profitable perspective.

With his investigations into the history of the Rangers, he took the right track and made rapid progress. As Llerena B. Friend points out in her well-executed essay on the subject, "Webb's writing practically began and ended with the Rangers."[73] It is true that Webb's *writing* practically began with the Rangers, but, as noted above, the origin of his ideas and concepts began much earlier. As a child of the plains, Webb's background and breeding had grounded him in the frontier long before he acknowledged his debt with the written word in the Rangers and works branching from this matrix. The Ranger research rekindled his desire to write in earnest and turned him back to the land he knew so well.

With the Rangers, Webb discovered that he had a saleable product on his hands. The first sketch, written on the early history of the force, sold to the *Dallas News*. This first check was a landmark occasion, what he termed, "the beginning of a long and happy relationship between me and editors." Webb shared his good fortune with his friend, Emil Sevario, then a teacher at Southwest Missouri State Teacher's College. Sevario sent Webb his congratulations and advised him to keep his "hobby" of the Rangers, for he felt the subject would lead him to future successes as a historian.[74]

Webb continued to reap profits from his relationship with this law force, sometimes through rather strange connections. He had begun his research during the era of the Texas oil boom, which brought with the black gold, certain characters with hearts of the same color—speculators who had no compunction against fleecing the unsuspecting public. An oil strike in a town generally predicated a sociological pattern characterized by: the convergence of a criminal element bringing in gambling, murder, and robbery; the Rangers who came in to purge the town of the criminals; and ultimately, the speculators who hoped to pick the pocketbooks of any money left behind. One means of achieving the last was to create bogus companies to make a hoax more believable. Webb acknowledged in later years that he owed a considerable debt to one of these fraudulent companies, for it was through his association with such an organization that he stumbled on the first of his original ideas.[75]

The man in charge of the concern, Owen A. Wood, of the Owenwood Oil Company and editor of *Owenwood Magazine* of Fort Worth, sent a letter to the university requesting that it be directed to a qualified writer who could develop a series of articles on the part the Rangers had played in cleaning up the oil towns. Webb leaped at the chance and for two cents a word started turning out articles for the versatile Mr. Owenwood. The first issue dated December 1921, and sub-titled "A Messenger of the Opportunities of the Great Southwest," sold for twenty-five cents a copy and featured the oil town of Mexia. For the May issue, Webb wrote an article entitled "How Mexia was Made a Clean City." (Upon the suggestion of the editors, he used the pseudonymn of Kyle W. Shoemaker, since the magazine featured another article by Webb on Big Foot Wallace.) The magazine's editorial description revealed its true intent as "a source of instruction and a guide for those who wish to make money in oil, without accepting any hazard or making costly mistakes." Soon the United States government became aware of its objective as well. Webb recalled that "This pleasant arrangement was interrupted by a United States marshal and judge who had quaint ideas about the uses of the mail"; not, however, before the series entitled "Texas Rangers—Riders and Fighters of the Lone Star State" had brought Webb several checks of between $45 and $50.[76]

The fringe benefits of this arrangement proved to be even more valuable, for in the process of his reading and research on the Texas Rangers, and his writing of the articles for *Owenwood Magazine*, Webb came across Emerson Hough's *The Way to the West*, wherein the author stated that the conquest of the West was effected with the horse, boat, axe, and long rifle. In this simple statement, Webb quickly determined a significant exception. His study of the Texas Rangers showed that these men used the six-shooter as an indispensable weapon, but Hough had mentioned instead the long rifle. Webb pondered the subject one cold February night as the rain beat a staccato on the roof. In a moment, the amalgam of research and reading crystallized into a coherent form, and a picture flashed clearly in his mind. He saw "the great western country, arid and treeless, as distinguished from the east with its rich forest of trees." He saw, too, that Hough's axe, boat, and long rifle were no longer effective when they were transported into the arid region—that the Colt revolver, so readily adapted to plains use by the Ranger, cowboy, and miner, epitomized the manner in which environment demanded adaptation. As Webb later explained, "It took a year to gather the proof of what I knew that night, and I sensed that something very important happened when the American people emerged from the woodland and undertook to live on the plains." From his orientation in the heartland of Texas, Webb saw that the early pioneers of his state—the colonists of Stephen F. Austin—had been the forerunners; the Rangers, the advance guard; and the Colt revolver, "an adaptation to the needs of a new situation."[77]

The excitement of that creative situation was so great that he had to share it with Jane. The scene remained imprinted on his memory, as many years later, he recalled the ecstasy of the moment: "With the roar of rain in my ears, I went to the front of the house to tell the most sympathetic listener I have known that I had come upon something really important, that I was no longer an imitator, parroting what I read or what some professor had said." If Jane did not share his enthusiasm she at least pretended to.[78]

That night Webb had drawn together years of research, reading, and observation, what he called "isolated bits of knowledge, united as if in an electric circuit to form a unified pattern." He began to ask himself: "What else happened? What other changes took place as these pioneers emerged from the woodlands? During the process of this intellectual inquiry, the Rangers, as he said, "became dull and prosaic fellows," and he determined to let them rest as he followed a new trail. He found himself reverting to the Keasbey methodology as he considered the interrelationships between a people and their surroundings.[79]

The first result of this discovery was the story of the Colt revolver as a tool symbolic of the many adaptations or modifications deemed requisite by a hostile environment. He took his paper to department chairman Barker, who suggested that Webb submit the article to *Scribner's* or *Harper's* commenting that he thought it "too interesting to be buried in the mosaleum [*sic*] of official publications,"[80] referring to the more scholarly journals. *Scribner's* accepted the article, providing Webb with funds to undertake "a tragic year" of study in a graduate school in the north. The department had been exerting what Webb termed "gentle pressure" for him to get the advanced degree. He had earned his master's in 1920, but this was merely a pitstop on the road to professional advancement; he had traveled to Chicago for a session that summer where he met and studied under William E. Dodd, who helped him decide to return there to continue work on the Ph.D. He corresponded with Dodd, telling him of his interest in pursuing a dissertation relating to an expanded study of the Texas Rangers; and his advisor, Frederic Duncalf, wrote to Professor Frederick J. Turner at Harvard about a scholarship there. Turner replied that Webb was too old, but Chicago was not so discriminatory and accepted him. Turner was correct, as Webb later realized; he was too old to be embarking in a Ph.D. program, replete with its seemingly meaningless ritualizing. Furthermore he already had an idea in his mind that made others seem extraneous; yet this was to be the unfortunate path he chose somewhat unwillingly to take. He still needed the security of credentials—his professional "union card."[81]

In order to ensure that they had adequate finances, Jane returned to teaching, and they managed to save about $3,000. That sum, plus the amount advanced on the *Scribner's* article (which would be four years in appearing), provided them with living expenses for their year in Chicago. The university regents granted Webb a leave of absence and assured him that a position would be waiting when he returned.[82]

During the period from 1915 to 1922, Jane had provided Webb with motivation and guidance, generally keeping him on course, except for the brief foray into business with Rees Optical Company. As she had predicted, his article on the teaching of history had been one of the most important things he did, for this essay read at the annual meeting of the Texas State Teacher's Association at Corpus Christi on November 26, 1915, in addition to another titled "How the War Has Influenced Teaching in San Antonio High Schools," had brought him to the attention of the University of Texas history department.[83] Her feeling and respect for the teaching profession, and her belief that Webb had a place in it, undoubtedly influenced the course of his life, as he so often admitted during this early period. And now in 1921, through her return to teaching she helped provide the monetary means for him to attain the Ph.D. But this quest would eventually become the most bitter setback the Webbs would suffer.

5

THE TURNING POINT:
THE UNIVERSITY OF CHICAGO

We Texans have been as insular as Kansas—God save the mark.

W. P. Webb to J. Frank Dobie, 1957

It was the year 1922. Webb was thirty-four years old, and he was not excited about leaving Texas. In retrospect, he felt that he would have done better by staying, but the tenets of academe ruled this alternate unacceptable. Upward mobility in the profession he had chosen had as its prerequisite the advanced degree. Thus, after "gentle pressure" he set forth in search of the "accursed" doctorate, taking with him the Great Plains concept. As a fellow graduate student observed, Webb "brought with himself a 'chunk' of Texas and a generous slice of the great, wide-open, Western Plains and he seemed to be in a hurry to get back there as soon as possible."[1]

Nevertheless, in the fall Webb took his wife Jane and their young daughter to Chicago where they rented a lovely two-bedroom apartment at 6350 Kimbark Avenue from Mrs. Pauline Day, who was leaving the city for an extended visit. The family had hardly settled into their new surroundings when Jane received word that an aunt was critically ill. Taking the four-year-old Mildred, she returned to Texas for a brief period. Walter Webb, in the meantime, registered for the autumn quarter, taking courses in "Early Constitutional History of the U.S.," "Problems in Recent American History," and "American Historiography." By the winter quarter, February 1923, he had studied "European History," "History of Civilization," another course in "U.S. Constitutional History," and audited a "Survey of the Renaissance." The first portion of the year passed pleasantly. Unfortunately for Webb, however, William E. Dodd, his major supervisor, went to Texas during this period as an exchange professor.[2]

Earlier, Webb had solidified his program with chairman of the department, A. C. McLaughlin, and with Dodd. He planned to minor in European history and pursue in expanded version his studies on the Texas Rangers. There is no indication that Webb changed his academic approach while there. Throughout his years of sporadic schooling, he consistently had a difficult time studying as he put it "in the groove" that his instructors laid out for him. He could never escape the habit of reading at random, and now, in spite of the work at hand, he could not forget the Rangers and the implications for plains history that his study of this force had revealed. One who knew and understood this facet of Webb's personality—since he also shared it—explained that he and Webb had a mutual admiration for the educational philosophy of Dr. Samuel Johnson, who did not acquire his doctorate in the modern manner. Newspaperman Hubert Mewhinney recalled, "Arriving at the University of Texas and discovering that fine library . . . I decided not to bother with those silly courses, just to read the books. I could not read them all, of course, but I did succeed in reading a hell of a lot of them." Mewhinney maintained that Roy Bedichek, J. Frank Dobie, and Webb "all felt the same way about it."[3]

Avery Craven, a graduate student at the University of Chicago when Webb was there, expressed a similar analysis of Webb's approach to graduate study. Craven, who saw him in classes and spent much time with him, talking and telling stories, noted that Webb had "an independent mind" and took from professors only that which fit into his predetermined pattern for the future. "He seemed to care little for mental discipline or differing points of view," according to Craven, because he had already established his plans and just was not interested. He therefore took only the courses he liked and ignored others which would be needed for the doctoral examinations. Webb told his friend that he "would read up on those subjects later." Craven attempted to reason with him, pointing out that "rules were rules," but to no avail. Webb went his own way.[4]

Among his peers, Webb was evidently held in high esteem. Members of the Graduate History Club elected him their president. The fact that he already held a university position and had

published a few articles added to his status. Webb appeared to
have a healthy opinion of his own capabilities, as well, and felt that
he was one of the stronger members of the group. He showed his
article on the Colt revolver to his supervisor, who was also duly
impressed. As Webb recalled, "My stock was pretty high, and it
was suggested that I should take the preliminary examinations for
the doctorate, even though my residence had been too brief for me
to guess what was in any prof's mind."[5] Webb appeared to be
making good progress; he had earned an even number of A's and
B's on course work and in December and January he passed his
language exams in French and German. As the result of what may
have been overconfidence and bad advice, he scheduled his
preliminary orals for February 20, 1923, after only six months in
residence. This was the first big hurdle, according to the system
then in force. The student was not allowed to take the finals for
nine months after successful completion of preliminaries.[6]

On the appointed day, Webb faced "the inquisition" and soon
determined that it was not going well. There were four or five men
on the committee, but William E. Dodd, who would have been "a
friend in court," as Webb termed it, was away in Texas. Medievalist James Westfall Thompson soon made it apparent that Webb's
weakness lay in his field. During the past autumn and winter
quarters, Webb had audited, rather than taking for credit, only one
survey course on the Renaissance. Thompson, who had a reputation
for giving "vicious hazings" to new students, capitalized on this
deficiency. James Lea Cate, who studied under Thompson at the
University of Chicago in 1928, and who survived to become a
well-known medievalist himself, admitted that he almost left
Chicago because of his mentor's rudeness. "Later when I knew
Thompson better," Cate explained, "he said he had given me a stiff
introduction because he did not believe anyone from Texas knew
anything about the Middle Ages. I have often wondered if he was
thinking of Webb."[7] As Avery Craven had observed, "Webb took
only courses that he liked," and medieval history was not included
—at least for credit. Webb himself, in his partial autobiography,
assumed part of the blame for his lack of preparation. Although
intelligent and original in his historical insights, he narrowly
focused his area of interests on the history of the United States and
the West.[8]

To close friends and family, however, Webb went into more

detail about the exam situation. He recalled that he had the
effrontery to disagree with the committee view that immigration
into Texas was motivated by Southerners seeking to create a slave
state. Rather, Webb argued that people moved to Texas for land,
with the result that the committee derided his view "as being that
of a biased Southerner." Webb responded by saying that it was
obvious that the committee did not want to pass him and that "he
didn't really give a damn."[9] Although generally soft-spoken, Webb
would have been irritated by such an accusation, for it cast
aspersion on him personally, on his origins, and on his historical
beliefs. If immigrants had not come to Texas for land, he would not
have been a Texan. Conceivably Webb took his examiner's rebuttal
as a personal affront. Furthermore, the department had no courses
in the West, indicating a general lack of knowledge and interest in
the field. Webb had expressed the opinion earlier that even the
work in the general area of American history offered at the
University of Texas was on par with that in Chicago, and regarding
the West, in particular, he doubtless had little respect for the
professors' opinions on what he considered to be *his* field.[10]

The fact that Webb never had much talent for oral exposition
did not help him in the exam situation. Throughout his college
career, questions from professors tended to leave him "flushed and
speechless." In later years, analyzing the academic process, he
reflected that he found it curious that colleges devoted years to
training people to write examinations, then made "the supreme
ordeal of the whole process oral." The lengthy discussion that
followed the quiz session indicated to Webb what the verdict
would be and he decided on a course of action. The chairman came
out and sympathetically informed him that the committee was not
satisfied and suggested that he take the exam at a later date.[11]

"May I speak to the committee?" Webb asked. Somewhat taken
aback by such a request, his supervisor consented. Webb entered
the room once again, so choked with emotion that the walls blurred
in front of his eyes. Selecting an advantageous spot, he addressed
the group:

"Gentlemen, I realize that I did not pass this examination. I
should not have attempted it at this time, but it was suggested that
I come up and I accepted the suggestion." He continued by
pointing out that he doubted that he could ever pass a satisfactory
oral examination; that he was not looking for a job, because he had

one; and that what had happened in no way affected his plans since they had been made for a long time in the future. He concluded: "I know what I want to do; have my program laid out, and expect to follow it." He did not ask for reconsideration.[12]

This failure was one of the hardest blows Webb would ever receive. As he walked back toward his apartment through the snow and cold, he equated the feeling of utter exasperation to that he had felt as a child when he had been dragged down the sandy road by his heels, and when he had thrown the tools out of the wagon in angry dejection. He later admitted to a close friend that the affair depressed him to such an extent that he contemplated suicide, but ultimately decided, "Hell, I'll go back to Texas and show 'em!" He considered leaving Chicago immediately, but determined that he must stay and finish his course work.[13]

Shortly after this trying experience, his young daughter, Mildred, took the flu, and Walter and Jane caught it soon thereafter. The entire family spent the week of spring vacation in bed. The baby recovered rapidly, but her parents were not so fortunate; both ran high fevers and were seriously ill. Mildred Webb still remembers the difficulty of those days—"Poppa lying in bed, staring at the wall, and cussing a streak." Illness and misfortune combined were almost too much to bear, and his family shared in the bitterness and unhappiness of this period, which had a tremendous impact on their lives. The bitter cold of the winter compounded their emotional and physical discomfort, and Webb had to purchase an electric reflector to supplement the heat. After all was said and done, they reached the mutual agreement that they would never again subject themselves to such a situation.[14]

While the family was still recovering, the landlady, Mrs. Day, returned from her visit, and the Webbs had to start looking for another apartment, a trying task in mid-winter with both of them still weak and a small child to care for. The management, in many cases, did not permit children. Webb could never forgive or forget the city where "dirty slovenly women" turned them away, saying, "No children allowed." Eventually they found a third-floor walk-up with a bedroom so small that one practically had to stand on the end of the bed to get into the closet.[15]

Webb remained for the spring and summer sessions, auditing courses in medieval history and taking additional courses in European and United States history. Although he hated Chicago now and the lectures he attended, he determined to have done with graduate work once and for all. Years later the embers of this low period still burned in his memory: "From February on to the end of August," he said, "I knew what hatred and bitterness meant and I sensed what it might do to the human mind. . . . My attitude toward the men was one of bitterness for my own and their bungling. I took their notes, but I would not laugh at their jokes, and I would not cultivate any acquaintance."[16]

In the spring, Jane and Mildred returned to Austin. The loneliness did not help Webb's emotional state and once again he decided to withdraw from school. But first he went to see W. E. Dodd, who urged him to stay and take the examination when he would be there. Webb made no commitment to take the exam, but he did remain until the end of the summer session. His mental attitude deteriorated, and his depression grew as he dwelled continuously on the details of the oral ritual and his failure. Finally, in a moment of clarity, he discovered what was occurring and realized he was verging on a nervous breakdown. He did some serious talking to himself and determined to better control his mind and think of other things. Only by overt effort and firm resolution did he survive this experience, an event especially humiliating to a man of his pride and conviction. For a man of Webb's caliber, this ordeal had been a test by fire and in the process his inner resolve was strengthened and tempered into steel. He placed his life in perspective, realizing that he was now thirty-five years old, no longer young, and that life was passing him by. Never one to accept rejection and injustice meekly, he set out to rectify himself beyond a shadow of a doubt.[17]

In spite of the general unhappiness of this year in Chicago, there were a few happy interludes. He witnessed a silent, but humorous, encounter on a narrow street between the drivers of a bus and a police car, which ended when the bus driver was forced to back away. He enjoyed reading Emerson Hough's *North of 36*, which had just appeared in serialized form in magazines, and provided him with additional understanding for the work he was developing on the Great Plains. And, too, he remembered a pleasant evening when Carl Sandburg climbed the stairs of his walk-up to visit him because of their mutual interest in the collecting of folklore. Sandburg had been to Texas gathering folk songs, and he had heard that Webb knew some his father used to sing. Webb recalled that

Sandburg strummed his guitar and sang "Lonesome Road" sad enough "to make a dog howl." Toward the end of July, he heard some additional good news through Jane and his friend, Charles Ramsdell. In his absence from the university, he had been granted a raise that placed his salary above the $2000 mark. To Jane this was a significant event after the deprivations and disillusionments of the past year. It made less of an impact on Webb, however: "There are many things," he said, "which for me stand out more prominently than that, for instance my first teacher's certificate, the San Marcos job, and other things."[18] For him, the gloom of the past year would not be lifted until he was back in Texas and working.

Prior to leaving, Webb and other students during these final days in Chicago staged a farewell dinner for Professor W. E. Dodd. Webb made arrangements for a private room at the Hitchcock Hotel, and Frank Graham, who later became president of the University of North Carolina, invited the guests. The party enjoyed what Webb called "a truly Southern dinner served by an immobile faced darky" who was the best waiter he had ever seen. "He did the service so well that one was not conscious that a dinner was being served," Webb declared. After several courses, consisting of shrimp cocktail, fish, spring chicken and corn on the cob, fruit salad, cake and coffee, the group engaged in discussion concerning the role of the southern historian.[19]

A spirit of comradeship prevailed as Dodd expressed the view that it would remain for a southern historian to write the truly great history of America. He explained his rationale saying that the southern man came closest to being the "true American," and the one who had best preserved American traditions and ideals. Because of the section's isolation, Dodd felt that the South had not been blinded as the North had by the industrial character of their region. He believed that industrialization tended to color the Northerner's outlook. Furthermore, the Southerner, according to Dodd, was better fitted to meeting all classes of people "on a plane of equality and friendliness," an important asset in research; and finally, he considered the Southerner to be a more effective writer, imbued as he was by an inherent "spiritual quality"—a "langorous slow fire" he called it—that was impressive, provided he stopped short of sentimentality. Dodd suggested to his students that state histories and biographies offered good starting grounds. Webb then directed the conversation to specifics: Frank Graham expressed an interest in the mountains, as Webb said, "similar to my purposes in the plains region"; while Mac Swearingin was interested in the Mississippi; Avery Craven wanted to do a number of things; and J. Fred Rippy planned to further develop a field in Latin American-U.S. relations.[20]

Dodd's inspiring conversation, occurring as it did at the end of a disastrous year while Webb was desperately trying to salvage his pride and chart a course to overcome the shame of failure, impressed him to the extent that he wrote Jane a report of the occasion word for word. He was a Southerner, and his Plains idea would fit into Dodd's assigned scheme. It would certainly be an opportunity to preserve the traditions and ideals of an important sector of America. As Dodd had stated, there was a wealth of work to be done in the South and in the West, and Webb resolved to do his part. Ideas on the Plains helped detract his thoughts from his bad experience. The year was coming to a close; the future held promise; and he was returning to Texas determined "to work on his own hook."[21] The Chicago affair proved to be the turning point in Webb's life and career. Through fate and misfortune, he was now well on his way to becoming a western historian, the first step in his development as a scholar of international renown.

After this year of educational "outbreeding" he took the train south, luxuriating in the soft talk of "cattle, cotton, and oil." The genial laughter and southern voices pushed away what Webb would remember as "the bitterness of the meanest year of my life." He returned to write history as he saw it "from Texas, and not from some distant center of learning." He was in debt, consequently, he vowed to recoup his finances, follow his own intellectual interests, and never to listen to another academic lecture.[22] Although the department expected him to return and take the Ph.D. at Chicago, as did his supervisor, William E. Dodd, Webb merely toyed with the idea, talking to friends about the possibility, and dreading the prospect. "The University of Chicago was very kind," Webb said, and suggestions were made several times during the ensuing years that he come up, take the exam and and get it over with, but he informed them that he was busy with the program he had outlined on that snowy February night. In the meantime, Webb forgot much of the material he would have needed to pass their examination. Furthermore, many of the men he studied under were now retired or had moved away. In response to a query concerning his thesis topic, "The Texas Rangers," he told them to remove it from their list since he was virtually through with his research on the project anyway and felt that no one could finish it before he did. He did not completely sever ties with Chicago, as he said, "not because I was not ready, but because I realized that at some time pressure might be put upon me to take the degree and I wanted to be in a position to do so if it became absolutely necessary."[23]

The degree dilemma was solved unexpectedly when department chairman, Eugene C. Barker, suggested that Webb use *The Great Plains*, published in 1931, as a dissertation topic. He said that the department had talked it over and decided that this was the sensible course to take. Webb wasn't too enthusiastic about the idea. He had not written the book as a dissertation and valued it more highly than that, but Barker advised that he go ahead and put an end to this unfinished business. In compliance with a few additional requirements, Webb wrote a paper to satisfy a credit needed for anthropology and passed the oral exam, although he did not do a particularly good job. Thus after what he termed "some mumbo-jumbo to satisfy regulations," the University of Texas granted him his professional "union card" in 1932 at the age of forty-four.[24]

The road to academic eminence for Webb had been strewn with obstacles, and as a result, he gained a great sympathy for graduate students. Of his own doctorate, Webb stated: "I did not earn it. I have sat on many doctoral committees, always spiritually very near to the cornered candidate, and I have never sat on one where I could have passed the examination." Webb further classified himself as "a pushover for people who have trouble answering silly questions."[25]

Ironically, the University of Chicago tried to redeem itself when, on December 19, 1958, it granted him an honorary doctor of laws degree. The citation read: "Distinguished historian, gifted writer, and well-loved teacher, whose challenging interpretations of the frontier have been applied fruitfully to the history of the Old Southwest, of the High Plains, and the whole of the modern world."[26] As early as 1946, but long after Webb had received notoriety with publication of *The Great Plains*, the University of Chicago invited him to return there to teach the summer session in 1947. Webb declined. Then in the spring of 1951, Avery Craven took the lead in urging the department to recommend to the administration that Webb be given an honorary degree. Nothing came of this initial attempt. Then in March and July of 1958, James L. Cate and Walter Johnson, when he was chairman of the department, tried again. With faculty endorsements, the Committee on Honorary Degrees accepted the recommendation that Webb be honored, as Craven had wished seven years before. By this time, Webb had been elected president of the American Historical Association.[27]

This second recommendation was warmly received; but President Lawrence Kimpton felt concerned that Webb might not accept. Cate therefore phoned Webb to see if he would, and when he agreed, the letter from Kimpton was mailed. In his formal letter of acceptance to Kimpton, Webb expressed appreciation for the honor, as he said "both for myself and as a mark of recognition for the University of Texas where I have spent my academic life."[28] The doctor of laws degree given Webb was the only honorary degree conferred at that Autumn Quarter Convocation. Those attending the functions preceding and following the ceremonies recalled that Webb was very gracious and complimented the university saying that their program was more impressive than that held in Oxford. Cate, who presented Webb in the ceremony, admitted feeling a bit of anxiety: "Knowing him," he said, "I was afraid he might have remembered earlier days, but he showed no antagonism."[29]

In spite of his gentlemanly conduct, however, Webb continued to consider himself the victim of a big graduate school on the make, even though he knew quite well and admitted that part of the problems he encountered were of his own making. At the time that Webb attended the University of Chicago, it was a young and liberal institution, but the department was well respected. Even so, the error in judgment concerning Webb, by 1931, had become all too obvious. James L. Cate summarized his opinion of the situation saying, "Any failure at Chicago was the fault of this university's, not Webb's. He was already a mature and excellent scholar, . . . with feeling for the land he grew up in."[30]

Webb's feeling for the land had been intensified by both his absence and the trauma of the Chicago episode. Now that he was "south of the tamale line," (as he called it), the ideas that had been amorphous fragments in his mind began to take form. It was really no wonder that he had made such a poor showing in Chicago as he admitted to his friend J. Frank Dobie not long after he failed his exam. "For the past two years my head has been generating ideas so fast that my hands have become confused, but I am at least making some notes while exiled in this academic desert."[31] Some of the notes he brought back with him or wrote shortly thereafter, read like rough drafts of the Plains book: "The history of a people can be understood only against the background of their environment and inheritance"; further on, "there is a law in human affairs higher than the law of man—it is the law of nature." In explanation of his rationale for the environmentalist approach he planned to use, he stated:

> To ignore the influence of the land in writing the history of the area west of the Mississippi would be to ignore one of the prime factors in its development. It would be like writing a history of the vegetation on the basis of soil, air and moisture, and omitting the influence of the life giving force of the sun. I do not mean to contend that writers have not recognized the land as a factor, but they have not followed the factor through or made the synthesis of all the phenomenon, a synthesis which makes the life and story of the Plains country unified and harmonious.[32]

The negative impact of this year developed in him an intensified sectionalism which became increasingly apparent as he searched for ways to build the image of his region and his own reputation.

6

CARRYING THE STANDARD: WEBB AND THE EMERSON HOUGH CONTROVERSY

Eventually there may come forth a writer or group of artists who have within them the distilled genius, spirit, and understanding to put in stone, on canvas, and in the printed word the realities, the verities, of the Great Plains. And perhaps by that time there will be a public with sufficient judgment to distinguish between a difference and an incongruity.

W. P. Webb, *The Great Plains*

With the advent of the 1920s, Americans were convalescing, feverishly trying to dispel the sense of disillusionment left by the war. Within the next decade resurgent nativism and "the Red Scare" would reach its zenith in the Sacco-Vanzetti incident and slowly ebb away to be replaced by the imminent reality of the Great Depression. In the meantime, much of America, like a businessman in need of a well-earned fling, felt the urge to play. New fads such as Mah-Jong, inventions such as the radio, and a siege of sporting events obsessed the American public. The Jack Dempsey-Georges Carpentier fight became the first million-dollar bout of the jazz decade; Babe Ruth batted his home-run record up to fifty-nine; Atlantic City sponsored its first Beauty Pageant; and women won the right to vote. A revolution in manners and morals occurred as the F. Scott Fitzgerald generation disrespectfully indicted their elders for ruining the world before passing it on.[1]

Novelists of the 1920s did their share by revealing the tarnished veneer of American society. The efforts of muckrakers and liberals of the Bryan-La Follette breed had stagnated; attacks were still being lodged, but not frontally. Critics of the "New Era" used the insidious weapons of satire, repudiation, and derision, comprising what Henry Steele Commager has called "the literature of revolt."

Whereas the critics of an earlier era exhibited sympathy and dignity in their attacks, lodged for the betterment of society, the new voices, negative in tone, directed their invective toward the middle classes rather than the rich, and their venom at the social, rather than the economic, sins of society. Authors such as Sinclair Lewis, painted sad pictures of an age, but only in a thin wash of watercolor with none of the rich texture of oil. The problems were presented, but the causes were not revealed. Babbitt, Lewis' societal caricature, attired in a businessman's suit and Rotarian lapel pin, came to life as the success symbol of the new era, "nature conformed to art." The derogatory attacks of the literati of the twenties cast aspersions on all facets of society, including the West of Walter Prescott Webb. Romanticism was a bad word; realism reigned supreme. In literary circles, the term itself—the West— evoked images of the romantic stereotype, and this was passé.[2]

By the end of the decade the Great Depression provided Fitzgerald's "sad young men" with quality cannon fodder. No longer would they have to conjure up ammunition to mount their attacks on society. With real problems to occupy their pens, they rejoined the main current of protest. They were no longer absorbed in the Oedipal exercise of searching their own lost souls, but could now turn toward "man's inhumanity to man."[3]

The middle generation, of which Walter Webb was a member, had not been so affected by the wartime neurosis. Although they, too, began to search for freedom in various ways, they had time prior to the outbreak of the war to build up patterns of conformity that were well ingrained. Webb's home state was in many ways anomalous, and in certain respects hardly reflected the "New Era." In Texas the national temper took on a regional hue. The revived Ku Klux Klan, by 1921 and 1922, gathered momentum as it permeated the eastern sector and infiltrated local politics. In 1924, Ma Ferguson became one of the few feminine officeholders in the nation, but she hardly epitomized the League of Women Voters' ideal. It was common knowledge that her husband and former governor, James E. Ferguson, conducted state affairs from the bedroom. Only in the economic sphere did Texas experience revolution. New lands developed; agriculture improved; and mineral extraction added wealth to both the state coffer and private pocketbooks. However, these changes did not result in a revolutionized view of society or ethics. As T. R. Fehrenbach succinctly concluded in his study of the Lone Star State, "Economic reform did not mean social or psychological change; the Texan had little difficulty in remaining a 19th century man."[4]

Webb in many ways personified the nineteenth-century gentleman. Victorian in outlook and in respect for women, and provincial in regional orientation and mores, he felt a natural pride in his home state and was becoming increasingly engrossed in its history and that of the whole Plains region. Back home on Texas turf, Webb settled into academic life in Austin, teaching his classes, and continuing his research on the Rangers. Jane was teaching again at the State School for the Deaf, and the Webbs had purchased their first car. Like many other Americans of the 1920s, they took to the road in an unattractive, but efficient Model-T Ford—that apotheosis of democratic equality that broadened the horizons of the whole nation, including the Webbs. By driving all day they could cover the 240 miles of mediocre roads leading to Weatherford where Webb's parents now lived. They had sold their land in Ranger and purchased a smaller farm on the outskirts of town. Here their modest home overlooked a fertile valley which produced fruit, vegetables, and grain in abundance, under Casner Webb's care.[5]

A specific reason for the purchase of the Ford was Webb's desire to take a trip in the summer of 1924 to the Mexican border. There he planned to visit the Ranger camps and witness firsthand the activities of the force as they attempted to control the remnant of frontier violence still in existence in that area. As Webb amassed his wealth of information on the Rangers, ideas relating to the Great Plains concept kept infringing on his studies, pushing his lawmen into the background.[6]

As he continued along his path of "intellectual stumbling," as he called it, he began to reap the fringe benefits of his research. In November 1923, *Frontier Times* printed his story of the revolver in revised form in an article entitled "Texas Rangers were First to Use Six Shooters." The following winter, *Sunset: The Pacific Monthly* became the first magazine to publish Webb's fiction with a story called "Jewelry." He had also signed a contract to do a series of stories on the Texas Rangers in the twentieth century for a state police magazine. Other fiction pieces during this period included "The Singing Snakes of the Karankawas" printed by the *Southwest Review* in Dallas, and "Rio Grande Rendezvous," in a western magazine of high quality called *The Frontier*. For J. Frank Dobie's book *Texas Legends*, he wrote "The Legend of Sam Bass," and he earned $60 for a piece called "The 13th Notch" that was purchased by *The Frontier* for their April 1925 issue.[7]

Webb was also writing for *The Texas History Teacher's Bulletin*. He had become a member of the editorial board in 1919, shortly after joining the University of Texas faculty. In May of 1921, he had been made managing editor, a position that he held until the magazine went out of existence. There had been no bulletin for 1922–23, the year he was in Chicago, but the following autumn Webb was back at work. Webb's association with this publication was significant in that it reflected his intense interest in the cultivation of local and regional history. It became his personal organ of communication as he encouraged Texas schoolchildren and teachers to perpetuate and preserve the history that was as close as their own backyards.[8]

Between the years 1923 and 1928 his interest in the promulgation of local history prompted authoring a section, "Talks on Texas Books," for Roy Bedichek's *Interscholastic Leaguer*. In it Webb attempted to persuade the public school system to establish a Texas Book Shelf in every school library. He also reviewed, in his beautifully simplistic and lucid style, relevant Texana books to encourage youngsters to read, enjoy, and understand their state and its culture. During these years he became acquainted with some of the men whose books he reviewed as well as with those who shared similar interests in the history of their state and region. Some, such as J. Frank Dobie, he had known before through university relationships; others, such as western novelists Andy Adams and Eugene Manlove Rhodes, he came to know through mutual interests. In his "Talks on Texas Books," he lauded some of the works of literary friends for their contributions to the history and literature of the Southwest.[9]

J. Frank Dobie, native-born Texan and occasional ranch foreman, had been educated at Southwestern University of Georgetown and at Columbia. His earthy personality and literary talent made him a natural to appeal to the likes of Webb, who dubbed his book on legends as having a permanent value for the Texas literary tradition. Dobie and Roy Bedichek, Texas naturalist and director of the Interscholastic League, became two of Webb's closest friends, eulogized in the colorful history of the University of Texas as "the

Texas Triumvirate." Webb also reviewed Andy Adams' *The Log of a Cowboy*. Adams had started out as a Texas trail driver, then ventured into the Colorado mining business prior to taking up his pen to tell of his experiences.[10]

Webb believed strongly in the value of good fiction to excite the interest of students in history, to make its study relevant, and to supplement dry textbooks. To Webb, Andy Adams' novel *The Log of a Cowboy*, filled the bill. As he said, "We have heard of the painter whose portrait of a curtain fooled an artist, and of the one whose portrait of grapes fooled the birds, and we have considered that such portraits must have been excellent. Andy Adams has written of cattle so well that he has fooled historians, novelists, and even cowboys." Webb thought the book even better than Emerson Hough's *North of 36*, and predicted that it would become a classic work on the western cattle drive.[11]

Webb next wrote about what he felt to be the most widely known Texas book outside the state, the collection entitled *Cowboy Songs* by John A. Lomax. Lomax, a native Austinite, had also lived and worked on ranches. In his review of this book, Webb quoted from Theodore Roosevelt who had complimented Lomax's work, saying: "Your subject is not only exceedingly interesting to the student of literature, but also to the student of the general history of the West."[12]

The works of Eugene Manlove Rhodes of New Mexico appealed to Webb for their fidelity to fact. He felt that both Adams and Rhodes had failed to receive the recognition their works warranted because of this very reality in style and content. The true-to-life characterizations projected by Rhodes and Adams did not mesh with the images conceived by Easterners. Ironically, authentic renderings of the West, such as those of Adams, Rhodes, and Hough, came under fire undeservedly because of the dime-western perspective of the eastern critics themselves. The western world *was* different. To the city-dweller, even the harsh realities of cattle drives, Indian attacks, and roundups appeared adventuresome and romantic when viewed from the security and safety of distance. The literature of the West depicted a primitive life of action, spectacular in nature, portrayed by characters equally colorful and picturesque. Given the most heuristic of literary renditions, the cowboy and his land appeared, to those unaccustomed to such a life, as fanciful exaggerations. This difference in experience and perception, according to Webb, accounted for many of the charges of romantic stereotyping directed at western literature.[13]

As he explained years later in *The Great Plains*, "The realities of the West, the far country, have created an illusion of unreality." There *is* a great difference between the novels of Zane Grey and Andy Adams, but a difference that the public hardly recognizes. Whereas Grey and Adams say to their readers, "Come ride with me to a Far Country" (the West), authors such as Hamlin Garland say, "I deal with a Near Country" (the Prairie Plains and the homely, mirror image of reality). Thus the "romantic" aspects of the Plains literature of Bret Harte, for example, versus the "realism" of prairie literature of Hamlin Garland, according to Webb, was a false polarization. Rather, the romantic view was generated "because of the distance from which the readers viewed the scene." In *The Great Plains*, Webb observed that the debate among critics over romanticism and realism—Wild West literature vs. Prairie Plains literature—resembled the spat between the Gingham Dog and the Calico Cat "who simply ate each other up."[14] On this topic, Webb was speaking from experience. After his return from Chicago he became involved in one of these futile dog-and-cat fights, futile in terms of dignifying the image of Western literature, but in no way futile for Webb, as it helped him determine the path he must take to resolve his own destiny.

The debate, known as the Emerson Hough Controversy, occurred when he was particularly sensitive to regional differences and full of pent-up anger and frustration, with himself and eastern intellectuals. The saga of what became a sectional duel between a representative of the literati of the East and chroniclers of the West began when a critic by the name of Stuart Henry scathingly reviewed Emerson Hough's book, *North of 36*. Henry's article was the third part of a series on stereotyped regional images as exhibited in literary works dealing with Canadians, Spaniards, and the romanticized West. He used Hough's book as an example of the latter. Webb had read the book in serialized form in Chicago and liked it, although he later admitted that Adams had done a better job in *The Log of a Cowboy*. Imagine his disgust when in November of 1923, not long after the Chicago debacle, he read a review of Hough's saga in which the critic labelled women of the West as "weazened, weary, and forlorn" and called the book a stereotype of the romanticized western. In essence, he charged that Hough had glamorized the grim life of the frontiersman with "bunk." To Webb, these were fighting words and with righteous indignation, he rallied in defense literary spokesmen Andy Adams and Eugene Manlove Rhodes. [15]

Webb's strongest support came from Rhodes who shared his anger at an Easterner with the gall to sit in his eastern citadel directing verbal jibes at a version of the history of cattle drives written by a native Westerner. What Webb and his cohorts did not realize at the inception of the dispute was that Henry had spent his early days in Abilene during this very era. Andy Adams, on the other hand, did not agree with Hough's treatment in all respects, so his ire was, to an extent, tempered. Webb later agreed that although Hough knew and understood the West and the history of the cattle drives, he had succumbed to the tenets of fiction writing and motion pictures, thereby marring a potential classic. Hough had traced the arduous journey of the trail herds in a historically accurate rendering, but he carried along with him what Webb called "too much excess baggage in the way of a fair damsel, a Negro mammy, a band of lovesick cowboys, and a convenient Texas Ranger." [16]

Regardless, the three men agreed that Henry's review was not merely an invective against the author, but an insult to their native region and its people. Henry, in turn, became the object of insults from Hough's supporters, one of whom was George W. Saunders, president of the Old Trail Driver's Association in San Antonio. Saunders, who had been contacted by Webb to verify certain aspects of cattle-drive history, referred to Henry, reputed to have European ties, as "that stupendous Parisian ass." [17]

Webb launched his defense of Hough by using testimony of men such as Saunders, then composed a questionnaire, which he mailed to Stuart Henry to test his knowledge of the West. Henry did not bother to respond, although he later made reference to the charges in the *Literary Digest International Book Review* for 1925, and in an addendum to his own book, *Conquering Our Great American Plains*. Ironically, Webb reviewed this book in the *Mississippi Valley Historical Review* in March of 1931. He did not choose to renew the controversy, but continued to believe that Henry's original article was an "unwarranted attack of Western people by an Eastern writer in an Eastern literary magazine." [18]

The significance for Webb of this engagement was the relationship that he developed with the two western novelists. He began to probe them regarding his own position and literary destiny. He knew that he had a fascinating idea in the Plains concept; he also enjoyed writing—fiction and nonfiction—but he could not determine the specific role he should play in promoting the traditions of his region. He questioned them regarding their writing philosophy and even suggested to Adams that he record his ideas on Western literature in an article. Rhodes gave Webb some hints on writing, and complimented his work, saying, "you have a clear call to write beyond a doubt."[19] Rhodes expressed what he felt to be the basis for their reactions in the Emerson Hough Controversy, saying that their own negative feelings resulted from a desire to perpetuate the contributions of their ancestors. As he explained, "You for your father,—I for my friends." This he saw as their personal effort to prevent on the national scale attempts "to Balkanise the American spirit, to Russianise our politics, to 'Levantise' our business methods, and to Europeanise our letters."[20] Webb shared with Rhodes his intense dislike for the Menckian diatribe spouted from the folds of *The American Mercury* and in his autobiography reflected on the days prior to the depression when "such flippants were in the saddle." H. L. Mencken, in Webb's opinion, had created "a school of brilliant insincerity," and made "suckers out of the American people and then laughed at them for their foolishness."[21]

Webb, Rhodes, and Adams all championed the attributes of their own region, but not at the expense of patriotism. In this respect they reflected the rise of regionalism as a significant cultural trend, particularly in the Southwest and the Trans-Mississippi West. To them Mencken's morbid hatred of democracy was intolerable. Webb personally mirrored the traditional Texas attitude, defense of state against all comers, but, first and foremost, defense of nation against foreign invaders. In the opinion of the western contingent, these "young intellectuals"—the Waldo Franks, Sherwood Andersons, and Harold Sterns—who maligned the common people of America as "the booboise," decried "faded moralism," "the Puritan tradition," and "Pioneer Culture," were more European than American. Historian T. R. Fehrenbach has analyzed this defensive characteristic of the Texan as a dominant mind-set derived from its brutal history of conquest and supremacy. Those who would have left their lands in possession of Indians or

Mexicans, when challenged, would not have expressed the imperial nature so vigorously. But these people had earned their right to Texas soil and played their part in carrying the American flag westward. They did not undergo a personality change overnight. Nevertheless, this pride in state did not negate pride in nation.[22]

Webb's reaction exemplified his regional orientation; he was very much a Texan and did not care to see his state maligned. For Rhodes, the controversy initiated a personal vendetta against the main current of national literary protest, an attitude that Webb and Adams shared, although to a lesser degree. Thus Webb, Rhodes, and Adams were attempting to defend their people, regional traditions, and the place of western literature in the national spectrum. In Texas, where the nineteenth century in many respects never passed completely from view, this attitude was not so surprising as it might have been elsewhere. To posit that their alienation from the national literary strain reflected the agrarian revolt against urban influence is not an adequate explanation. To be sure Texas had remained basically rural in outlook and politics, despite enormous economic gains during the twenties decade. But the regional awakening of this period could be seen in other fields—arts, crafts, and architecture as well. Webb's personal alienation can best be explained in terms of his historical orientation.

When viewed from the historical perspective, the controversy occurred at a time when the study of local history was growing in importance on both national and state levels, a trend that Webb strongly supported. Works on regional history, such as Hough's book, were merely one step beyond the local and becoming increasingly recognized in the historical field as an area open to investigation. Webb's own research spanned the local to the regional at this stage. He was also experimenting with fiction as well as historical writing; however his friend, poet Albert Trombly, did not encourage Webb's endeavors in this field. Pointing out that Webb had the whole state in front of him for a field of investigation, he encouraged him to capitalize on the area in which he had been trained. The fact that Webb had sold fiction articles did not mean that he should go this route, according to Trombly.[23] His friend's advice influenced him to take the historical approach in his writing. Andy Adams even more directly laid the burden squarely on the young professor's shoulders. He advocated continuing their fight for recognition of the West's literary contributions and for preservation of regional traditions. He championed Webb's stand, urging him to "awaken the dorment [sic] values that are pleading for expression," those that would provide a true literature of the West.[24]

The major basis for Webb's reaction to the whole inflated affair rested upon the fact that Stuart Henry's criticism, even against a fiction-based-on-fact treatment of the cattle kingdom, was also an attack on the area of specialization that Webb had chosen for his own; an attack belittling to his own people, and to the importance of the Great Plains concept germinating in his mind. Furthermore, this incident followed on the heels of his rejection in Chicago on similar grounds. Webb's temper at this time is reflected in a letter to Rhodes wherein he stressed the need for belief in America and resolved "to fight these University intellectuals in general and in particular." "Fighting," he said, "is half the strength of the Mencken crowd. . . . I believe a little 'intellectual' fur will prove an attraction."[25] For Webb, the Chicago crisis had provided the resolve, and the Emerson Hough Controversy a sense of direction. It was the consensus among the three that the West needed a spokesman to establish its rightful place in the national spectrum. By writing *The Great Plains,* Webb carried the standard.

W. P. WEBB:
IDEA MAN AND SEMINARIAN

I don't think you find an idea . . . by looking for it. When you begin to look for it, you have already found it. It comes to you unawares, and like Carl Sandburg's fog, on little cat feet. . . . It is a case of serendipity, once defined as a combination of serenity and stupidity. . . . Once it comes the facts fall into ranks and form patterns of meaning.

An hypothesis is an intuition of something which may turn out through investigation to be true or false. . . . If the facts seem to sustain it, the scholar develops it and finally he may announce it through publication [or] teaching. Once it enters the public domain, other scholars seize upon it, test it, and seek to destroy it. This is known as academic courtesy.

W. P. Webb, "Learning and Wisdom:
The Relevance of History"

Webb liked to tell a story about his Model-T Ford that illustrated how the Great Plains hypothesis took possession of him. He knew little about cars, but he did know that he could never get his Model-T to run properly. It was a four-cylinder job and prone to sputter, backfire, and balk. He took advantage of the guarantee on it and made numerous trips to the garage. The mechanic would tinker with it, then send him away. Finally, the exasperated man reached the limit of his endurance: "Don't bring this car back," he ordered. "There's nothing wrong with it."

"But it doesn't run right," Webb said, "It misses."

"Well, O.K. The damn thing ain't supposed to run until it gets hot." (Then Webb would make his point.) "And so, after much sputter and backfire, I got hot. I wrote *The Great Plains* defending my first hypothesis in four and one-half months."[1]

Although the actual writing of Webb's first major work had taken place in the short span of a few months, the development of it had been a much lengthier process. Starting with his childhood observation and experiences he began to build a memory bank of inert knowledge. He saw the impact of nature on the first settlers; he saw how they adapted their tools and mode of living accordingly, and how new institutions arose to replace the old. Living as he did, on "the hem of the garment of the frontier," as he liked to say in literary imagery, he noted that the 98th meridian had created an imaginary fault line separating one environment from another. A simple geography text and a brilliant professor helped to clarify his thinking and provided him with a tool and a methodology for analysis and investigation. Research on the Rangers revealed to him the importance of the six-shooter as a special adaptation to the demands of a hostile land; then the night came when he read Emerson Hough's book, *The Way to the West*, discussing the tools implementing the conquest of this region. This bit of information and Webb's recognition of what Hough had omitted was what was necessary to release that flash of insight—the magnet needed to draw the many particles of knowledge into a coherent matrix, formulating a meaningful pattern.

In a single moment all the living, reading, and research coalesced as he saw in the Plains phenomenon the "compelling unity" of the westward experience. This panoramic view encompassing the harmony of the integrated whole would occur again years later during the genesis of the Great Frontier concept as he viewed both Europe and the Great Frontier as units without regard to subdivisions into nations or continents.[2] Thus the basis for Webb's broad perspective was to see each area under investigation as a complete entity.

A friend recalled the first time he heard Webb voice the Plains concept. It was in the spring of 1922. Webb was an instructor in history and Rupert N. Richardson an instructor in government. Both were sitting in on one of E. C. Barker's classes. Barker began developing a topic on westward expansion and, pointing to the map, commented that the advance slowed as it approached the plains. "Does anyone have a reason to suggest?" he asked. Two or three comments were made, then Webb spoke up. "These people came from a timbered country and had developed a timber civilization; when they reached the land where forests ceased they were confused and did not know what to do. Before they could occupy the country they had to develop a new way of life, and it took them decades to do it." Richardson remembered that he was impressed by the statement, but did not realize at the time that he had heard the crux of the Great Plains concept.[3]

Soon thereafter Webb set aside his research momentarily while he went north for the advanced degree. He found, however, that the idea remained very much with him. As a result of the trauma at Chicago and his involvement in the Emerson Hough Controversy not long after his return, he had gained new resolve and motivation to vindicate himself and his region, and after searching, decided that he could do it by writing *The Great Plains*. He had the idea, but the proving of its precepts remained. In a somewhat unorthodox fashion, for a historian at least, he had reversed the process of investigation. Rather than compiling data to develop a conclusion, Webb had started with an a priori idea and worked in reverse. While this may not be the typical modus operandi for the traditional historian, it is not unique to "idea men." In a sense, of course, this statement must be qualified, for data absorbed through experience and observation is certainly a part of the preliminary groundwork.

Comments from friends and students helped to fill the gaps of the Plains thesis. He synthesized such information as a comment by his friend, Edward Everett Davis, that barbed wire and the windmill were instrumental in the development of the West. Andy Adams' *Log of a Cowboy* and his rendition of a cattle drive north broadened Webb's environmental perspective of the Plains region. He used another statement by a student that in the East, "civilization stood on three legs—land, water, and timber," and when its inhabitants moved westward, they found two of these legs withdrawn, and "civilization was left to stand, or topple."[4]

Webb borrowed these ideas, incorporating them into the whole. A suggestion from C. H. Thurber of Ginn and Company encouraged him to set aside his Ranger project and begin work in earnest on *The Great Plains*. Thurber pointed out that no one was likely to beat him on the Rangers and that his work on the Plains would make a "notable and important contribution to the history of our country." He also predicted that the book would earn for Webb honors in his field.[5]

As a result of a chance meeting in Barker's office with editor George H. Moore in 1927, a fortuitous association with Ginn and

Company had developed. When Webb mentioned that he was
working on the Rangers and Plains history, Moore exhibited polite
curiosity and at Webb's invitation went down to his office "to fry
some fat or burn a hole in the skillet." The unacademic terminol-
ogy of the invitation seemed to shock the eastern editor, Webb
recalled, but it must have added to his interest in the man and his
subject, for he soon had a contract to write a book for them. This
experience made him an advocate of the philosophy that it was
easier to sell a publisher on an idea, rather than a completed
manuscript. With contract in hand Webb felt a freedom to write as
he wished; he was not obligated to tailor his style to suit a
particular publisher.[6]

Webb was forced to withdraw for a time from the textbook series
that he had been writing with William E. Dodd and Eugen? C.
Barker. Two or three years prior to the publication of *The Great
Plains*, E. C. Barker, or "the Chief," as he was called, had
suggested that Webb join him in writing textbooks and the junior
faculty member was happy for the opportunity. This relationship
enabled him to get to know "the Chief," whom he came to admire
and respect greatly, even after their political views diverged. He
also found pleasure in the fact that textbook writing provided the
means for improving his financial status. Through the years he
collaborated with Barker, W. E. Dodd, Marie Alsanger, Frances
Cavanaugh, and Henry Steele Commager in the Our Nation history
series. He also helped construct outline maps and exercises to
accompany texts. In 1928 and 1929, however, Webb dropped out of
the series to a large extent as work on *The Great Plains* took
precedence.[7]

Fortune seemed to be in Webb's favor. Not long after the Ginn
contract was consummated, W. M. W. Splawn, president of the
university, approached him regarding a local history project that
Webb had been promoting in the Texas high schools. Representatives of the Rockefeller Foundation had become interested in
research projects underway at the university, and Splawn had
thought of Webb. He informed the president that he had underway
a project that he considered to be more important, then proceeded
to explain the nature of the Plains book, and told him that he
already had signed a contract. As a result of this encounter, the
Rockefeller grant was made, and Webb received a half-year leave
of absence for the spring of 1928 to devote to writing. With

financial assistance allotted through the Fund for Research in the Social Sciences at the University of Texas, and time now to devote solely to creativity, Webb began to live "in imagination on the plains." This was to be the happiest half year of the first part of his life. Two months before he was to go on leave, he returned to his office in Garrison Hall late one night and wrote the outline for the book. By this point, he had the complete story in mind with the exception of a section on land and water law.[8]

In order to save time he made arrangements to have books brought to his office as he needed them. He paid a library page to gather the books and deposit them at his office in Garrison Hall. Then Webb would compile additional lists of books needed from the bibliographies of those he had previously perused. The page, Ralph Parker, who eventually became librarian at the University of Georgia, would supply Webb each day with new material, thereby saving him much time. He did not make notes from these books, but learned to scan them quickly, developing what he called a "magnetic" attraction to relevant material. He would read for approximately ten days on one subject, marking the pertinent pages with cards and placing the books in stacks around the room, much to the janitor's despair. In this manner, he would progress from subject to subject and stack to stack in his development of the book. Previously he had never been able to compose using the typewriter, but after the first week he developed a severe writer's cramp. Unable to get rid of it, he resorted to the typewriter for writing quotations and soon discovered that he had made the transition from longhand.[9]

In developing his environmental approach, he relied heavily on John Wesley Powell's *Report on the Lands of the Arid Region of the United States*. His procedure was to trace one eastern institution, then another, as it was transported into the arid region and observe the modifications demanded by the new environment. During this period, Webb spun around himself a "mental cocoon" and was undisturbed by banging doors or noisy students that filled the corridors. As he recalled, "I was . . . building a world into which all the pieces seemed to fit. I was working creatively as well as historically, breaking a lot of precedents."[10] He found himself surrounded by buffalo, Comanches, and immigrants going westward. The real people around him did not exist, only the people of the plains. He worked according to an established pattern, four hours during the morning, followed by a nap in the early afternoon, then three more hours of work, occasionally returning at night to extend his working day into a twelve-to-fourteen hour stretch. Many times, he would go home exhausted mentally and physically, only to wake the next morning to find himself still intensely involved. With eager anticipation, as he said, "I would return to the task as a man to his mistress."[11]

Long before the book would be revised and polished into final draft form to be sent to his publishers in July of 1931, Webb added another stage to his development of the Great Plains concept, and in so doing initiated a mode of inquiry that would become a Webb trademark. During the fall semester of 1929, he offered for the first time a course on "The Great Plains and the Rocky Mountains."[12] He decided to take his students into his confidence, presented them with the thesis, and set them to work on certain facets of it. Although Webb would not become a member of the graduate faculty until 1933, he turned his course into a seminar and an indulgent department chose to look the other way.[13] As he recalled, "I did not rate a seminar, and I did not know enough to lecture. . . . I surreptitiously converted this class, and succeeding ones into a seminar—into hunting answers to my questions." He found his students to be "good hunters" who "dug holes all over the Great Plains." He frankly admitted that he "stole from them," but in return they received intellectual challenge and insight, as witnessed by the testimony of former students.[14]

Indeed Webb's development as well-known historian and innovative teacher was to be linked inextricably to his development of seminal ideas and to the problem method of presentation rather than the straight lecture format. Very early in his career he had tested the validity of this method of teaching and found it to be effective. A paper presenting the results of his experiment, "Increasing the Functional Value of History by the Use of the Problem Method of Presentation" gave a good preview of the seminar methodology that Webb later used. In this paper the beginning evidence of his ability as a challenging teacher was obvious. In it, for example, he traced the development of the mind in three stages: first, perception, when facts are gathered and material assembled; secondly, a short transitional period, when perception and imagination come into play; and finally, the critical stage, when causes are sought and proofs established. In general, it became characteristic for Webb to advocate use of the problem method of presentation, to omit memory data, and what he called other "medieval methods" that fill the student's mind with isolated facts.[15]

Webb had originally introduced the "problem method" for use in the high schools during the early years of his public school teaching career. The major ideas in this paper foreshadowed his teaching philosophy for graduate students and were similar to views expressed in his presidential address at the Forty-Eighth Annual Meeting of the Mississippi Valley Historical Association in 1955. According to Webb's analysis, the historical seminar should consist of an "outer shell" and an "inner spirit" without which the seminar becomes merely "a trade school in historical mechanics." The outer shell he expressed as the process of reading, collecting, analyzing, and organizing; the absolute essence of the seminar—the inner spirit—he saw as the driving force that expands the bounds of knowledge.[16]

Webb geared his own seminars in much the same manner, employing the problem method, but using his own original ideas to form the inner spirit or driving force. Around each original idea he organized a new seminar, used it to clarify his own thinking, and exposed his students to the challenge of the historical quest. The fact that his students did not rebel against his approach resulted from Webb's openness. They responded to his desire to work alongside them, as he said, "like a camping party exploring an unknown land." He described the library as the forest, and the classroom as the campfire; each student would be sent to hunt out information, then return to share his offering with others. He deplored the professor who, under careful subterfuge, used his students to do the "pick-and-shovel work" for some professional article or book which would advance his career. If he used his students' research, he very carefully gave them full credit for their findings. The intellectual stimulation he provided them, according to former students, could not be measured. He maintained his seminars until the book was published, then abandoned the topic for another. As he summarized briefly, "No idea, no seminar."[17]

Webb became famous for his seminars on the subjects of "the Great Plains" and "the Great Frontier," in which he fathered two major historical concepts and numerous seminal ideas and hypotheses for others to explore. After returning from Europe in

September 1938, two years after the genesis of the Great Frontier idea, he organized his seminar around this theme. The Frontiers and Democracy seminar was to last fourteen years and centered on the effect of the discovery of three new continents on world civilization around 1500, the impact of this acquisition of land and wealth on the individual, and on institutions such as absolutism, democracy, and religious polity.[18]

A former student described this last seminar on the Great Frontier as truly memorable, a sort of *"tour de force."* For this finale, Webb handpicked and interviewed most of the people chosen to participate. A very interesting group was selected which included a lawyer from England, who had come to Texas especially to study under Webb, and a Count from Rumania. The year-long seminar culminated at Friday Mountain Ranch, Webb's hill-country retreat, where he cooked steaks for the students over a charcoal fire, fed them homemade biscuits, and discussed with them a possible subtitle for his book. All received A's.[19]

Not the typical platform lecturer, he was an innovative teacher, yet his appearance was deceiving. Described as being of slightly better than average height with brown hair surrounding a balding pate, Webb would walk into a room:

> shuffling like an old-time farmer who has walked countless miles behind a Georgia stock, peering like an old desert rat who has tired his eyes looking too long at the sun in his wanderings. . . . His voice is low. 'I am Walter Webb,' he says. *Walter Webb?* Walter Prescott Webb? . . . Author of 'The Texas Rangers' and 'The Great Plains'? It's hard to believe. Somehow he should be different, sun-browned, robust, full of life, with a rolling voice.[20]

Nevertheless he was effective. His ability to hold an audience rested upon content rather than flamboyant speaking style, and upon the knack of teaching his students how to think, evidenced by the imprint of his influence on their minds.

He was not a great teacher in the classical sense. A former assistant, Rex Strickland, felt that his lecture courses could not be classed as inspirational. When the class bell would ring, it was his practice to assemble a handful of dog-eared notes and amble down the hall to his lecture room. In the Great West course, which this former student attended, Webb would "bumble along," giving the pages of his lecture with little elaboration; but he did exhibit a great sincerity and assisted the few rare students who had the ability to enlarge "the horizons of their understanding by the application of his principles of historicity."[21] Considering his lack of lecturing expertise, it is logical that Webb was more effective in the person-to-person atmosphere of the seminar situation.

Another former student and associate, Joe B. Frantz, observed that "he raised more questions than he answered and his classes were full of incomplete sentences and incomplete thoughts." When Frantz took History 80, Frontiers and Democracy, one middle-aged student who had a father fixation, often used the seminar as a forum to reminisce about "Daddy" and her girlhood in the Indian territory. Frantz was struck by Webb's kindness and solicitude in dealing with her. Unlike some professorial types who use their position as an excuse for bad manners, Webb was very genteel with her, merely saying, "We have to hear from someone else now." The course itself was unstructured, except that it was geared around the idea of the Great Frontier concept. He sometimes, according to Frantz, made statements that would not stand examination such as, "There is no such thing as a disagreeable sound made by Nature." These Webbisms, filled with sentiment and lore, reflected his distaste for the cacophony of modern living. He assigned landmark books such as *Das Kapital,* and the works of Adam Smith, and William Graham Sumner, whom he greatly respected.[22]

Others recalled that it was Webb's practice to explain the nature of the work expected in his seminar in "a measured, resonant, impressive tone, quite lacking in Texas drawl . . . 'There will be no daily assignments and no examinations in this class,' he would say. . . . 'Grades—for whatever they're worth—will be determined entirely by the papers submitted. You are a group of mature men and women, and you will be expected to work under your own initiative. That's all for today.' "[23] In Webb seminars, students could select, as one female student noted, but they also had to be selected. On one occasion, Webb firmly declined a pretty young girl with an invitation to return at a later date. Turning to his student, Edith Parker, he explained that he felt the girl was not mature enough for serious scholarship, as Miss Parker admitted, "a disability he could not see in me." In this student's analysis, Webb's seminars should best be classified as "a community of scholarship" and "a challenge to self-development through freedom of expression."[24]

Webb's daughter Mildred, who graduated Phi Beta Kappa from the University of Texas, took four courses under her father despite his warning that "he wouldn't give her an *A* if she made it." On at least one occasion, the grader came to her rescue and informed Webb that "if he gave anyone an *A,* he would have to give her one." Webb was always very careful not to give her special preference, but Mildred remembered one time when he "slipped." She had joined his class during the first summer session at the University of Wyoming in 1937. While they were there, Webb's parents customarily sent collect telegrams, one of which arrived in the middle of a lecture session. The messenger needed $1.69 in payment, but Webb had only a $10 bill and the boy could not make change. Turning to his daughter, Webb said: "Baby, lend me a dollar." Mildred recalled, "The class just yelled."[25]

Webb concluded his Plains seminar after the book was published in the summer of 1931. Approximately six months later, he received a call in the middle of the night from the editor of an Austin paper, asking if he had written a book called *The Great Plains.* Webb answered that he had, whereupon the man informed him that he had been awarded the Loubat prize of $400. "The what prize? Webb asked. "The Loubat prize of Columbia University," the man answered. Webb said that he had never heard of the Loubat prize. "Well" answered the editor, "I've never heard of *The Great Plains.*"[26] Soon, the book would become well-known, especially in historical circles, and Webb could feel that he had justified the faith of his benefactor. Publication of *The Great Plains* signified the end of a period of striving in Webb's life. Doors would be opened by this major success and he would begin to reap the profits of a job well done.

After an initial disappointment due to a negative review by a friend, Webb was pleased to find that the book was generally well accepted. To this point, he had not taken any visiting professorships due mainly to the illness of Jane's father. Following his death and publication of *The Great Plains,* Webb accepted an assignment for the summer session at Duke University. The Webbs had just purchased the family's first big car, a Studebaker, and in this they made the four-day trip east, stopping in Boston to meet with Mr.

George H. Moore of Ginn and Company. The Webbs registered at the Statler about 1:00 A.M. The next day, when he went to the publisher's offices located at 15 Ashburton Place, the editor met him in high spirits saying that he had something to show him. Then he opened a desk drawer to reveal the book section of the *New York Times*. There, spread across the front page, was an impressive review of *The Great Plains* pronouncing it to be "a new interpretation of the American West."27

Other favorable reviews followed. William McDonald of the *New York Times* lauded the book for its sound scholarship and industrious research, complemented by an easy style and "abundant evidence of first-hand acquaintance with the conditions of Western life." Henry Steele Commager in the *Books* section of the *New York Herald Tribune* called it "One of the most original, suggestive, and thoughtful contributions to the science of history in recent years"; and Rupert N. Richardson in the *Southwestern Historical Quarterly* credited Webb with constructing "a thesis which in originality and boldness has scarcely an equal in recent historical literature." The college editor of Ginn & Company labelled it "one of the three most distinguished publications in the college field" and placed it in the same category with Shakespeare's plays and William Graham Sumner's *Folkways*.28 Webb enjoyed the fruits of his first big literary success, but he was not to escape criticism. Other reviewers declared him guilty of writing largely from secondary sources, summarizing existing information, and of limiting his chapter on literature to the contemporary. However, the most severe and publicized criticism came from Fred A. Shannon.

In 1939, the Social Science Research Council selected the book as the outstanding contribution to American history since World War I, which Webb considered as "rather silly" since he did not believe there was "any best book." Regardless, Fred Shannon was asked to perform the critique of the book at the Conference of the Appraisal at Skytop in Pennsylvania. Webb's reaction, after receiving Shannon's damaging summation, is best described in his own colorful terms:

At any rate after the selection the book was handed to a Kansas Jayhawker for what they call an appraisal. This Kansas boy tore the book asunder in preparation of making a good splash before this Committee [sic] of distinguished scholars which is to assemble on September 9. They had me in a pretty tight spot trying to defend my own book. I refused to accept the Jayhawker's work as an appraisal of *The Great Plains* and thought that would probably stop the show. The officials insisted that I come on. I made the terms, namely, that I would not accept the Kansan's opinion as an appraisal and the Committee accepted. I then made a brief report which I think takes care of the Kansan pretty well. At any rate I am going.[29]

At Skytop, those present included representatives from various disciplines, since Webb's book covered several fields. Sociologist Louis Wirth, anthropologist Clark Wissler, and economist Edwin G. Nourse, were accompanied by such well-known historians as Arthur Schlesinger, Sr., Roy F. Nichols, and John D. Hicks. Although valid in some of his criticisms of Webb's book, Shannon, in general, engaged in sarcasm and nit-picking with the result that the Plains thesis emerged intact. Proceedings of this council were published in book form as Fred A. Shannon's *An Appraisal of Walter Prescott Webb's The Great Plains: A Study in Institutions and Environment.*[30]

This, in turn, was followed by a rebuttal from the Webb faction led by John W. Caughey with his "A Criticism of the Critique of Webb's *The Great Plains,*" published in the *Mississippi Valley Historical Review.* In general, Webb felt that his critic did not understand the book since he was not an expert in the field, and other historians such as Caughey of the University of California at Los Angeles, and Avery Craven of the University of Chicago agreed. Years later when it became Webb's duty as vice-president of the Mississippi Valley Historical Association to introduce Shannon as the president-elect, there was some trepidation on the part of the audience. But Webb's speech, couched with humor but imbued with sincerity, resulted in the friendship of the two men. Shannon died in February 1963, before he could accept Webb's invitation to teach a session at the University of Texas.[31]

Criticism from friends and associates mainly evolved around his treatment of the Spanish period. His friend, George Fuermann, wrote, "To call our Spanish period 'thin and of little consequence' seems to me to put you on thin ice, but here you have the voice of inexperience." He continued by calling Webb's attention to the

William E. Hinds. *Courtesy of the Archives Division, Barker History Center*

Casner and Mary Kyle Webb. *Courtesy of the Archives Division, Barker History Center*

Walter Prescott Webb as a young man. *Courtesy of the Archives Division, Texas State Library*

Jane Elizabeth Oliphant as a young woman. *Courtesy of Mildred Webb Bugg*

Jane Oliphant Webb with Mildred. *Courtesy of Mildred Webb Bugg*

Walter and Jane Webb. *Courtesy of the Archives Division, Texas State Library*

Walter and daughter Mildred. *Courtesy of the Archives Division, Texas State Library*

Mildred Webb Bugg. *Courtesy of Mildred Webb Bugg*

William Bradford Bugg. *Courtesy of Mildred Webb Bugg*

The Webb Home in Austin. *Courtesy of the Archives Division, Texas State Library*

Walter Prescott Webb in Oxford Garb. (Webb standing, second from left)
Courtesy of the Archives Division, Barker History Center

Friday Mountain Ranch. *Courtesy of the Archives Division, Texas State Library*

Participants in the International Symposium on The Great Frontier. (Left to right,
Aaron Copland, Bentley Glass, H. Max Gluckman, Terrell Maverick Webb, Loren
Eisely) *Courtesy of the Archives Division, Texas State Library*

Joe B. Frantz, Rodney Kidd, C. B. Smith, Sr., and S. Spurr (left to right) at the
International Symposium on The Great Frontier. *Courtesy of the Archives
Division, Texas State Library*

Walter and Terrell Webb at Friday Mountain Ranch. *Courtesy of Mrs. Walter Prescott (Terrell) Webb*

fact that El Paso was a prime example of the permanence of Spanish culture.[32] Others concurred that Webb had erred in his contention that the Spaniards, although successful explorers, were unsuccessful as colonists. The founding of Santa Fe shortly after that of Jamestown, plus other examples of the impact of the Spanish make this a valid criticism; yet a partial basis for this interpretation rests upon vantage point. Webb, for example, viewed the approach of the Spaniards from a position within the Great Plains and saw them colonizing the fringes, but circumventing its heart. He noted that if a Spaniard wanted to go from San Antonio to Santa Fe, he skirted the Great Plains by taking the Camino Real, south to Durango, then around the mountains to Santa Fe. He observed, too, that even after 1821, there were Spanish settlements bordering the Plains but none situated on it. He therefore saw the Anglo epic as an east-west sweep across the nation with the Spanish on its fringes.[33]

On the other hand, those specializing in Borderlands history such as Herbert Eugene Bolton, departed from this view and featured a unity of new world development as the basis for interpretation of American history. To Bolton, the Borderlands were not merely geographic regions, but areas where Spain's cultural baggage bears witness to the permanence of her influence. Bolton, therefore, dispensed with the traditional view that he claimed came "from mistaking the tail for the dog and leaving the dog out of the picture." Accordingly, Bolton's "dog," included all the area between the Rio Grande and Buenos Aires, while the remainder north of the Rio Grande was merely the tail or fringe areas of Spanish occupation. Rather than teach American history in isolation, Bolton advocated a comprehensive view that saw the western hemisphere as a cohesive historical unit composed of the two Americas. In comparison, Webb's treatment of the Spanish advance in *The Great Plains* was more traditionally Turnerian and Texan and his perspective was geographically different.[34]

In the opinion of Webb's associate and former president of Hardin Simmons University, Rupert N. Richardson, "Webb did not purposely minimize the influence of the Spaniard and Mexican, he just dealt with other matters and left them out of his thinking." Referring to Charles Hackett, a contemporary colleague of Webb's at the university, as well as to Carlos Castañeda, Richardson observed that "Webb wrote about and admired the Anglos; the

other men did the same for the Spaniards."[35] John Francis Bannon,
Borderlands specialist, noted that "Webb's departmental associations at Austin would have rubbed out any serious anti-Spanish
bias," but, he added, "Webb was a Texan, and they do have their
anti-Mex feelings."[36] Odie B. Faulk, student of Boltonian David
Vigness, claimed that "Webb never really understood or appreciated Spanish contributions in the Southwest, and it is my belief,
he never really studied the period."[37] Regardless of criticism of
certain facets of the Plains book, others such as W. Eugene Hollon
of the University of Toledo, maintain that the "Great Plains thesis
is holding up as well as any original thesis that has been
propounded by historians of the West since and including Frederick Jackson Turner."[38]

Despite the fact that Webb's special interests restricted him to
Anglo emphasis in his writing and research, he actively supported
efforts of fellow faculty members to improve research facilities in
the Latin American field as a part of his efforts to adopt a more
aggressive attitude for the university in general. Three years after
publication of *The Texas Rangers*, while serving as Harkness
Lecturer in London, he promoted through correspondence with E.
C. Barker, the development of a Latin American Institute at the
University of Texas. He hoped that Hackett would renew his efforts
in this direction as he felt that "the time was ripe" and that
financial assistance from the government and the Rockefeller
Foundation would be available.[39]

After completion of *The Great Plains*, Webb returned to work on
the Texas Rangers. Knowledge that the anniversary of the force
was approaching in 1935 to be followed the next year by the Texas
Centennial celebration spurred him to activity. He realized that
this would be an opportune time for publication and resolved to
finish the book by 1935. The Ranger history was a far cry from his
first idea book on the Plains, for the history of this force was
episodic in nature, and Webb had to search to find a thread of unity
on which to relate the multitude of incidents in which they had
been involved. He finally decided that the only recourse was to
center the book around the Ranger leaders. He knew that it would
be tempting to dwell on the heroism of the Rangers and therefore
decided on a factual rendition that would allow the romance to be
revealed through their deeds.[40]

In addition to pouring over records and original documents, he became personally acquainted with Ranger personalities such as Sam Gholson, W. M. (Major) Green, Dan. W. Roberts, Frank Hamer, and Tom Hickman. Webb thrilled to their exploits and was intrigued by the quality of courage the men exhibited. He realized that in order to understand the psychology of the men, this personal contact was necessary. Consequently, he also began attending meetings of the Ex-Ranger's Association at Weatherford, Ranger, and Menard. From these oldsters he gained some insight into what he called "the spirit of courage which has become a tradition of the Texas Rangers." After analysis, he decided that these men lacked a quality that most men have. As he explained: "Instead of having something—in this case courage—that most lack, they lack something that nearly everybody has. They lack fear."[41]

In order to learn about the activities of the present-day force, he toured the border camps with Captain R. W. Aldrich. Adjutant General Thomas F. Barton granted Webb an official Ranger commission and the "jewelry" to go with it, a forty-five calibre Colt revolver. J. A. (Arch) Miller of the Texas Big Bend area was detailed to accompany the Ranger Historian on his tour of the upper border. Webb also had some memorable sidelight experiences with the Rangers, one of which took him to a greasy-spoon restaurant in a small West Texas town. When time came for the waitress to present the check, the Rangers said, "Give it to the professor, give it to the professor!" The waitress did as told and everyone had a big laugh. Webb tried to make the best of the situation as he fished out two wrinkled dollar bills. "How much will you take off for cash," he asked. "Everything but my shoes, Baldy," the girl shot back. Needless to say, the Rangers laughed all the way back to Austin and for years later. By riding with the Rangers, sharing their campfires, and drinking their camp coffee, he received a special understanding of the contemporary Ranger force and recorded their activities in what is known as the definitive work on the Texas Rangers.[42]

Midway in his pursuit, Webb learned some discomfiting news involving his friend, J. Frank Dobie. Webb had confided to him his plans concerning the Ranger book; yet, not long after, he learned that Dobie planned to do an introduction for a rare reprint edition titled "A Texas Ranger." Webb was deeply hurt by this discovery and felt that Dobie had preempted his claim. Dr. Barker, whom Webb had turned to for advice, urged him to pass up the whole matter. When Dobie learned of Webb's feelings, he came to see him, treating the whole affair "as incidental." In fact, Dobie reminded Webb that he had given him the book to read in the first place. The outcome was that Webb told him to go ahead with his introduction, but the episode shocked his conception of professional propriety, and in view of their friendship, he failed to understand Dobie's actions. Nevertheless, the momentary breach healed and the two remained friends.[43]

The manuscript was finished by 1934, and Webb began to shop for a publisher. With one good book to his credit, he felt that the going would be easier. He knew that as a trade book, *The Texas Rangers* would not interest Ginn and Company since they functioned as a textbook firm exclusively. Meanwhile he had been collecting photographs of the Rangers, but decided that some would not reproduce satisfactorily. Although Lonnie Rees, the daughter of his former San Antonio employer and a talented artist, was not well-known, Webb liked her work and decided that she was just the person to do the illustrations for the Ranger book.[44]

Opportunity again presented itself as time approached for him to market his manuscript. He heard from a former friend of San Antonio days, an employee of Dun and Bradstreet, who wanted Webb to come to New York, examine errors made by his employees in their report writing, and then develop a course in composition for them. The fee mentioned, as Webb said, "made my summer salary look like pocket change." He readily accepted the offer. He knew, too, that this would be the perfect time to find a publisher for the Ranger book and secure a contract. In preparation, he wrote to several publishers, then limited the field to two who showed a definite interest. One was Houghton Mifflin of Boston. Webb became very much impressed with the firm's editor, Ferris Greenslet, a gaunt, leonine-looking man who had the ability to conduct an immense amount of business in a very brief period of time. When Webb went to see him, without preliminaries and without seeing the manuscript, Greenslet told him that he wanted the book and would make a one-third advance at the present time, one-third on delivery of the finished manuscript, and the final third when the book was published. Greenslet agreed to spend an equal amount on advertising and promptly brought out a contract. When they reached the clause covering moving picture rights, Webb wisely requested that they increase the commission by five percent, giving that extra sum to the agent who negotiated the deal. With this incentive, he felt that he was increasing his chances of selling the book to Hollywood. With a signed contract and a big check in his pocket he took the train back to New York.[45]

When the editors read the manuscript, they decided that it should be published in two volumes because of its length, but Webb disagreed and requested that the book be returned in order that he might shorten it. He accomplished this without harming the story. On another trip, he took the Lonnie Rees drawings with him. Greenslet was skeptical as to their suitability, but his staff artist was not. Webb arranged the drawings all around the room for better viewing and when the artist responded with an enthusiastic "Grand!" Webb's Texas artist had earned her berth.[46]

Despite the fact that he had started making money, it seemed that he was always broke for one reason or another. Of course, these were the depression days, and times were generally tough. Webb had planned to attend the American Historical Association Convention, but discovered that his bank balance had hit bottom. He was also faced with other obligations around the first of the year. Feeling very low, he informed Jane of the sad state of his financial affairs. She could not believe that the picture was as bleak as he had painted it, but he told her that the convention was definitely out of the question and dejectedly made his way to his two o'clock class. He was tired; "the bottom had dropped out," as he termed it, and he wished that he could just forget it all.[47]

As he approached the door to Garrison Hall 102, he saw a boy in a blue uniform coming down the hall toward him to deliver a telegram from Boston. After signing the receipt and tearing the message open, Webb discovered in amazement and with rapidly rising spirits, that Paramount had chosen his Ranger book to feature as the Texas Centennial picture. Houghton Mifflin had accepted the offer, subject to Webb's approval. After signing a contract of "impressive dimensions," which he said renounced "everything except the fact that he had written a book," he went out to purchase a new suit and attend the American Historical Association Convention in style. Eventually Paramount staged a gala premiere in San Antonio, featuring a film that bore little resemblance to the Ranger book, and the author was not invited. Webb noted that Texas politicians received all the "glory." When he inquired as to why the company had used little else than the title, the producer replied, "Protection."[48] The $11,000 received in payment for the motion-picture rights, of which Webb received eighty percent, enabled him to try his hand at investing in his own community where he soon discovered the benefits of credit and buying on margin.[49]

Published in 1935, *The Texas Rangers* was not one of Webb's favorites; he much preferred his idea books on *The Great Plains* and *The Great Frontier*. In fact, he referred to it as "a potboiler" full of dry facts, and favored a later edition written for youngsters that eliminated some of the scholarly appurtenances. Two years after publication of the Ranger book, Webb came forth with a work of considerable political impact, *Divided We Stand: The Crisis of a Frontierless Democracy*. Not an idea book in the manner of *The Great Plains* or *The Great Frontier*, it was, nevertheless, what Webb called "an adventure in interpretation and otherwise."[50]

The conception of this idea took a period of years, but it was the crisis of 1929 and its results that enabled him to make the synthesis. He had been gathering material, filing it away, never quite able to reach the point that he could start writing. Webb, who contended that "a compelling idea was the essential ingredient to provide unity and inspiration in historical writing," found the necessary spark one morning in February 1936. He learned that the Supreme Court had struck down the Triple A (Agricultural Adjustment Act), a law that afforded economic protection for farmers similar to that enjoyed by business for a century. To Webb, this was an inequitable tragedy. With this knowledge, he started writing and continued into the early morning hours. In six weeks, he had completed the first draft. It was ragged and lacked the necessary compilation of statistics, but the major task had been accomplished.[51]

Webb's story, rewritten several times, contended that practices of the modern corporation contributed to the sectionalism which was still evident in the United States—a sectionalism by which the North made the South an economic vassal, robbing it of wealth and power. The resulting domestic crisis was, according to Webb, a product of the closing of the frontier. He saw corporations reaching out from the North to attach their tentacles to the natural resources of the South and West. He saw the crisis occurring when the common man found himself pressed by corporate power and faced with the lack of a frontier. His story of two young Texas entrepreneurs and their treatment at the hands of northern interests created a stir of controversy. The destruction of their small milk bottle factory at Santa Anna, Texas, resulted in a federal investigation and indictment of the firm for monopolistic practices.[52]

Webb knew that he would need a liberal publisher for this book and thought he had selected one, but discovered that the firm would not allow him to use the word "milk bottle" at all. It seems that the Hartford Empire Glass Company of Connecticut owned ninety-five percent of the bottle machinery in America and all patents on it. Thus lawyers pointed out that it would be obvious that Webb was talking about this specific company. Webb also learned that a family connection existed between the publishers and the Hartford Empire family. A heated correspondence took place during the course of which Webb informed the publishers that several of the professors at the University of Texas owned stock in the Knape-Coleman glassworks.[53]

Prior to the book's first appearance, which contained only a sketchy account of the destruction of the small company, all the faculty stockholders received a check for their investment, some netting a fifty-percent increase in worth. Webb owned no stock, and unfortunately, as he said, had not been "paid off." The second edition of the book, reissued by Webb personally, contained "The Story of the Texas Milk Bottle" in devastating detail. John Crowe Ransom in the *Saturday Review of Literature*, said of the book, "Here a distinguished professor of American history produces a book of which the merit and the boldness alike consist in examining the Great American inequality as a historian and a geographer. . . . His argument is realistic and valid, it is inevitable, it is long overdue."[54]

Described by Carl Sandburg as one of "the great modern American pamphlets," and acknowledged by Webb as a "political tract," the book influenced President Franklin D. Roosevelt to issue the "National Emergency Report on Economic Conditions in the South," declaring the region to be the nation's number one economic problem. By the time the book reached its fourth edition, it had sold some 15,000 copies. Gayle A. Waldrop listed it as one of fifty highly recommended books for editorial writers, and one Texan purchased 1400 copies, which he distributed at the National

Education Association. Despite its controversial aspects, the book became greatly respected, especially in the South, although it is now dated.[55]

While writing chapter six of *Divided We Stand*, the chapter which would provide the book's subtitle "The Crisis of a Frontierless Democracy," Webb experienced the moment of synthesis which would result in *The Great Frontier*. This time he would follow the frontier to its logical conclusion. Armed with the idea, he attacked the problem in much the same manner as *The Great Plains*—by using the theme for a seminar. The driving force, in this case, he explained as "the insatiable curiosity" to determine the meaning of the Great Frontier in contemporary times. For the next fifteen years he would investigate its many ramifications and slowly the idea would fully develop. By 1950, he completed an outline, though he had previously written some fragments while at Oxford in 1943. He did not intend the book to be a definitive study; rather he saw it as an introduction to lines of future investigation, and as such it succeeded brilliantly.[56]

Published in 1952, this book was Webb's fourth historical adventure, and one that he felt might ultimately prove to be his greatest. In what he called "the boom hypothesis," he proposed that new lands discovered by Columbus and other explorers precipitated a boom in the Metropolis (Europe). Accompanying the boom came the rise of modern civilization, great wealth, and new institutions such as democracy, capitalism, individualism, and the acceleration of progress. By 1900, the new lands disappeared, the frontier closed, and new institutions were placed under stress. With depressing clarity of expression and a hint of prophecy, Webb analyzed contemporary questions and attempted to alert society to problems of today and tomorrow. He suggested that the frontier and its wealth had created an abnormal period of prosperity for western civilization. Since it had ended, society was faced with adjustment. Despite the fact that we continually search for new frontiers, these very words being adopted as a slogan even by a young presidential candidate, Webb bluntly proclaimed that most of these frontiers were "fallacious." In the fifties, such gloom-spreading was considered un-American and resulted in a half-serious effort for his dismissal. Webb himself realized that *The Great Frontier* could not be judged by standards of his times, but suggested that around 1990, the "thinking public" would reevaluate the boom hypothesis.[57]

In addition to its depressing prognostications, the book evoked criticism on other accounts. Even so, Clifton Fadiman, a member of the Pulitzer Prize committee, regarded it highly enough to nominate it for that coveted award. Henry Nash Smith in the *New York Herald Tribune* classified the work as "bold, speculative, and rich in hypotheses, some of them buttressed with evidence, others thrown out as guideposts to further inquiry." He also posited that Webb relied too heavily on the safety-valve theory of free land. David M. Potter, author of *People of Plenty*, questioned Webb's conception of the frontier as the only significant source of wealth, while E. De Golyer, writing for *The Dallas Morning News*, bluntly stated that "Professor Webb has not proved his thesis. His great synthesis covers too much territory."[58]

Critics also condemned the work as an extension of the Turner thesis, a charge that Webb himself attempted to explain during his presidential address to the American Historical Association in 1958. He admitted that he didn't really mind being classed as a member of the Turner School, and in fact, considered it an honor. However, he maintained that he had developed his thesis independently of Turner, although both theses were based on the historical philosophy of the same European scholar. Webb's mentor Lindley Miller Keasbey, had translated the works of the Italian economist, Achille Loria. Turner had quoted Loria in his frontier essay of 1893, indicating a mutual source of influence.[59]

Biographer Ray Allen Billington provides more detail concerning the relationship and influence of Loria on Turner, claiming that Turner had indeed either read or heard the *Analisa della Proprietà Capitalista* and that it had provided inspiration in the formulation of his ideas. Billington concurred that Turner borrowed from Loria, although it is his opinion that the historian could have written his frontier thesis without having done so because he had already synthesized such a mass of material on the subject.[60] Thus the similarity of concepts can be explained to a large extent by the similarity of sources.

Although Webb spent a summer of study at the University of Wisconsin in 1916, his correspondence does not reveal any mention of Turner or his influence. Turner, of course, was not there at this time, having transferred to Harvard during the years from 1910 to 1924, with time out in 1916 and 1917 to go to Washington to do his share in the war effort.[61] On the other hand, it would be unreasonable to assume that Webb knew nothing of Turner. In fact, the *Webb Papers* at the University of Texas Archives include a set of notes pertaining to Turner, but these are undated.[62] Webb's educational grounding did not include specific course work in history of the West; thus it is conceivable that whatever insight he had into the field was developed independently. It is also feasible that the impression of Turner gleaned from a lecture or class notes could not compare in Webb's mind to the imprint of Keasbey's dramatic teachings. Therefore, Webb felt no obligation to the frontier historian.

In the autumn years of his life, Webb toyed with what may have developed into still another great idea book, although his trial balloon in the form of an article, "The American West: Perpetual Mirage," created such a furor that it might well have become less acceptable to the general public than his other controversial works.[63] What came to be termed the "arid lands thesis," ironically reflected that Webb's intellectual journeys had taken a path similar to that of Keasbey during his elder years. Although Webb in 1931 failed to understand the bent Keasbey had taken, he too, by the mid-1950s had begun to search for the answers to "Why" and "Wherefore." Having covered the approach to the Great Plains and the how, when, and where of its conquest, he now began to seek the "Why" of the matter. In October 1956, he answered his friend, George Fuermann's query concerning the depression Webb's last letter had conveyed, explaining that it was due to his "inability to put on paper what I want to say about the West." Again Webb was experiencing his old malady of the doldrums, that period of frustration and futility accompanying gestation of an idea. By January of 1957, he felt that he was getting nearer to the inner spirit of the West and contemplated putting these ideas in book form. Whereas in *The Great Plains* he had explained the approach to the West, the proposed book would tell *"what* is there and *why."* "For three years," he said, "I have been groping towards this key, and now I think I have it."[64]

Instrumental in the development of this new synthesis had been his reading of a book on the West by Lucius Beebe. After reviewing Beebe's book and concluding that it treated the region artificially, he had decided that the distinguishing feature of western history is that there is so little of it; that in fact, the entire character of the American West had developed as a result of deficiencies. Its unifying element and "over-riding influence," Webb decided, was the desert, and because of its aridity, the land and its society learned to survive by adaptation and by pridefully upholding what they had. For this reason, according to Webb, historians of the region depicted cowboys as "noble knights," wrote biographies of outlaws and bad women, and considered western artists such as Charlie Russell and Frederick Remington as the equal to Michaelangelo. According to Webb, the West had developed a special talent "for making the most of little." In so doing it had produced a schizoid western society: one revealing goodness as in the case of the Mormons of Utah, "a rejected people with a bizarre religion," whose industry earned them permanence and prosperity; the other revealing the negative features illustrated by Nevada, whose depletion of minerals and natural resources had forced it to solve its dilemma by creating what he called "an oasis of iniquity and license in a sea of moral inhibitions."[65]

When Webb revealed his thesis, John Fischer, editor of *Harper's*, responded enthusiastically saying, "I am angry with myself for not having seen your 'simple and revolutionary idea,' which has been lying right in front of my eyes all these years." He saw the idea as "a theme which is central both to the history and to the future of the West, not to mention its present, and which no one else has ever been willing to face."[66] Western Congressmen and Chambers of Commerce were not so broad-minded. They were, in fact, irate. After reading the *Harper's* article, Roy Bedichek commented on the "cries of horror" emitting from Mike Mansfield and the various Chambers of Commerce. "For a quiet, unassuming peaceable soul," he told Webb, "you certainly stir up a lot of hell."[67]

The article and responses to it were written into the Congressional Record, and Congressmen such as Barry Goldwater, urged people of the Far West to "rise in defense" against Webb's remarks, and rise up they did. *The Denver Post* led the attack, urging Webb to take off his glasses and his Ph.D., saying, "You've picked yourself a fight." Another individual wanted to visit Austin and "spit" on Webb's building. Still others saw it much as Webb had intended, as an attempt to call attention to "some really dangerous social and economic illusions in the West." As one admitted, "the C. of C. mind is incorrigible," and he further noted that such blind optimism refuses to see conservation problems inherent in arid regions.[68]

Webb, who loved the desert in all its austere beauty, was disturbed enough by the public reaction to explain himself further in an article in *Montana, The Magazine of Western History*. He explained that the desert thesis had been the result of his personal quest to reveal the special character of his own country. In order to arrive at his conclusion, he had traveled during the summer of 1955 across the southern desert states. In 1956, he drove the length of the United States from the Canadian border to Mexico. He began to perceive that the desert was the heart of the American West, providing both unity and special problems. Answering what he termed "a civilized critic" from Nevada, he expressed regret if he had offended the people of the West, whom he greatly admired for their courage, integrity, and "adventurous spirit." His purpose, he concluded, "was to help them understand their country and themselves," for he loved it too.[69]

All of Webb's idea books were destined to attract controversy, and therein lies part of their greatness. His works elicited not only passive esthetic enjoyment, but stirred emotions and urged men to action. In all his major works can be found the thread of the frontier, as he said, "dominant in three and present in the fourth." After tracing its impact to a logical conclusion in *The Great Frontier*, he turned inward to find in the desert the geographic basis for the spirit of the West and its people.[70] Considering that Webb developed four largely original ideas in his life span (four more than most people), it is remarkable that he also found time to function effectively in numerous other spheres. During the germinative periods for his great ideas, he found time to make contributions not only to his profession, but to his city, state, and nation.

8

W. P. WEBB: ADMINISTRATOR

God so loved the world that he did not send a committee and for that we should all be thankful.

W. P. Webb, "A Letter to a College President"

After publication of *Divided We Stand* in 1937, fifteen years would lapse before Webb produced his last major work. He had made his mark as a historian with three important books published in rapid succession and at this point he began to build his reputation in other spheres. With his publications came recognition in the field and invitations to teach at prestigious universities during the summer sessions. Visiting professorships included a session at Harvard the summer of 1935, the University of West Virginia in 1936, and the University of Wyoming for the first session of the following summer.[1]

American University in Washington attempted to lure him away from Texas permanently, but Webb declined the offer. His esteem had undergone a gradual rise on his own terrain and administrators made arrangements to keep him.[2] By the mid-thirties, his quiet but firm stand on academic matters had earned him a reputation as a respected member of the faculty, a reputation that would become even more deserved with the passage of time and controversy. In many respects, Webb seemed to attract controversy, as most individualists do. It resulted not only from his written works, but also because of his involvement in the political workings of an institution with a turbulent history and through his association with friends such as J. Frank Dobie.

In the early twenties Webb had helped Dobie return from his exile at Oklahoma Agricultural and Mechanical College in Stillwater to rejoin the Texas faculty. Dobie had frankly asked him "to pull whatever wires" necessary to facilitate his return. Webb

125

obliged, advising his maverick friend "to quit knocking the Ph.D.," pointing out with empathy that they were both "in a hole" when it came to the degree matter. In 1925, Dobie returned as adjunct professor. Some twenty years later, Webb would again go to bat for his friend, who was, even more than he, "a mustang in the groves of academe."[3]

Webb himself could never be classed as the traditional academician, for his interests, pursuits, and opinions extended beyond the narrow confines of the university, involving him as a welcome member of both town and gown. His intellectual curiosity and his universal concern for people from all walks of life would allow no other recourse. While most university circles rotate in social and professional grooves, established according to rank, age, and department, Webb crossed these lines with ease.[4] Without appearing patronizing, he could deal with young people, regardless of position on the academic ladder, establish rapport with the local taxi driver or bellhop, or hobnob with politicians or plutocrats, all with the same sincere demeanor and innate courtesy. He could not fathom those who did not share his gift. Speaking of one such unfortunate associate, he once told Joe Frantz, "I'll bet that man never goes downtown unless he has to buy a pair of shoes."[5]

Chancellor Harry Ransom explained Webb's rapport with people as being "Old Texas," and "rooted, like the word, in a good heart." Ransom continued, "Webb savvies all kinds of academic brutes (including even administrators, whose motives he insists often mystify him)."[6] Content to play his part as faculty spokesman, Webb was considered by some as presidential timber, but he showed no interest even in the department chairmanship. When his young protégé Jim B. Pearson became Assistant Dean of Arts and Sciences, Webb called him into his office and sternly stated: "I have just heard that you have joined the brass collar boys." Pearson explained that it was only an assistant deanship, but Webb admonished him "to go no lower by taking another title."[7] Yet Webb himself became an able administrator, who chaired nearly all the committees the university could boast. Greatly respected within the educational complex for his clear thinking and decisiveness, he exhibited little patience when progress was impeded by divergent viewpoints or the inability to compromise.

The year 1937 was an important one in the annals of the history of the University of Texas, for on May 10, the "golden" decade of the Benedict administration came to an end. With the death of Harry Yandell Benedict, whose administration had been identified with academic freedom and general goodwill, the university was hard pressed to find a successor. Students and faculty alike mourned the death of beloved "Dean Benny." During the Benedict administration, prosperity had faded as the depression took its toll. In Texas the economic picture was not so bleak as in other states, but its impact was felt and reflected in the Hoovervilles blighting the outskirts of urban areas, in the increasing number of hitchhikers, and in the files of the unemployed. Although the Wall Street collapse had hit in October of 1929, Texas suffered a delayed reaction. Not until 1931, when European markets for Texas exports dried up, did the state feel the crunch. Even then, Texans en masse experienced only a light attack of the capitalistic crisis. The majority of the population was still agrarian in orientation and would recall more vividly the disastrous drought and dust storms of the 1930s than the depression itself.[8]

During the thirties, exploitation of natural resources in the state (sometimes referred to as industrialization) continued and with it came expansion of the University of Texas. While the nation suffered, the university, in general, prospered because of its rich oil holdings. Under the Benedict tenure, the student body had grown from 5,000 to nearly twice that number with a corresponding increase in faculty from 330 to 500.[9] Awareness of these facts became a prime consideration in Webb's mind when in 1937, the search for Benedict's successor got underway. Webb stressed that the new president must not only be an educator, but an executive of good business sense. In a classic editorial, "The Regents vs. Diogenes," Webb showed his concern for the future of his university.[10] As if by some gift of foresight, he addressed the problem that would be a major factor in the downfall of a future president, Homer Price Rainey: the conflict between wealthy business interests in the state, well-represented on the Board of Regents, and the president's stand for academic freedom and tenure. In his role as faculty advisor, Webb would be frequently called upon to employ the power of his pen. His gift for writing with clarity and sincerity stood him and his compatriots in good stead.

The following year, Webb interrupted his tenure at the University of Texas to accept an honorary assignment as Harkness

Lecturer at the University of London. Despite the fact that Hitler was already issuing ominous threats, the Webbs embarked for Europe on the *Berengaria*, February 3, 1938. The trip started out on a somewhat sour note as Webb had tried to persuade Jane to make the trip a holiday affair for the two of them alone. He saw it as an opportunity to mend the wear and tear of time and divergent interests that had affected their relationship. Their daughter, Mildred, now nineteen years old and a student at the University of Texas, was capable of caring for herself. Webb suggested that she should remain in school for the spring semester, which would give her a taste of being independent, then follow them to Europe in the summer. Jane, however, had grown very close to her daughter through the years and would not consent to this plan. Because of ill-health as a baby and an eye problem, Mildred had required special attention, and Jane found it difficult to relinquish her role of maternal solicitude.[11]

On February 4, 1938, the Webbs celebrated Jane's birthday on board the *Berengaria* by having dinner with the captain, Curtis Nunn. Six days later they landed in England. They spent their first ten days at the Cumberland Hotel in London, then moved to Carleton Mansions, a private hotel frequented largely by visiting university professors. The guest list while the Webbs were in residence included William S. Taylor, dean of education at the University of Kentucky; Anna Pearl Cooper of the University of Washington; Dr. and Mrs. L. F. Stock of Wisconsin; Miss De Long of Sweet Briar, and Dr. and Mrs. L. Payne of the English department at the University of Texas. Room and board cost $300 a month, indicative of the expensive and taxing year in several respects.[12]

The eight months Webb spent in England were largely unhappy; as he noted, "all the people everywhere were unhappy; preparing for the doom of Europe and the world." The desire for peace in 1938 was still strong, and Webb had a first-class seat on history as world leaders attempted to maintain it. In his mind's eye, he saw Winston Churchill, "The growling bulldog of Britain, straining on the leash of public disapproval," and going unheard. He saw Anthony Eden attempting to ward off Mussolini's attack on Abyssinia and being sacked for his efforts. He witnessed the resultant protest rally in Trafalgar Square. In September 1938, he was not surprised when Neville Chamberlain went to Munich, "carrying an umbrella in his hand and the softness of a whole nation in his portfolio." To Webb, appeasement at Munich merely reflected the public sentiment he had witnessed in England. With myopic vision, Europeans appeared to place the fear of Communism in front of the more imminent threats of fascism. Stealthily the war clouds gathered.[13]

Webb's teaching assignment during this time included the presentation of several month-long lecture series. He had been scheduled to lecture in Prague, but Hitler took over Austria in March 1938, and the atmosphere on the continent was tense. Uncertain what to do, Webb consulted with the American Embassy, who urged that he go only at his own risk. He changed his plans and in June rented a car and drove with Jane and Mildred to Devon. There they visited Professor and Mrs. W. N. Mendicott, who feted them with parties, then went on to Scotland for a month.[14]

In London, Webb met a friend from Texas, W. Eugene Hollon, whose reports of his tour of Germany, Austria, Italy, and Czechoslovakia reinforced Webb's concern that they might be overstaying their welcome in Europe. Hollon had listened to Hermann Goering speak in Berlin, and Mussolini in Italy, and had seen Hitler's military machine practicing their goose-steps down the *Unter den Linden*.[15] The portents were not reassuring as crisis after crisis developed. Webb himself would have enjoyed traveling on the continent, in spite of, or perhaps because of, the excitement, but he had his wife and daughter to consider. He also received worrisome telegrams from his parents urging him to return home as soon as the lectures were over in order that they could "look upon his face once more."[16] Messages such as these added to an already distressful situation, particularly since Jane wanted to stay. The sightseeing tours, antique shopping, and lacemaking made for a thoroughly enjoyable visit on her part. She seemed unaware or perhaps uninformed of the gravity of the situation as Europe prepared for war. Finally, when Webb received confidential information that Hitler would strike as soon as the crops were in, he made arrangements to send Jane and Mildred back to the United States. This news created a crisis on the domestic front as Jane felt that he should share his news with other visitors. Webb attempted to explain that this was impossible since the news was confidential and also because it might precipitate a panic. When Jane threatened to release the information herself, a quarrel ensued during which bitter words were exchanged, and Jane accused Webb of being a coward. This event marked a low point in their marital relationship. As he admitted a few years later, writing in the third person, "This single experience embittered his whole outlook."[17] On August 10, Webb booked passage for his wife and daughter on the *Aquitania*. After arrival in New York, Jane and Mildred spent two or three days at the Hotel Astor, then on to Chicago, and home to Austin by August 31. Webb stayed behind in London to preside at the Anglo-American History Conference.[18]

Although this quarrel had been the direct cause of estrangement, other factors had contributed to the gradual build up of tension. A very strong-willed woman, Jane insisted upon economic independence and Webb had provided it for her through separate ownership of property when he became financially able. As he explained, this meant that "he now could not provide for her wants because she could do it herself, and he began to feel a little less necessary and essential." He also began to be quite lonely, as he admitted, "because she always seemed to be busy with the family, or with other interests." After the quarrel in London, Webb felt that they were both entrapped by circumstances. As he explained, "It was the sort of situation that the stage loves when preparing for divorce or tragedy, which the woman considered synonymous."[19] Correspondence indicated that Jane did not take the incident as seriously as Webb, or if she did, she wisely attempted to mend hurt feelings, writing from Illinois en route home, "I had been thinking about you all day and feeling lonesome for you. I wish it were so we could have the trip home together."[20]

After returning to Texas, Webb threw himself into his work, but found his creative efforts to be as dull and heavy as his heart. He soon found other productive outlets for his energies in his real-estate ventures, in his role as faculty advisor, as editorial consultant for "The Way of Life Series," which involved considerable traveling, and as Director of the Texas State Historical Association.[21]

As the "Oldest Learned Society in Texas," this organization had grown out of a meeting held in the Old Main building on the University of Texas campus in February of 1897. The first annual meeting followed in Austin on June 17. President-elect Oran M.

Roberts listed as the Association's objectives the promotion and preservation of historical material relating to Texas. They planned to publish the products of their research in a companion *Quarterly*. Despite the "uphill struggle" of its early years, the organization and its publication flourished under the stewardship of the University of Texas history faculty.[22]

George P. Garrison, the chairman of the history department prior to the days of Eugene C. Barker, ran the association in his spare time, with the assistance of Lester Gladstone Bugbee. Both men worked on a voluntary basis, at times supporting the organization from their own pocketbooks, and spending their vacations soliciting members. In 1910 Garrison died, while editing for the *Quarterly* from his sickbed. Eugene C. Barker took over as editor the following year. Barker had become an active member of the group when his friend, Lester Bugbee, was forced to resign because of ill-health. (Bugbee died of tuberculosis at the young age of thirty-two.) In June of 1911, Herbert Eugene Bolton wrote to Barker from California suggesting that the name of the publication be changed to the *Southwestern Historical Quarterly* and its scope expanded to include the wider region. Bolton offered to serve as coeditor or associate editor. Barker agreed, and on March 2, 1912, the Council met and changed the name officially. For the next twenty-six years, Barker would remain at the helm of the association with Bolton assisting from California. Upon Barker's resignation in 1937, he was succeeded by R. L. Biesele, Walter Prescott Webb, and Charles W. Hackett. Webb became the Association's new director.[23]

The relationship between Walter Webb and historical associations extended back to 1915 and his days as a public schoolteacher when he had realized that professionalism would be necessary for advancement. His participation in such groups had been instrumental in shaping his career. Papers read at teacher's association meetings on methodology had earned him the attention of members of the University of Texas faculty and subsequent employment by the university in 1918. In 1938, after his return from Europe, Webb resumed the TSHA directorship. As he admitted to his friend, R. D. Mason, "This has been a very tough year for me. I have not recovered from the European orgy, and it will require at least another year before I am on my feet."[24]

Nevertheless, his association with the historical organization was to be rewarding for both parties. He was again providing a service for his region and able to apply his talents for the benefit of both state and profession.

Despite needing time off to recuperate physically and financially, Webb had other irons in the fire. Problems with relatives compounded his responsibilities. On December 19, 1937, Leslie Wright, his sister's husband, had been crushed in an elevator accident. His death left Ima with four dependent children, a responsibility that devolved upon Webb as the only brother. He determined to see that the older children were educated and the family cared for. When his oldest sister, Alma Hewlett, died in 1917, she had left two daughters, Lucille and Oletta, a charge that the elder Webbs assumed. Lucille, a rather difficult child, was sent to live temporarily with Jane and Walter in 1924. As Ima Wright recalled, "Webb was the responsible older brother and tried to make something of all of us."[25]

Now that his parents were gaining in years, Webb knew that they would soon be in need of assistance themselves. Realizing the responsibility in store for him, he purchased five acres of land on the east side of Austin and planned to move Ima and her family there. His instinct for good business had come to the fore in the selection of this piece of property; he hoped that a large gravel pit on the acreage would produce an adequate amount to meet expenses for the upkeep. He planned, too, to bring his mother and father there when they sold their farm at Weatherford. Casner, whose eyesight was failing, asked his son to take charge of the money from the sale of the farm and invest it as he saw properly. During these years, Webb kept a sharp lookout for investment opportunities in order to build his personal estate.[26]

Meanwhile, Webb was fortunate in having an excellent staff to man the ship at the Texas State Historical Association while his energies were scattered by other obligations. He thought highly of his people and commended them for their efficient handling of the various association projects. With the true leader's natural ability, he delegated responsibilities effectively. Staff members of the Texas State Historical Association during these years included Miss Llerena Friend, whose primary function was the promotion of the *Handbook*, and Miss Betty Brooke Eakle, who, as Webb said, "puts the *Junior Historian* to bed." Both dealt with the publication headaches of the *Quarterly*, when H. Bailey Carroll, Webb's assistant, was not present. Other staff members included Deena Anderson, and Dorman Winfrey, whom Webb called "the general factotum who does everything any of the others asks him to do, does it cheerfully and well." E. C. Barksdale, later to become chairman of the department of history at the University of Texas at Arlington, and Coral H. Tullis also assisted during the Webb years with the Texas State Historical Association.[27] Llerena Friend became librarian at the Eugene C. Barker Texas History Center, prior to Chester V. Kielman's term, and "the general factotum," Dorman Winfrey, functions cheerfully and efficiently as director of the Texas State Library in Austin.

This was the staff that assisted Webb in the engineering of such projects as the "Texas Collection," his "odds and ends" addition to the *Southwestern Historical Quarterly*. The Collection had been started as a file built up by accretion from letters of inquiry. If the letters included items of interest that might be used, the staff then set them aside for future use. Although the section carried Webb's by-line, he did not author all inclusions. As he admitted, his "historical conscience" hurt him each time he assembled his department because much of the information he compiled in creating the "Texas Collection" he merely "borrowed" without credit or quotation, or staff members wrote it themselves. As an example of some of the borrowed paragraphs that reached his desk, he cited one humorous note that helped break the monotonous routine of editorial work. The following gem was posted for posterity:

> Please send me information on the Spanish.
> Yours truly,
> John Doe

The answer—unmailed, of course—read:

> Please meet the next freight train at the station. We are shipping you the Garcia Library.
> Texas State Historical Association[28]

One of the most impressive undertakings during Webb's tenure as director was the comprehensive *Handbook of Texas*, begun in 1939. Webb strongly believed that the *Handbook* would become an indispensable aid to the students of Texana. At the time of its compilation, he considered it to be "the most educative process going on in the social science field in Texas" and one that brought to light new and interesting factual information about the state. As an example of one such fact, Webb liked to tell about a Texas railroad, the Bartlett and Western, abandoned in 1935. This railroad, it seems, had stations named Matthew, Mark, Luke, and John, in each of which was a copy of the appropriate gospel.[29] The *Handbook*, when completed in 1952, was an immense two-volume collection of data and an indispensable research tool for students of Texas and the Southwest.

Promotion and funding for such an expensive undertaking proved to be a large task. Webb enlisted the aid of sympathetic newspaper editors who touted his grandiose idea, gathering support, yet at the same time eliciting criticism from those who felt the project too ambitious. Webb found that university administrators—at least President Homer Price Rainey—were on his side. With Rainey's support, the Forty-seventh Legislature appropriated $4,750 to initiate the project. After 1943, the annual budget for the *Handbook* was set at approximately $12,300, where it remained until its completion.[30] A portion of the financial aid for this and other Texas State Historical Association projects came from the Rockefeller Foundation. On June 26–27, 1942, as part of his fund-raising activities, Webb participated in the Conference on the Northern Plains in Lincoln, Nebraska, where he presented "A Summary of Projects Recommended by the Texas State Historical Association to the Rockefeller Foundation."[31]

Webb had a talent for fund-raising. Another of his memorable activities in behalf of the organization included a stint as empresario. H. G. Wells, the famous British historian, had been asked to speak in San Antonio, and the Brewer's Association had invited Webb and a hundred others to listen to him. After hearing Wells, Webb decided to invite him to speak in Austin as a fund-raising device for the Texas State Historical Association. There was only one catch. Wells charged $1500 per engagement. Traveling on a hunch, Webb followed the British historian to Dallas where he offered him $1000 to come to Austin to speak. According to their agreement, the Association would get the second thousand and anything in excess would be divided 50-50. With this bold maneuver Webb placed himself in a financially risky position. The Association had no speaker's fund; Webb was not authorized to make such an offer in the first place; and he had to guarantee Wells the $1000 personally. When advance sales for the lecture amounted to only $500, Webb began to count his losses. Fortunately, however, the lecture pulled what Joe B. Frantz remembered as "the largest non-athletic crowd at Gregory Gymnasium since Will Rogers." The total income from the affair came to $2700. Webb's fund-raising gamble paid off.[32]

Another of his successes while Director of the Texas State Historical Association, possibly the most far-reaching, was the founding of the Junior Historians, a student branch of the organization. Webb had long been interested in making history relevant to young people as well as in the promotion of research in local history. With the founding of the Junior Historians in 1939, he accomplished both. These interests can be traced to his work on the *Texas History Teacher's Bulletin* as a newly arrived adjunct professor at the University of Texas in 1919. As managing editor of the *Bulletin* in 1922, he had initiated a drive to encourage investigation into local history by both teachers and students. For Roy Bedichek's *Interscholastic Leaguer*, he wrote his "Talks on Texas Books"—reviews geared to interest schoolchildren in Texana, and he had initiated the Caldwell Local History Prize for the best writing on relevant topics. Bulletins 11 through 14 launched his publicity campaign and listed the rules and regulations for the contest, standards for judging, and suggested topics. C. M. Caldwell, a University of Texas regent from Abilene, provided money for the prize. In the October 1924, *History Teacher's Bulletin* Webb proposed a Library of Texas Books and encouraged the establishment of a Texas Bookshelf in every public school. At the Texas State Teacher's Association Convention in San Antonio in November of that year, he spoke on "Opportunities for Research in Local History in Texas." With such a longstanding and active interest in the promotion of research on local history and in stimulating student participation, Webb's development of the Junior Historian arm of the Texas State Historical Association was a natural outgrowth of his past activities.[33]

He announced the founding of the Junior Historians in the "Texas Collection" section of the *Southwestern Historical Quarterly* in October of 1939. With the assistance of the colorful Texas cowboy type, H. Bailey Carroll, the first five chapters were formed by January of 1940. Stating his aims for prospective young members, Webb hoped that they would "acquaint themselves with

Texas history and literature and thereby develop a richer culture upon the great Texas heritage." He foresaw the organization serving as a training ground for "future historians of Texas." By January of 1941, there were twenty-one active chapters in the state high schools. The first issue of the *Junior Historian* magazine carried a Webb editorial, "Salute to Youth," which stated as its purpose the fostering in young people of a "love of their own state" by developing their knowledge of it.[34]

Webb designated H. Bailey Carroll to guide the new Junior Historian organization. With his Stetson hat and cigar, Carroll soon captivated his young members and excited their imaginations. Much like a figure from the historical past he discussed, Carroll, as Dorman Winfrey remembered him, was "a combination of cowboy Gary Cooper and John Knott's 'Old Man Texas.'" (Knott was a well-known editorial cartoonist for the *Dallas News.*) Another well-known name in the early history of the Junior Historian movement was author Paul Horgan, who sponsored the only Junior Historian chapter outside the state. Horgan headed a chapter at New Mexico Military Institute in Roswell. In an editorial published in the organization magazine in March of 1943, he advised young people to "write about anything that is truly related to the land of your birth and being . . . if you can feel truly about the facts of your historical past, and if you can get that into the works for others to feel with you, you will solve the problem of what to write about, and how to write it."[35]

Webb, of course, agreed with Horgan's philosophy, since he had an ongoing love affair with books. In this vein, to promote good reading and financial stability, he initiated the Book Auction held at the annual meeting of the Texas State Historical Association. One of his favorite auctioneers was Will Timmons of the University of Texas at El Paso. Webb maintained that Timmons "got the best prices." In keeping with his philosophy that books should be made available to the largest possible audience, he attempted to keep publications of the Texas State Historical Association within a reasonable price range in order to prevent "rich Texans" and collectors from being the only purchasers.[36]

As with most organizations of any size, there were bound to be problems, and the Texas State Historical Association was no exception. Some members still recall suffering through a period in association history referred to as "the bloody days." Never one to sit out a fight, Webb, although no longer the director, became involved. In 1943, he had decided to step down and allow his assistant, H. Bailey Carroll to take over. Carroll, who had been one of Webb's most competent assistants, ran the Texas State Association during the 1950s. As time passed, he became a controversial figure due to his purported acceptance of support from wealthy Texans, particularly the Dallas oil and cattle people. There was also some question concerning methods of administering association funds. In accordance with orders given during a meeting in Carroll's office October 20, 1953, Coral H. Tullis, gave Walter McCaleb access to the association books, sparking additional controversy. To compound matters, Bailey Carroll was suffering from ill-health. With all good intentions, Webb offered to arrange for Carroll a year's leave of absence with pay and suggested that he consider choosing a successor. Carroll, perhaps due to illness, reacted in a hostile manner. In much the same way, Fred Cotten, first vice-president who was next in line for the association presidency, also managed to offend him when he asked Carroll whether he was training a successor. It soon became obvious that Carroll felt that there was a plot underway to undermine his position as director.[37]

By 1961, the internecine controversy reached the point where Webb felt obligated to step in, and after evaluating the situation, decided that Cotten was on the right side of the dispute. By thus declaring himself, Webb earned Carroll's bitter animosity, which he expressed in no uncertain terms in a letter to Fred Cotten. In this letter Carroll asked Cotten to resign from his succession to the presidency and included some remarks regarding Webb's record as director—none of which were complimentary. Mrs. J. Bruce. (Merle) Duncan of Baylor University was president of the association at the time. Webb did not disapprove of Merle Duncan's reelection to the presidency for another term. He considered her as one of those exceptional women who managed, as he said, "to be feminine without being feline." He simply believed that custom should prevail, that Cotten should move into the president's slot according to tradition established through the years.[38]

At this point, Webb decided to take a stand and, in a typically bold and biting talk entitled "On Personal Privilege," chastised Carroll and admonished the whole group. He did not make a defense of himself, stating that most members knew the truth of the matter anyway. Instead he chose to speak of Fred Cotten, who had been a working member of the association for fifteen years. Cotten, an authority on local history in the Parker County and Upper Brazos areas and an active supporter of the Junior Historians, was well-qualified to fill the post. Webb considered Carroll's attempt to pass over him a gross insult to the man and to the precedent established by the association in years past. Webb pointed out, that Cotten's chief crime seemed to be that of asking the director for an explanation of items he failed to understand. Cotten, never a "rubber stamp" character, had refused to endorse programs already in effect or to sanction expenditures of association funds without knowing the services or goods received. As Webb stated, "He has sat on the Board of Directors of Banks and other institutions, and is accustomed to having questions answered. He probably did not know there was anything wrong with it."[39]

Since Carroll had chosen to make a "direct challenge" in his attempt to reinstate Merle Duncan, Cotten felt that he had no choice but to let his name remain on the ballot. This meant that the whole affair would have to be resolved by the council. In Webb's speech, he pointed out that, in effect, the council itself was now on trial and asked that the voting be conducted openly. "I trust no one will want to hide his identity behind a secret ballot," he said. He then reemphasized that it was the custom of choosing the successor from among members of the council, explaining to them in blunt terms that this meant that the person scheduled for the nomination was now among the council members. Webb continued:

> I would like to ask you who are eligible for this honor, if it is an honor, whether you would accept it under such dishonorable circumstances. If you do accept it, as I doubt you will, you will have to live with your conscience for the rest of your life. The pedestal you mount prematurely will rest on shifting sand, and everytime a member sees you, he or she will turn away with involuntary nausea at what you have been a party to.[40]

At the business meeting of the association the following day, the full membership would have an opportunity to vote on nominations recommended by the Executive Council. Carroll, however, had threatened a floor fight if Cotten were nominated. Webb stated that he was not so concerned with this possibility as he was with immediate council action. He admitted to the council that Carroll may have made enough prior preparation to defeat Cotten on the floor. If this happened, Webb predicted that it would be a great loss by killing the man's usefulness and service to history across the state. Webb concluded by saying if this were the result, he wanted the privilege of writing the epitaph, which would read:

> HERE LIES FRED COTTEN, HISTORIAN
> His Career was cut off by
> a Combination of Malice
> and injustice
> He was stung by pismires and
> Kicked to death
> By Grasshoppers.[41]

And with that humourous note, he concluded what was in actuality the high point of seriousness in the controversy. The upshot of the whole affair was that in 1962 Cotten was instated as president for a two-year term after an interregnum during which Merle Duncan completed her service.[42]

This episode, and Webb's participation in it, exemplified his characteristic reaction on matters where he felt principles and justice were at stake. At the risk of damaging his own career he traditionally stood as a bastion of integrity against regents and administrators alike. Consequently, he was well-respected among his peers although they might not share his views. Among Webb's worthy contributions to the Texas State Historical Association, one stands above all others. J. Frank Dobie summarized it very well:

> I don't know but that when Webb gets to St. Peter, he may not have more credit there for the Junior Historians of Texas than he will have for the books he has written, because the far-reachingness, if I may use such a word, of this Junior Historian movement can't be determined at all.[43]

9

BATTLEFIELDS: AT HOME AND ABROAD

Tranquility, thou languid Goddess, rise!
Stretch thy rheumatic limbs, and rub thine eyes;

Free Enterprise! God save the Status Quo!
Down with that Man! and Don't Forget the Alamo!

Two mortgages closed down Kerrville way.
Three copies (freshly marked) of U.S.A.
Four dummy profs to set up as decoys,
Five dinners, seven movie picture passes—
Prizes for all who want to kiss their a____!
Proud of his cohorts, Woodward hails the Queen.
And smiles with slitlike mouth upon the scene;
"While we have power," he cries, "to fight for thee,
Justice shall ne'er disturb Tranquility!"

Anonymous, "Tranquility, A Poem" quoted in
Homer Price Rainey, *The Tower and the Dome*

In August of 1942, Walter Prescott Webb received a cablegram from the registrar of Oxford offering him the Harmsworth Professorship of American History. This was an endowed chair and entailed a five-year appointment if the recipient so desired. Chancellor Lord Halifax, as well as the American Ambassador to England, and previous Harmsworth recipients Professors Samuel Elliot Morison and Allan Nevins, all encouraged Webb to accept the position as "a great public service." From Harvard, Morison wrote: "The English interest in U.S. History is at an all time high. I urge you to accept. . . . It will be an interesting experience."[1] With the assignment couched as a duty to country in times of peril, Webb felt obligated to accept and requested a leave of absence for a period of not less than one year. As Webb informed his department, "I believe that time spent in England and under present conditions will be of considerable value and will make my future work in this country more effective." On this second trip to

Europe, Jane would not be accompanying him. She served as president of the Albert Sidney Johnston Chapter of the United Daughters of the Confederacy from 1940 to 1942, and in 1943 the Daughters of the Republic of Texas elected her their state president. She also had been a regent of the DAR and had obligations in all associations.[2]

Webb's personal rationale for accepting the assignment, as he candidly admitted, rested upon the fact that it would be an excellent opportunity to vindicate himself in the eyes of his wife. It was wartime; danger would be present; and "It was his chance to prove that the woman he had loved so much had misjudged him. He left in a bitter mood, actually glad to be gone to see whether the wounds would heal or prove fatal in foreign climate."[3]

It was in this frame of mind that Webb returned to England after a near catastrophic flight across the Atlantic. The plane had skimmed the ocean three times trying to take off and in the process had picked up an excess cargo of sea water. The crew manned hand pumps continuously during the flight and managed to reach their destination. After circling for more than an hour to permit rescue launches to take position, the captain brought the plane in for a somewhat anticlimactic safe landing. On this flight, Webb had as his traveling companion, Henry Steele Commager of Columbia. The two professors reached Paddington Station in London at 8:30 P.M. in the middle of a blackout and found that their hotel reservations had been cancelled because of late arrival. With forty pounds of baggage to lug, finding new accommodations was a major feat finally accomplished by midnight. The next day Webb drove through bombed-out sections of London, amazed to find the damage less than he had expected due to the fact that repairs had gone on continuously. On October 10, 1942, he boarded a train for Oxford, where he rented an apartment overlooking a courtyard housing a dormant fountain. The bitter damp and cold of the English climate induced Webb to don long woolen underwear in an attempt to keep out the chill. Since the use of coal was "unfashionable," he often interrupted his work to do a bit of walking to restore circulation.[4]

Not long after his arrival and admittance as a Fellow of Queen's College, the department notified him that he would be expected to give an inaugural lecture on "The Significance of the Closed Frontier." Since he had not been able to bring books with him and lacked the time to find his sources in the Oxford libraries, he relied on his store of knowledge to compose this first lecture, which he made at the Great Hall at Queen's College on October 27. During the Michaelmas term, he lectured twice a week, surveying topics in American history. The next term, Hilary, he gave two series of lectures, one relating to the Civil War and the second on his specialty, the American West. The final Trinity session, he offered one series of lectures on contemporary U.S. history. The war had disrupted life at Oxford, but interest in the United States had increased; consequently he classed attendance at his lectures as "comparatively good." He also presented invitational lectures to various undergraduate groups, a practice highly encouraged in England. At these gatherings, discussion would follow his presentations, although this was not customary after formal class lectures.[5]

Aside from his professorial duties, Webb began to write again. As Harmsworth Professor, he was expected to promote better understanding between the American and English people. In order to meet this obligation, he wrote approximately twenty articles about "England in Wartime," to be serialized in the *Dallas News*. Some of the personal bitterness he suffered began to wane as his creative urge returned. In January 1943, he wrote to Jane and Mildred, "The best news is that I am again writing, the first time I have felt like it since I finished *Divided We Stand* in 1937. It sure feels good to have the old tingle that enables me to sit down to this blimey machine and do something that I think is good."[6] He was referring to the series of true Ranger sketches he was writing, using Friday Mountain Ranch for background and atmosphere. Soon he found that he was able to write five to six hours a day and began making plans to continue his productivity upon return to the states. He planned to work in earnest on the frontier book, provided he could be released from some of his responsibilities connected with the Texas State Historical Association. In order to facilitate his efforts, he requested, in somewhat dogmatic manner, that certain arrangements be made for him at home. He itemized his needs, which included a comfortable place to sleep, eat, and work. For the latter, he specified that the small north room be prepared since it was cooler than the hot room on the west. Secondly, he ordered that differences of opinion among family members be adjourned for a period of two years with any disagreements being settled by quiet discussion rather than "stronger measures." He also ruled that each person should consult the other prior to making obligations socially or financially. Anxious to return and write productively on his own terms, Webb admitted that he felt the European trip to be "a good thing by enabling all of us to get a little better perspective."[7]

Gradually he became more embroiled in his work. Conditions were favorable for creativity with little else to disturb him other than the hum of bombers flying missions into the darkness of the night. In addition to his Ranger sketches and features for the *Dallas News*, he began writing fragments of what would become *The Great Frontier*, but the most therapeutic of all his projects was the writing of what turned out to be his partial autobiography. He reflected on the past and his struggle to succeed, realizing that although he had gone far, his success had "brought no happiness." With the catharsis of writing and remembering happier, younger years, the woman he loved appeared, "and in writing he recovered temporarily the sense of that love." As he explained this feeling: "For the first time in years he saw how beautiful she was to him when he first saw her and how beautiful she remained, and how much she meant to him in the years before they were married, and in the years when they were making their way in confidence and affection together."[8] Under his characteristic cover of expressing himself in the third person, Webb revealed that his bitterness had largely passed and that he could return home in harmony with self.

Ironically, Webb had reconciled his personal battles to rejoin those on the academic and political front. When he returned to the University of Texas in 1943, the Rainey Controversy was in full swing. During a get-together at Friday Mountain Ranch, President Homer Price Rainey informed Webb and other guests that the regents were out to get him.[9] Webb, although regarded as a liberal, did not have the radical connotations that some Texans had. He was one of the few professors who managed to get along with both the business community and academic circles, partially because he was respected as being a successful individual in both areas, and also because he was recognized as a level-headed individual who believed in communication and compromise.[10] In the current affair, Webb sided with the Rainey faction. As he wrote W. Eugene Hollon in November 1944: "We here at the University are fighting a battle for a principle which if preserved will protect every educational institution in the State, but if destroyed, will unloose the forces that destroyed us in all the smaller institutions."[11]

When Harry Y. Benedict had died seven years earlier, Webb had recognized the need for a man who could satisfy requirements of the university both as an educator and as a businessman and had advised that such a man be selected. Little did the men who chose Homer Price Rainey realize that he would not fill the bill, for his paper credentials were impeccable. He held a doctorate in education from the University of Chicago, had presided over a college in Indiana, Bucknell University in Pennsylvania, and had served as director of the Rockefeller-funded American Youth Commission in Washington. Rainey was also an ordained Baptist minister, which should have been an asset in the middle of the Texas Bible belt, but this was not the case.[12] There were those who felt that Rainey considered education "a crusade to elevate the moral and economic security of the race." Joe B. Frantz saw him as "a Baptist evangelist at heart who wanted to save Texas. Not all of us wanted to be saved," he concluded.[13] Rainey personally viewed the clash with the regents as fundamentally a conflict between the "dominant business culture" and "Judaeo-Christian ethics," between the old world of the frontier and the modern world of the industrialist.[14]

The Texas Board of Regents, preponderantly reflecting the dominant and conservative monied interests of the state, began to square off against Rainey's humanitarian liberalism, a liberalism characterized by such crass contentions as "Negroes had souls," and instructors had the right to hearings prior to being fired. Rainey's hopes of making Texas into a university of the first order soon suffered serious setbacks. W. Eugene Hollon, who at the time was teaching at Schreiner Institute in Kerrville, Texas, wrote Webb of an encounter with Regent Scott Schreiner. Schreiner told Hollon that the Board and the president represented "two entirely different schools of thought and that one or the other must go. I have no intentions of resigning now or later and am sure that none of the other members do either." Then, according to Hollon, "he started all of the old crap again . . . about communism at the University and how it should be wiped out completely even if it took the whole economic and government departments with it. He makes no distinction between teaching communism and teaching about communism."[15]

To Rainey's way of thinking the communism issue was merely a smoke screen in the attempt to purge the university of New Deal radicalism. This issue represented merely one of numerous incidents that precipitated the actual break between Rainey and the regents. Origins of the controversy could be traced back to the election of W. Lee "Pass the Biscuits, Pappy" O'Daniel as governor in 1940. That election had been synonymous with conservative support for Texas industrialists. After a number of professors had openly opposed O'Daniel during his bid for election, he decided that educational institutions in Texas needed revamping and in a meeting with a group in Houston announced plans to do just that. When Chairman of the Board of Regents, Major J. R. Parten, completed his term in office, O'Daniel replaced him with oil magnate, Dan Harrison. Then he filled the remaining vacancy on the board with Orville Bullington, also a wealthy oil man and Republican candidate for governor. By these appointments, the governor tailored the board of regents to function as a corporate board of directors which would tend the affairs of the university according to his dictates.[16]

To Pappy and his followers, the New Deal was an anathema and anyone who had sympathy for it was a radical. Rainey fell into this category. Attacks against him took on personal coloration, charging that he presided over a hot bed of communism at the university, sheltered homosexuals, and loved Negroes. These charges had little substance since the FBI had kept a close watch on alleged communists and had investigated the university when the Navy ROTC program was implemented. It could also be substantiated that Rainey had cooperated fully with an investigation concerning homosexuals on the campus.[17]

The real issues included a motion made by Regent Lutcher Stark to eliminate Dean Shelby, Roy Bedichek, and Rodney J. Kidd from the extension division of the university for changing an interscholastic league ruling affecting the athletic eligibility of his two sons. Rainey proposed a hearing, but refused to fire the men. Other incidents concerned the removal of John Dos Passos' *The Big Money*, the third book in his trilogy, *U.S.A. An Omnibus*, from the reading list of a sophomore English course due to its "obscene" content; the firing of four economics professors for making a public statement after a labor meeting to the effect that it had been stacked; and the attempt by Regent D. F. Strickland to impose a patriotism test on the faculty. But the most dangerous of their actions, according to Rainey's way of thinking, was their attempt to dispense with tenure in order to get rid of professors they did not care for. On the other hand, as conservatives pointed out, some of the issues, such as the dispute over a location for the medical school and John Spies' position as its dean, had nothing to do with academic freedom. Rainey would not bend and neither would the board.[18] As one observer phrased it: "It is the kind of board that would take no dictation from Jesus Christ himself, and Dr. Rainey's action was not calculated to soften [its] temper."[19]

The event that precipitated Rainey's public stand against the regents also brought Webb into the fight. Regent D. F. Strickland, in a phone call to Vice-President Alton Burdine, urged the firing of a young graduate student. In the process of the conversation Strickland charged Rainey with "running all over the country making speeches to religious groups." He indicated that this activity would have to be curtailed, and that in fact, the university could manage without him.[20] When news of this exchange leaked to the press, the front page exposé of this astonishing conversation staggered the entire community and triggered a chain of events that created turmoil throughout the state. The announcement of his impending demise motivated Rainey to present the situation, as he viewed it, to the public. This was considered injudicious by some, who felt that he should have handled the matter in a private confrontation with the board rather than before the faculty.[21]

Feeling that the issues at stake were larger than personal consideration, Rainey indicted the regents on sixteen different counts at a meeting held in the Geology Building. The faculty responded by giving him an ovation and a vote of confidence. Ronnie Dugger in his account of the controversy analyzed the faculty spirit: "People living their lives mostly in their minds seldom get to have the illusion they are heroes, but this was their Alamo."[22]

The regents reacted violently to Rainey's charges and after a meeting in Houston, fired him on November 1, 1944. Soon the conflict became publicized nationally. Observers such as Bernard de Voto considered the situation indicative of a national danger. He regarded the Texas crisis and attack on academic freedom as "the first of a new model precipitating waves of reaction that will strike at Yale, Stanford, and other places." Stressing the larger brotherhood of the academic community, he noted that when Texas had lost its freedom, "we have lost ours." In response to

Rainey's firing, students boycotted classes for a week and marched through the streets of Austin bearing a black draped coffin labelled Academic Freedom which they laid to rest at the Rotunda of the Capitol. Faculty committees formed to bring about reconciliation between Rainey and the regents, but to no avail.[23]

An investigation by the Texas State Senate followed Rainey's dismissal. Many witnesses were called to testify during this twelve-day inquiry and at the start of questioning, each was asked if they knew who had revealed to the press the conversation between Burdine and the regents. All had answered "No." Then one evening when the Chamber was crowded and stuffy and the hearings seemed to drag on and on, Walter Prescott Webb was called to the stand. He answered the routine questions in a low murmur:

"Where do you live?" "Austin."

"What is your vocation?" "I teach history at the University."

"Do you know who revealed that story to the press?" "Yes," he stated. The reaction was immediate—a sudden stirring and increased interest as the crowd listened intently for his answer to the next inevitable question.

"Who gave the story to the press?" "I did," Webb said. The truth was out. Vice-President Alton Burdine, troubled by the news that the regents planned to fire Rainey, had called Webb and relayed this information in confidence. For some time thereafter, Webb wrestled with his conscience, then decided that "Public Good outranks private obligations," and called the editor of the local paper.[24]

The beneficial consequence of these events was the drafting and acceptance of a new rule defining academic freedom and tenure. A facet of this ruling provided for a committee called the Council on Academic Freedom and Responsibility, a committee on which Webb served with fearlessness and compassion. The committee provided counseling services for all members of the university community who encountered problems. Webb's value in this capacity, according to one who served with him, lay in his ability to hold convictions, yet "gracefully lay them aside when circumstances require."[25]

Webb believed that the entire controversy could have been averted or patched up if Governor Coke Stevenson, who had succeeded O'Daniel, had appointed a board of regents who represented the people of Texas.[26] Stevenson, however, chose to reinstate members of the old guard. Dudley K. Woodward, described as the "white-haired oracle of the plutocracy of Texas" became chairman of the board. As one of three members of a search committee to select a new president, Webb, along with others, agreed not to seek the presidency personally. When committee member T. S. Painter, after meeting with regents in Houston, came back as president, thereby negating his pledge to the faculty, Webb was irate.[27] According to his view, this act of hypocrisy was inexcusable and helped establish his role for the future. In a letter marked "Personal and Painful," he wrote to his friend Bedichek:

> Tonight I attended a caucus in Garrison Hall, and made the mistake of saying something. Result: I was appointed as one of a committee of five to draw a resolution of no confidence in Painter. I went to my office and wrote out what I would say. . . . The whole committee accepted it and turned their guns on me to present it. . . . Had I known the turn events took, I would have remained away.[28]

The whole affair was extremely disturbing to Webb. He expressed his feeling of personal frustration and inadequacy to his friend, Rupert N. Richardson: "Richardson," he said, "I am not worth a damn; the only excuse I have for accepting my salary from the University is that I have been underpaid for so long." His friend had never seen his morale so low, and learned that "his problems were not his own problems but those of the University." Webb saw himself on the opposite side of the fence from people he admired and respected, people such as Eugene C. Barker who shared with him a deep love of and concern for the university. Barker placed the blame for the affair on errors of regents, president, and faculty. He did not see the threat to freedom and tenure that Webb saw and felt that the faculty's reactions had been hysterical. Neither did he see any value in reelecting Rainey nor did he feel that there would be any benefit in a pledge of noncooperation. Thus, he turned to Webb, requesting that he use his position and influence as a dominant member of the faculty to restore calmness to the university. Calling his attention to the fact that the state legislature controlled the apportionment of endowments and building funds needed by the university, he urged Webb, as a leader of the "excited and bitter organized majority" to "consider the best methods of getting the University out of its turmoil without regard to Rainey or any other individual."[29]

Webb's election as spokesman in this instance was particularly painful. He respected Barker greatly, but felt that Rainey was more in the right than in the wrong. Bedichek sympathized with Webb's position praising him for his action and the courage to voice the resolution indicting Painter for breaking faith. Others were not so brave under the spotlight of public opinion, and the vote of censure failed.[30] As Webb wrote to Jane and Mildred who were away visiting relatives, "I see little but turmoil for two or more years, and of course the University is the one that will suffer."[31]

Webb's predictions were accurate. The American Association of University Professors censored the university for a period of nine years and the Southern Association of Colleges placed it on probation for one year.[32] When it became apparent that Painter would not receive the support needed to function effectively, the regents developed a "super-presidency" called a chancellorship. The man they chose to place in this position was James P. Hart, a slow-speaking Lincolnesque man of character and former member of the Texas State Supreme Court. Hart, not long after his appointment, questioned Chairman Dudley K. Woodward as to why Webb had not received the title of Distinguished Professor, a designation that he should have been awarded many years earlier. He found out that Webb had been passed over time and again because he had managed to ruffle the feathers of one regent or another. Hart resolved the inequity when he bluntly declared that Webb *would* receive the honor, or the regents would receive his resignation.[33]

When Webb learned by the process of "academic osmosis" the facts of what he referred to as "the Case of the Distinguished Professor," he wrote Hart saying that he had heard of his efforts in his behalf and what he called, "the extreme length you might have gone in order to maintain a principle." He told Hart that he hoped that the "principle won would compensate for the risk taken," which just happened to remind him of a story about Jeff Vaughn, a Texas Ranger in the Alpine area. As Webb told the story, two Negroes got in trouble, barricaded themselves in a boxcar and were holding off all the local citizens, who decided to send for Jeff Vaughn. When the Ranger arrived, darkness having fallen, he called out: "This is Jeff Vaughn. You boys come on out." One Negro then turned to the other and said: "Come on, Bill. The boss is done come." Webb concluded, "I think the whole University faculty is beginning to feel just like those Negroes, and the recent incident, I trust, will strengthen that feeling."[34] "Boss" Hart did much to erase the stigma of the Rainey controversy, but as Webb had predicted, there were still troubled times ahead.

J. Frank Dobie, called by one reporter "a problem child" at the university for thirty years, became involved in what would be his final hassle with University of Texas administrators.[36] After dismissal as president, Rainey had entered politics and was subsequently defeated in his bid for the governorship. Dobie reacted to the new regime on both political and academic fronts by exiling himself to England, in accordance with what Webb termed his "maverick nature." Webb described this characteristic as running "free and easy with whatever crowd takes his fancy," then separating himself from the herd if the crowd grows "objectionable."[36]

During Dobie's absence, a ruling was passed which provided that a sabbatical could not extend beyond two academic years except in cases of military service or illness. A few months later, Dobie applied for an extension on his leave citing the need to finish a manuscript and stating also that he suffered from hayfever and could not return during Austin's allergy season. The English department recommended the extension for health reasons, but opposition from other quarters was strong, and the extension was denied. There were those who saw no need to welcome the likes of Dobie back into the fold. Liberalism, in the opinion of some, perpetrated the "rampant and undisciplined spirit in the student body" evidenced by the riots disrupting University of Texas registration. To this faction, J. Frank Dobie personified vocal liberalism in Texas.[37]

Others felt that Dobie was "a teller of tall tales" who deserved to be fired for teaching "damaging social propaganda."[38] J. Evetts Haley, in reference to Webb's defense of Dobie as the man and "the maverick," said that he had no objection to him being a maverick. "Neither do I deny his perfect right to make a jackass of himself for purposes of publicity, . . . though I do think it rather offensive to people of good taste, and hence of no benefit to the University of Texas." Furthermore, Haley objected to what he termed Dobie's "dishonest nature" which he noted Webb had previously experienced.[39] E. C. Barker, in reference to the so-called "Dobie rule" maintained that it had no connection with the Rainey controversy. He pointed out to Webb that, after all, the rule had been passed in due process and did not fire Dobie. Rather, he said, "its universal application simply created the impasse by which Dobie fired himself." On the other hand, Barker, like Webb, recognized Dobie as a distinguished member of the faculty, who had brought the institution recognition, "along with some embarrassment." Barker suggested writing to Painter requesting half-time reinstatement for Dobie as a compromise gesture.[40]

Webb, who believed that the university should be a host to "all sorts of people and ideas," did his best to secure his friend's return, but without success.[41] In this instance, Dobie had walked into a trap of red tape, laid by the administration and applied by the regents. The rule stated that professors on leave must return within the stated period of time. Dobie did not, and Dobie was fired. Exceptions could not be made for the idiosyncracies of individual professors, regardless of fame.

Another repercussion of the Rainey controversy was the postponement for a time of the expansion of the University of Texas Press. Founded in 1922, the press limited itself to publishing university publications and some subsidized works. By 1944, agitation for a press capable of publishing books of general interest resulted in the appointment of an advisory board to study the problems involved. Faculty members such as Webb realized that University of Texas scholars enhanced the reputation of other university presses by their publications when they could be contributing to the University of Texas if the institution had adequate publication arrangements. As a member of the Press Advisory Board, Webb helped initiate the move for expansion, and in October 1947, President T. S. Painter presented the issue to the regents, recommending the employment of a part-time editor.[42]

Opposition to the proposed expansion was based largely on the expense involved. Others saw it as a means of building up the state's political, social, economic, and general cultural development. Webb observed that university presses provided the answer for the many worthwhile scholarly works which would be unacceptable commercially because their limited appeal made them economically unfeasible. The major problem the advisory board faced was to find a man capable of directing the planned expansion.[43]

In November of 1949, the board settled on a candidate by the name of Frank Wardlaw and invited him to come to Texas to interview for the slot as director. Chairman of the Committee, Reginald Harvey Griffith, an older, stately gentleman, and members of the administration occupied Wardlaw's first day in Texas. The prospects did not seem too appealing, Wardlaw admitted. The next day he met Walter Prescott Webb, who took him out to Friday Mountain, introduced him to his picturesque ranch foreman, Hub Garret, and eventually got around to inquiring about his credentials. Wardlaw felt that the fact that he had no degree would nix his chances of employment. He told Webb that he had dropped out of college during the depression with almost enough hours for a degree, although they "didn't add up to any degree known to man." He added that he could probably get one if it were necessary, but Webb told him not to think of it, commenting that there was increasingly less distinction every day in having the Ph.D., whereas there was "real distinction in having no degree at all." Wardlaw and Webb ended the day by going to Roy Bedichek's house, where he listened to them "insult each other" for an hour or so. By the end of the second day, Wardlaw had a more positive attitude. In fact, he had decided to come to Texas.[44]

Although the power and influence of Walter Webb pervaded the University of Texas at Austin, the business world, as well as the academic complex grew to respect him. He took an active interest in promoting his community and associated with fellow historians and professional businessmen alike. At the request of Charles Green, editor of the *Austin Statesman*, Webb and Cecil Bernard Smith, Sr., served on a civic committee responsible for organizing the Headliners' Club in Austin. A social club for business and professional men, Webb designed for it a dual membership policy. Businessmen paid a substantial initiation fee and annual dues, while professors and members of the news media paid a lower fee more in accord with their economic means. In Austin Webb could also be seen at meetings of the Town and Gown held at the Driskill Hotel, where he shared a table with Dobie and Bedichek, or eating out at Harry Akin's Night Hawk or at Caruso's. On other occasions he would seek out the peace and quiet of some lesser known haunt.

C. D. Richards of Arlington once invited Webb and E. C. Barksdale out to eat on one of their visits. Webb suggested that they drive out the old Austin-Dallas highway past the insane asylum to the Chicken Shack where "there weren't any god-damned music boxes to beat his ears off." Richards recalled that "He had the damndest places to eat."[45]

Webb earned a solid reputation as a shrewd businessman, making some very wise and farsighted investments in real estate from which he reaped substantial profits. C. B. Smith, Webb's former student, explained that Webb knew the value of land for the same reasons he understood its history—he was a product of his environment, "close to the soil, and he recognized that the influence of nature and business is closely tied to the law of supply and demand."[46] He appeared to have an uncanny ability, an intuitive sense for discovering and developing not only natural resources, but human resources, as well. Rodney Kidd, Webb's associate and current owner of Friday Mountain Ranch, described him as "moving about like a bird dog" whether in search of an historical fact or a good investment.[47]

The money earned from sale of the movie rights for *The Texas Rangers* had provided Webb with the means to make his first major investment. Harbert Davenport, who at that time was practicing law in Brownsville, Texas, advised him to invest in his own community. Webb took the advice seriously, studying the city sprawled over the hills and envisioning its future growth. Realizing that the depression was a good time to go in debt, he boldly borrowed an advance on royalties from text and trade books and turned the money into real estate. He invested in land lying strategically between the university and the capitol, built six studio cottages for rental purposes, and even purchased a church, which he converted into an office building. Later on he bought land fronting the old Austin-Waco-Dallas highway. This fringe property is now the corner of North Lamar and Airport Boulevard and houses a shopping center.[48]

Through the years C. B. Smith maintained a profitable and friendly business relationship with his former professor, starting in the mid-forties when he initiated a series of leases on this land from Webb and his daughter. As a successful Austin real estate investor and auto dealer, he traded cars and ideas with Webb, as well as land. Typical of business conducted during an earlier era, many of their agreements and those he arranged with his partner, Rodney Kidd, rested upon mutual respect, trust, and verbal agreements. Introducing Smith to a group of university and downtown businessmen, Webb remarked, "Smith was an undergraduate and graduate student of mine at the university. He is also a tenant of mine. For a long time, I have bought all my autos and trucks from him and I am beginning to think he is reasonably honest."[49]

Business correspondence often contained typical Webbisms or a pertinent anecdote. He enclosed a check to Smith with the comment that he now felt like his yardman had felt toward him regarding his indebtedness. Somehow this man had always managed to keep ahead of him and had a marvelous knack for putting him in the wrong. One day Webb said, "John, how do we stand?" John, being very formal, replied, "Well, Mr. Webb, I doan know unless I sees my books, but I thinks I'se about rid of you."[50] Of all his real estate investments, the purchase of the Old Johnson Institute some seventeen miles outside of Austin, renamed Friday Mountain Ranch, became the most gratifying, if not the most profitable.

10

W. P. WEBB: ENVIRONMENTALIST

*There is something infectious about the magic of the Southwest. Some
are immune to it, but there are others who have no resistance and
who must spend the rest of their lives dreaming of the incredible
sweep of the desert, of great golden mesas with purple shadows, and
tremendous stars appearing at dusk in a turquoise sky. And I am
one of these.*

W. P. Webb, "Today's Southwest in Fact and Fiction"

Walter Prescott Webb had an abiding love for the Southwest.
From childhood days he had learned to appreciate the beneficence
of nature and as an adult, he sought to preserve the beauty and
abundance of natural resources through his writings and his actions.
He had a special interest in desert regions of the Southwest and in
the Big Bend country of western Texas in particular. He visited the
wild and untamed area for the first time the summer of 1924 while
going through the Texas Ranger border camps. Webb had never
seen such desert country—the craggy canyons slicing into the rocky
terrain dotted with an occasional scrubby mesquite, and the
grotesque forms of weathering and erosion—all of which had for
him an indefinable charm and made a lasting impression. Even the
names of the landmarks intrigued him: names like the Contrabanda
Trail, Robber's Roost perched high "like an Eagle's eyrie," Boot
Spring, Strawhouse Trail, and of course, Terlingua, supposedly a
corruption of *tres lenguas* or "three languages," referring to the
tricultural influence of the Indian, Spanish, and Anglo-American
inhabitants of the region.[1]

With the geographer's eye, he noted that three life zones existed
between the base and the summit of Chisos Peak to entice nature
lovers. But more than that, he saw the human interest value
emanating from the fact that it comprised a meeting place for two
contrasting civilizations. Here the Rio Grande constituted a line of

155

demarcation, but not a barrier. The bold history of the locale had been engraved in the geographic surroundings and in the minds of border men: Rangers, border patrol, river guards, game wardens, and cowmen, who sat around their campfires and shared with him their reminiscences. These border lands separating two nations, whose histories were so interwoven, made a powerful appeal to his imagination. He saw in this wild country "a place of temporary escape from the world we know," a place "where the spirit is lifted up," and he admitted that he felt an "almost irresistible desire to see it again and again," a desire akin to homesickness.[2]

In 1937, somewhat dissatisfied with his situation at the university, he considered leaving academe for full-time employment with the National Park Service, but ended up by accepting a position as consultant. His duties as Consulting Historian included the writing of general descriptive narrative dealing with the Trans-Pecos area and particularly the Big Bend, providing an historical interpretation of the effect of the region on its people, and recording the location of its various landmarks, and the origins of their names. Soon after his appointment, he made two trips to the region to investigate the historic sights and tourist possibilities since the Park Service was considering opening the area to tourists. On these trips, he stayed with Pete Crawford who had a cabin on the Cartledge Ranch at Castelon.[3]

The Santa Helena Canyon area, channeling a fifteen-mile stretch of rapids and eddies, attracted his interest. He learned that its treacherous course had been surmounted previously by only one expedition, that of Dr. Robert T. Hill in the late 1800s. Other parties had attempted the journey but with disastrous results. Webb's flair for the dramatic came to the fore. He began to imagine possibilities of creating public interest in the preservation of the area through a well-staged and well-publicized boat trip down the Santa Helena Canyon. With the sanction of the Department of the Interior, Webb gave his exploratory nature free reign as he planned his adventure carefully, writing press releases to be aired at appropriate intervals, making arrangements for the construction of special aluminum boats, and collecting photographic equipment to make a pictorial record of the feat.[4]

The fact that civilization had not seriously disturbed the Big Bend area recommended it as a national park site, according to Webb's way of thinking. He wrote of the region in words that painted an inviting picture: "There it lies in its gorgeous splendor and geographical confusion, almost as it fell from the hands of its creator. Man has marked it, but he has not marred it."[5] The press had a field day with the antics of "that crazy college professor" who thought he was going to run the rapids of Santa Helena Canyon. Jane, who had heard of the treacherous currents, was also fearful. The fact that the boats were being specially constructed with air chambers did little to allay her fears. She remarked that the *Titanic* also had air chambers, to which Webb's partner, Thomas V. Skaggs, replied, "Yes, but we have no icebergs in May. I will put it another way: There is no danger in capturing a rattlesnake if you keep out of reach of its fangs. There is absolutely no danger in this trip if we portage around those deadly rockslide obstructions."[6]

Originally, the team slated to make the trip—Webb, Skaggs and Joe Laney of McCamey, and William R. Hogan, Associate Historian for the National Park Service—planned to make it in two steel rowboats, one to be christened the *Big Bend* flying the American flag, and the other to be called the *Cinco de Mayo* flying the Mexican flag. Ultimately they decided that additional equipment would be needed to get the boats around the rapids area and postponed their venture while a third boat was constructed.[7] The boats had to be shipped to Alpine, the only common freight terminal for the area. Here Webb stayed at the Holland Hotel near the rise of the Davis Mountains, and it was here also that he heard from Jane the shocking news of Dr. Benedict's death. Other preparations were being carried out at Lajitas, where they planned to embark.[8]

On May 15, 1937, the party left for the canyon, hoping to start by Sunday and to complete the trip by early Monday the 18th. Webb wrote Jane not to worry; "We have taken all precautions and will portage around the one bad place."[9] Where the party entered, the river ran smooth. At the point where the canyon made a sharp turn to the left, the boats had to go straight ahead, landing on the Mexican side of the river. Just beyond the bend lay 200 yards of heavy boulders obstructing the passage. Once past this dangerous spot, the remainder of the trip was smooth sailing. The coast guard plane flying above kept close watch on the progress of the party, informing Mrs. Webb at 10:15 in the morning, "Expedition will complete trip through canyon in about two hours everything apparently OK." Webb wired that the party arrived safely at noon on May 18, as planned.[10]

He failed to complete his report on the trip for the Interior Department until just prior to sailing for London to serve as Harkness Lecturer. Typically, he had postponed this final detail until the last minute, necessitating that he stop in Washington, get a public recorder, and work all night. "Procrastination," according to his daughter Mildred, "was Poppa's middle name." She recalled another occasion when he attempted to catch a train for New York. The family had arrived at the Austin station just as the train was pulling out. Webb cancelled his ticket, had the agent phone ahead to the next stop for new reservations, then everyone got in the car and chased the train to Taylor. Mildred noted that this character trait became the bane of publishers who would wire him, wine him and dine him, and send representatives to encourage him to meet his deadlines. Joe Frantz, who had a father-son relationship with Webb, observed that he seemed to need deadlines to motivate him.[11]

Seldom was it ever lack of interest that caused this disposition to postpone things, particularly in the case of the Big Bend, for his interest in this part of the country lasted throughout his lifetime. In January 1941, he seriously considered purchasing land fronting the river at the mouth of the Santa Helena Canyon. The land itself had little value, approximately fifty cents an acre by valuations of the early forties, but it did have value as an access route to the canyon for tourists. Webb proposed that a syndicate of ten people contributing $1000 each could purchase the land and develop the property into a winter resort. He wrote to a prospective partner, "I confess that I am not interested in it from a monetary point of view. I love that country and want some excuse to get out there as often as possible. Should we establish a camp at Santa Helena I am sure I would live there at least two months out of the year. I find that I need something different from desk work if I am to continue to do desk work efficiently."[12]

The state had already assumed sections bordering the area, but Webb felt that it would take them another ten to fifteen years to officially set up a park. In the meantime, he thought that their group could "have a world of fun and pleasure and perhaps make a little incidentally." He commented that he had seen "a good many engaging playthings, but nothing quite so alluring as this, provided it can be acquired at a reasonable price." He advised those interested to take a week off and investigate. He also suggested that they contact Jack Wise, a one-armed man and the sole occupant of the place, who lived in a tent on the property and made his living, as Webb said, "by showing dudes how to get back to their automobiles."[13] Plans to purchase and develop this portion of the Big Bend were shelved when the group learned that the both the House and the Senate had passed an appropriation bill to add this land to that set aside for a state park—a park that Webb's activities had been so instrumental in creating.[14]

In time, Webb's reputation as an environmentalist came to be increasingly recognized. In February 1949, Texas Senator Lyndon B. Johnson wrote to the Secretary of the Interior requesting that a scientific study of the water problem in Texas be conducted in hopes of developing a comprehensive water program for the state. The Bureau of Reclamation conducted the study, and Johnson appointed Webb to investigate and report on the problems of water conservation and water resources. By the time the study was completed, one of Texas' periodic droughts had struck and people needed no prompting to concern themselves with water deficiencies.[15]

In 1953, shortly before Washington granted federal relief to harder hit portions of the state, Webb published *More Water for Texas: The Problem and the Plan,* a popularized version of the government report titled *Water Supply and the Texas Economy: An Appraisal of the Texas Water Problem.* In this timely book Webb stated in nontechnical, but urgent terms, the problem and the solution as determined by the Bureau of Reclamation. The suggested plan included the construction of an inland canal to carry water to the lower Gulf Coast area, emphasized the need for revised water regulations to prevent exhausting the store of underground water, and advocated stricter controls over water use. Johnson and Webb agreed that the long-range plan would increase the economic and industrial potential of the state. Webb's efforts reflected his active concern for his state and his belief in the importance of preservation of natural resources for the future well-being of the country.[16]

He promoted his conservation standards not only in books and articles, but also in speeches to such diverse groups as a conference on water law, a Houston garden club, and the American Society of

Range Management. To many of them, he explained his view that the advent of civilization with its advanced technology heedlessly destroyed valuable grasslands and other resources, in the process guaranteeing man's ultimate poverty and misery due to his own profligacy. He liked to illustrate the impact of man and machine on nature by telling the story of a bright Indian boy who won an essay contest by describing a photograph in the *Farmer-Stockman*. The photo showed a desolate wind-swept field and an abandoned farmhouse. The boy's prize-winning essay told how and why the farm came to be this way:

> Picture show white man crazy. Cut down tree. Make too big tepee. PLOW HILL, *Water* wash. *Wind* blow soil. Grass gone. *Door* gone. *Window* gone. *Squaw* gone. Whole place gone to hell. No pig. No *corn*. No *pony*.
>
> *Indian no plow land. Keep grass.* Buffalo eat grass. Indian eat buffalo. *Hide* make plenty big tepee. Make moccasin.
>
> All time eat. *Indian no hunt job. No work.* No *hitch-hike*.
>
> *No ask relief. No build dam. No give damn. White man heap crazy!*[17]

From this figurative example in miniature, he would then ask his audience to consider the ramifications of an entire civilization indulging in mass wastefulnesss from the year A.D. 1500 to contemporary times. The end result of this macrocosmic view of a world of continual over-indulgence was the somewhat depressing picture he verbally painted in *The Great Frontier*. Speaking as a fellow of the Texas Institute of Letters in 1951, he remarked, "Science has not been creative—up to now. At least, it has destroyed more than it has created. . . . You have only to compare the world of 1500 A.D. when we had forests and the minerals and all the other natural resources. Then look at the depleted earth of 1951."[18]

As an example of constructive action he lauded the efforts and philosophy of his former schoolteacher, Charles Pettit, who had become a wealthy oil man. Pettit, according to Webb, felt that he owed a debt to the state of Texas since it had provided the source of his wealth in oil, an exhaustible resource. He acknowledged this debt and attempted to repay it in part by improving his own land.

At his Flat-Top Ranch at Walnut Springs, Texas, Pettit utilized an extensive system of dams, lakes, and water systems to transform barren ranchland into a sea of grass. In so doing, Flat-Top became recognized as a model of conservation procedures and produced more grass and water per acre than any other in Texas. Webb recorded the story of Pettit's accomplishment in a limited-edition book called *Flat-Top: A Story of Modern Ranching* published by Carl Hertzog of El Paso.[19]

Webb realized that all citizens could not practice conservation on the grand scale of Charles Pettit, but he did feel that individuals of lesser means could make contributions in different ways. He urged the members of a Houston garden club to encourage their husbands to buy small farms, not to make money, but to "hide some income from Uncle Sam" and preserve a bit of nature at the same time. Webb himself practiced the philosophy he espoused when in 1942 he purchased a 630-acre tract of land in the hill country southwest of Austin.[20]

From the start, he regarded this property as more than a money-making proposition. He had purchased Friday Mountain with other goals in mind. Writing from Queen's College in England to his wife and daughter, he said; "I am glad all of you are enjoying Friday Mountain Ranch. I want all in the office, any of the poker crowd, Bedi, and of course any you may choose to use it and enjoy it. That is what it is for, the pleasure it will give."[21] Those who knew him best observed that Friday Mountain entered into the very fibers of Webb's being. As he admitted himself, "I think of that ranch all the time. At whatever cost, I am going to develop it, restore it, and see to it that it is preserved as it should be, if that is possible. . . . I am going to write a book about it and spend all the money the book makes on the ranch."[22] And restore it, he did.

The land housed what had previously been a boys' academy called the Johnson Institute. When Webb first acquired the place, it was desolate and sickly-looking and barren of all the native grasses, with the exception of a few clumps of buffalo grass and broom-weed. The topsoil had been eroded or blown away. Webb set about reclaiming the land and nurturing it back to productivity. He hauled refuse from the cotton gins east of Austin and commercial fertilizer to revitalize the leached earth. He nursed it through the drought that began in the late forties and continued until 1957. Eventually Friday Mountain became something of a show place covered with grasses of various types, and Webb was intensely proud of it. To him, it was "the most charming and beautiful place I have ever seen," and he could not fathom his luck in owning it.[23]

In many respects, Friday Mountain provided for Webb a sense of place and a sanctuary from the demands of an industrialized and structured world. He recognized what he called the necessity for "that doubtful aspect of civilization symbolized by the city," but felt strongly that a love of the land should be "inherent and implicit in every healthy human heart, . . . whether an individual is lost among the masses in the dreary man-made canyons of New York, or happily at home on the limitless grasslands of the Staked Plains of Texas." Regardless of location, in country or in town, he saw this love for one piece of ground as "a stabilizing, gyroscopic influence that helps keep a man on an even keel." While still in England he wrote:

> I have a hell of a lot of time to think here and feel that this place [Friday Mountain] may contribute much to enabling me to escape too frequent recurrence of a sense of utter futility. I have tried my best to develop some enthusiasm for this job, and I have succeeded only a little better than I did previously. I simply can't adapt myself to the immobility and the proprieties of academic life. I've really never been able to do it in Texas, where the world is young, and I certainly stand small chance of doing it against the inertias of eight centuries of immovable tradition.[24]

Friday Mountain became the source of great happiness for Webb. He loved the pastoral beauty of it and the opportunity it provided for companionship with people he enjoyed. Here he tended his small part of the world as he thought it should be tended and here he escaped temporarily "the proprieties" of his profession, a respite necessary for a totally unacademic, but thinking man. In a revealing letter to W. Eugene Hollon, he said:

> I got a shipment of Louisiana bullfrogs the other day for my creek, and anybody who is fool enough to order bullfrogs is not going to jump out of any towers. Bullfrogs are a great comfort, and so are cows and armadillos.[25]

An additional source of satisfaction was the fact that Friday Mountain afforded Webb the opportunity to develop not only natural resources, but human resources as well. It was here that he forced Roy Bedichek into the realm of writers and established a camp for boys, a prime concern during his later years.

Bedichek, Director of the Texas Interscholastic League and a renowned philosopher and naturalist, had served as friendly advisor to Webb in his efforts at restoring Friday Mountain. He shared Webb's concern for living things and for conservation. As Bedichek neared retirement age, Webb and other friends decided that it would be a great loss if he did not put his wisdom in printed form. With the help of J. Frank Dobie, Webb began making the arrangements that would enable Bedichek to take a year's leave of absence. They contacted several wealthy individuals and corporations, as well as the Rockefeller Foundation and the Texas State Historical Association, in their attempt at providing a grant commensurate with his salary.[26] Webb was to provide the hideaway. There was some discussion among those contacted as to the political views that Bedichek would voice in the proposed book. After being reassured that he would write as a Naturalist, rather than as a Liberal, they were willing to grant their support. The Humble Corporation, for example, said that they would contribute $500 to a naturalist's study quite willingly, "but not 5¢ to sponsor an interpretation of Texas' natural objects in the light of liberalism." In other words, "a scientific description of the cowbird would be fine but calling a cowbird a regent would not be."[27]

For Bedichek, this was the offer of a lifetime. As he wrote to Webb in the summer of 1945;

> Your proposal in the lobby of the Stephen F. Austin Hotel has been subjected to the digestive juices of my enfeebled mind, and I imagine now and then even in this withering August heat that I feel the stir of glands I had forgotten I had, and I catch myself dreaming that maybe after all conception and birth is possible in exceptional cases long after the mental menopause.[28]

With arrangements completed successfully, Bedichek started moving out to Friday Mountain "in installments." Here he set himself up in an upstairs room that boasted neither plumbing nor electricity, parked his typewriter on a round oak table that had been confiscated by the Rangers during a gambling raid, and began his first book. The result of this literary exile was *Adventures of a*

Texas Naturalist, the first of four books he produced after the age of seventy.[29]

While Bedichek was still camping out at Friday Mountain, Rodney J. Kidd, assistant director for the Texas Interscholastic League, paid him a visit. He was much impressed with the historic limestone building, and the giant oak trees, and mentioned to Bedichek that it would make a "beautiful spot for a boys' camp." When Bedichek relayed this comment, Webb decided that the idea was much in keeping with his goals for Friday Mountain. He suggested that Kidd meet him at the Night Hawk Restaurant on South Congress to discuss the matter further.[30]

Here on a cold and rainy November day in 1946, they mapped out the plans for the establishment of a boys' camp. Webb would make the necessary repairs, lease the property to Kidd for one dollar a year, then they would split the profits after expenses had been met. Thus evolved a verbal agreement that existed for seventeen years. They had been partners for quite some time before Kidd found out that Webb had borrowed $10,000 to repair the premises and provide other necessities to set up the camp. Webb later admitted that he failed to tell him about this "minor detail" on purpose because he was afraid that he would back out.[31]

Webb left the running of the camp entirely to Rodney Kidd, but he did take an active interest in the restoration of the soil and the farming and ranching schemes cooked up by his manager, W. H. (Hub) Garret. Webb advised Kidd to do the communicating with the parents and children, while he communicated with nature. "There is no back talk from my project," he would say.[32] Webb began investigating the establishment of boys' and girls' camps in other areas not long before his death. In 1961, he considered setting up a girls' camp at Eagle Rock, a property belonging to C. B. Smith. He also took a trip to Rockport in southern Texas where he considered establishing a coastline ranch on land belonging to Minor James—until he discovered that the place was infested with rattlesnakes. In the summer of 1962, he thought of organizing a boys' expeditionary camp in the northern wilds. He envisioned young men learning the habitats and ways of the wild animals under the tutelage of an Alaskan trapper.[33]

Friday Mountain, however, was his working success. It became the scene of many informal meetings and much outdoor enjoyment, not only for youngsters, but also for Webb's expansive circle of friends that included many of Texas' best conversationalists, songsters, musicians, and prevaricators. Kidd noted that "when sufficiently inspired Frank Wardlaw will sing 'Frankie and Jonnie' with the touching refrain, 'He won't come home,'" and illustrate the latter. Visitors included J. Frank Dobie; Bill Kittrell, the Eastland County peanut grower, who informed the group of "the low-down on the political high-ups"; John Henry Faulk, talented writer and humorist, straight from his battles with the New York networks; and others equally gifted in other areas. On a typical typed invitation to one of these shindigs, Kidd relayed Webb's instructions to the effect that "Dr. Webb specifically requests that no one tell him how young he looks or how long he will live. He says he will have plenty of evidence that there are liars in the group but he does not want their talents wasted on him. He also requests that no one bring him a present unless it can be consumed on the premises. Likewise, he warns that you had better praise his grass."[34]

Dorman Winfrey, director of the Texas State Library, recalled that the highlight of his undergraduate career at the university was the receipt of one of these invitations. On another occasion after Winfrey was married and had a family, Webb invited his six-year-old daughter to ride the horses. Shortly thereafter, they met him on campus and his daughter, Laura, began telling Dr. Webb how much she loved visiting Friday Mountain. Winfrey remembered that "He put her up on his lap and with the greatest kindness in a man's eyes I have ever seen said; 'I have Friday Mountain Ranch for young folks just like yourself.'"[35]

According to Webb's own daughter, Mildred, if Webb had a hobby "it was young people." He liked to be around them, enjoying their presence and the potential he could see in them. Mildred, as a page in the Daughters of the American Revolution, frequently hosted friends and members of this group at buffets and dances at the Webb home in Austin. On one memorable occasion they held a dance for twenty-six people. The group adjourned to Thornton's Watermelon Garden, taking the orchestra along with them, shot fireworks, danced on the grass, and then went back to the Webb home for more dancing. On other occasions the festivities were held at Friday Mountain.[36]

At these gatherings Webb would frequently ask Deacon Jones, a barbecue chef, to preside at their cookouts. Jones, a bit of a character in his own right, would in turn generously invite Webb and his friends to come down and visit his own restaurant in the

Negro section of Austin. "Come right on in," he would say, "We don't practice no discrimination in this here establishment." And sure enough, as C. D. Richards remembered, "There would be as many white people as blacks there."[37] When a smaller group visited Friday Mountain, Roy Bedichek would often serve as cook, burning the steaks, while J. Frank Dobie contributed his wife Bertha's deluxe potato salad, and Bailey Carroll presided at the coffeepot.[38]

A good portion of Webb's enjoyment from Friday Mountain stemmed from his friendship with the ranch foreman, Hub Garret, an interesting man with a great amount of native ability but little formal education, and a true expert in the use of profanity. Webb spent many evenings with the Garrets, eating the meals Mrs. Garret prepared especially for him, playing dominoes, telling stories, and speculating on moneymaking in the cattle business. As Kidd observed, their moneymaking schemes rarely succeeded. "Friday Mountain produced more good stories than good steaks," but it served purposes perhaps more worthwhile by providing enjoyment for people of all ages. Webb declared that he preferred spending his money on the ranch rather than at a country club. During the summer of 1962, he accepted a teaching position in Alaska. While there word reached him that the man he described as "the bull of the woods" had passed away. With Garret's death, much of the enchantment of Friday began to wane, and Webb's interest in farming and ranching diminished.[39]

In February 1963, Webb once again contacted his partner, Rodney Kidd, with business on his mind. Meeting at the Night Hawk, where they had first made their plans to set up a boys' ranch, Webb informed him that he intended to sell him Friday Mountain. They arranged to sign the agreement on March 9, but the day before, Kidd learned that Webb had been involved in an automobile accident near Buda. He had been killed instantly, and his wife, Terrell Maverick Webb, was in critical condition. (After the death of his first wife, Jane, in 1960, Walter Webb had married the widow of New Deal Congressman, Maury Maverick of San Antonio.) Fortunately Webb had written a letter to Kidd in February stating his intentions to consummate the sale. As soon as she was able, Mrs. Webb instructed her son, Maury Maverick, Jr., to make the letter an addendum to her will and Friday Mountain was left in good hands.[40]

11

THE AUTUMN YEARS:
TERRELL, TEACHERS, AND POLITICS

Though it is difficult for me to realize it,
time is also getting important. Already, as
in the words of a licentious poet,

> *At my back I always hear*
> *Time's winged chariot hurrying near.*

Here's hoping he wrecks the damned thing before
he overtakes you.

W. P. Webb to Alton J. Burdine, 1958,
The Graduate Journal

The autumn years for Walter Prescott Webb were filled with valleys of sadness, yet his life ended on a high plain of happiness. He had reached the retirement age of seventy in 1958, but in no way did he retire. In many respects these late years were the most involved and fruitful of his long career. At the stage when many men are content to sit and rock, Webb began taking on a more active role in the political and professional spheres.

Honors long overdue began to accrue. The American Historical Association elected him their president; the American Council of Learned Societies bestowed on him a $10,000 cash award for a lifetime of distinguished scholarship; the University of Chicago granted him an honorary Doctor of Laws degree; and Ex-Students of the University of Texas named him as one of their four most distinguished alumni. After his so-called retirement in 1958, he served as professor at Rice University and taught at the University of Houston.[1]

Webb had started his professional career as a public school-teacher, and during the later years he renewed his interest in the promotion of good teaching at all levels. He had become concerned with the growing gap that seemed to exist between the public schoolteacher and the university professor, and in 1958, while president of the American Historical Association, he determined a way to do something about it. He traveled to St. Louis, Missouri, at his own expense, as he caustically pointed out, to address the organization on problems related to the teaching of history in the high schools. He knew that the Ford Foundation had allotted $148,000 to establish a Service Center for Teachers and he hoped to return to Texas with a share of it for use in his own state.[2]

He left in a malignant mood due to a situation that perfectly illustrated his cause for concern; namely, the lack of interest at the university level for quality education in the public schools and general disinterest in problems of the people of the state. In his address to the group, he told how his own request for travel expenses to attend their meeting had been denied due to the fact that his paper entitled "Historians and the Teaching of History" did not constitute original research. Had he been involved in any other part of the program than the one on teaching, his expenses would have been paid for by the university. As Webb stated, "I was to talk on the vulgar subject of teachers," a subject that the state had paid him a salary to talk about throughout his career. The money he hoped to obtain would be used to improve relations between the university and its constituents. From this experience, Webb decided that the state needed the whole amount.[3]

In his biting bid for financial support and aid, he struck at the tender spots of most institutions of higher learning, indicting them for emphasizing research at the expense of good teaching; depriving the freshman and sophomore students of quality instructors because they could not advance the professors' private research projects; and taking them to task for what he deemed to be an inherent inferiority complex that prevented them from hiring their own graduates. Webb noted that if one did manage to gain admittance to the inner sanctum, he had to work twice as hard to gain recognition. "To this I can testify," he concluded. He placed the blame equally on progressive educators who had diluted the quality of history teaching in the high schools by considering the school as "an agency for social conditioning" rather than as a means for intellectual development.[4]

Belatedly, he noted, the University of Texas was attempting to rectify its mistakes by establishing a Service Center for Teachers in

Texas; hence the need for funding. His trip was successful and he returned to Texas to implement his plan. The university persuaded Dr. James Taylor of Southwest Texas State Teachers' College to take a leave of absence from February through May 1958 in order to make a study of the problems of history teaching in Texas. Taylor's study resulted in an upgrading of history requirements in the high schools. Webb then turned to a young protégé, Professor Jim B. Pearson, to act as a liaison man between the high schools and the university. Pearson, who had just purchased a home in Arlington, decided to accept Webb's offer and returned to Austin, where he remained from 1958 to 1971.[5]

Pearson's duties included visiting high schools across the state and offering a course called "Teaching History in the Public Schools." He was appointed consultant to a Texas Education Committee which was studying new requirements for history in the public schools, and he also promoted a conference for the Texas Council of Social Studies. Webb provided assistance and guidance whenever called upon, and Pearson recalled that this occurred frequently.[6]

As an educator, Webb earned a reputation as a pioneer in the field, actively promoting projects to solve teaching problems and raise standards in various ways. One of these entailed encouraging talented students and teachers to publish. He admitted to being "always on the lookout for those who have a talent for writing, a feeling for words, a gift for the telling phrase." "I really want students who will write books," he claimed, "not those who are willing to stop with themes, theses, and dissertations."[7] He voiced disgust with professionals who taught students that attempts to be interesting lead to "scholarly perdition," that a textbook author was akin to a "prostitute," and in general, that "there is something historically naughty about good writing."[8]

Webb himself rarely published in professional journals, preferring popular magazines that would reach the lay public. On one occasion, he was supposed to have held up a manuscript and asked his student audience whether he should publish his article in *Harper's* for $5,000 or give it to a scholarly journal. When the students voted that he should submit it to the journal, Webb informed them in his typically bromidic manner that "he wasn't interested in teaching a bunch of damn fools," turned around, and made a pretense of leaving.[9]

He often personally sponsored the writing and publication efforts of talented students and teachers. One of his favorite stories concerned a grade-school teacher who wrote an admirable master's thesis for him entitled "Thirty Years in the Third Grade" with chapter headings such as "Papa's on the School Board," and "Hi-o, Ma-dei-ri-o, the P.T.A." Webb felt that she was one of many talented people who could create closer understanding between schools and universities. In this vein, he encouraged students and teachers to write and to publish "anywhere."[10]

He returned two letters from a friend and former student saying:

> These letters are remarkable for their human interest, for the vividness of the imagery, and because they make simple things, such as getting five kids to bed and retrieving the coffee so fascinating. Your figures of speech, such as 'the wash of years' and 'a bale of time' would delight Carl Sandburg.[11]

With these confidence-building compliments, Webb encouraged the young man to cultivate his talent and "do more of this sort of thing." He suggested how the two letters could be combined into a story and promised to help in getting it published.[12]

In another case, he revised a former student's article to the extent that she suggested a joint authorship, but he rejected her offer saying: "The fact that I made some revision does not affect the matter, although I had anticipated that you would raise the issue on account of the revamping. . . . Let's don't argue about this. We all get such help and we make it up by helping others." He suggested that she send the article to *The Yale Review*, but, as he said, "To get it in a history mag., [*sic*] the footnotes would have to be restored (damn footnotes)."[13]

In 1953, he also took time out to help a fisherman's wife get a manuscript ready for publication. For some time he had been searching for an interested graduate student to do a history of the Texas coastal area when he heard that the wife of an old friend had written a book she called *Stringing Along With Florida*, later published as *The Stubborn Fisherman*. Webb had first met Florida Roberts in 1939 when he went with Eugene C. Barker and Bill Couzzens on a fishing trip to Port Aransas. George E. Roberts, as he was officially known, captained a fishing boat off the chain of islands extending the length of the Texas Gulf Coast for some two hundred miles. Florida took his living from the sea and from the tourists like Webb who came to fish. On board his boat, Florida was master and Webb was much impressed with the seemingly carefree and colorful life of his barefooted host. He liked to recall the picture of him standing on deck, the sun reflecting off his brown face and, with a container in his hand, making a toast:

> Here's to the girl that I love best,
> She looks so sweet in her gingham dress.
> But when she's in her pink silk nightie,
> Jesus Christ, God-Almighty.[14]

Webb observed that this was one of the few that could make it past the censors.

Florida married "a little Yankee woman" named Elda May and eventually she wrote the story of their life together—the saga of a man and a woman against the sea. Not long after Webb heard that she had completed her manuscript, he and his wife Jane drove to Port Aransas and on to the Roberts' cottage. Twenty years had passed since Webb had first met Florida, who was now in ill health, but his wife had continued the tourist trade by selling shells. After buying a large quantity, the Webbs returned to Rockport with a car full of shells and a copy of a beautiful manuscript that portrayed the humor, the pathos, and the struggles of this couple. He found the story so intriguing that he began reading aloud to Jane. Both of them shared with the author the difficulties of rearing three sets of children, surviving the floods that washed away all their possessions, going broke, and running away from each other only to return. "I am not sure what literature is," Webb concluded, "but I like to think of it as a piece of writing that portrays some aspect of human life and struggle in such a manner as to give the reader the illusion of reality."[15] To Webb this was a human history of the coastal area and as such had great relevance. Characteristically, he appreciated the art as well as the information revealed. He felt that history was made more meaningful to the general public by the manner of writing.

Webb's innovative ideas for improving the teaching of history and making it relevant included not only helping individuals, but also encompassed such schemes as the establishment of a school for historians, and the assembling of a team of scholars to reinterpret the history of the United States, particularly since the 1930s. He advocated the improvement of teaching and learning through the use of scientific and technological equipment such as radio, television, and the computer. To implement one such idea, the Ford Foundation awarded him a grant so that he could record and tape the contributions of twenty distinguished historians, each a specialist in his field. With the $91,300 funded, he masterminded a series of television lectures called "American Civilization by the Interpreters," which was videotaped by the university's radio and television studio under the direction of Robert D. Squier. In his conquest of the frontier of educational television, Webb engaged such illustrious guests as Arnold Toynbee, David Potter, Allan Nevins, Rodman Paul, Samuel Bemis, Ray Billington, Richard B. Morris, Carl Bridenbaugh, and Thomas D. Clark among others. The course carried college credit and received national distribution. After Webb's death, Joe B. Frantz completed the series.[16]

During the late years, Webb not only forged new frontiers in the teaching field but in politics as well. In January 1959, at the age of seventy-one, he accepted a challenging job as part-time special consultant to Senate Majority Leader Lyndon B. Johnson. Never a cloistered individual, the new position nevertheless exposed him to more excitement than he had ever known, the world of Washington politics. Whereas he had observed and interpreted the forces of history, he now found himself participating in history in the making. His schedule was hectic: he taught three days a week at Rice Institute in Houston, interspersing his duties there with flights to Washington.[17]

The Washington scene was quite a change from the academic life. After following politicians around for a while, Webb concluded that "God must give them a second wind." He found himself watching Lyndon B. Johnson as he termed it, "through a cloud of dust, most of which is raised by those scurrying around him trying to figure out what he will do next." In Webb's opinion, Johnson had something of the "audacity" of Franklin D. Roosevelt and a great belief in the future of America, a sentiment that Webb shared.[18]

As legislative consultant, Webb concerned himself with the future of the South, an area that he felt had great potential if its populace would act positively. In 1937, he had written *Divided We Stand* in which he portrayed the South as "the sick man of the nation." Two decades later, he saw the North losing some of its economic control as the South gradually came into its own. Of all the sections, he now felt that the South had the brightest future *if* it was not deterred by the traditional outlook of its people. With its trilogy of oil and gas, water, and sulphur, the South possessed all the necessary requisites for a vast petrochemical industry. According to Webb, however, the region had to become more aggressive in capitalizing on its wealth, rather than leaving it to be exploited by northern concerns. In numerous speeches across the South he attempted to alert the people to their new potential and opportunity. At the same time, he warned them that their future, enhanced by the silent technological revolution, would come to naught if they did not cast aside the absorbing racial issues that directed their energies away from economic considerations. The South, he said, "cannot afford to make the same mistake twice. It cannot afford to be diverted by a cause already lost."[19]

Webb admitted that he felt in some respect responsible for the upswing of the South's future prospects. His book, *Divided We Stand,* had encouraged President Franklin D. Roosevelt to declare the area the nation's major economic problem, thereby placing much needed emphasis on a neglected facet of American society. The situation had gradually improved, through no real effort of its own, according to Webb. As he explained, "It would be a mistake to say that the South, like Br'er Rabbit, has fortunately fallen into the brier patch of opportunity. It is more accurate to say that the South has stood still and the brierpatch has grown up around it." He advised the region to make the most of it.[20]

Of all the southern sector, he felt that Texas had exhibited the most progressive outlook and the most success in overcoming the blight of the Civil War and the depression era. Texas itself exhibited dual characteristics and two different sectors—the more progressive western and central areas, on the one hand, and the east, which Webb termed "a corner of the old south," on the other. He saw the success of Texas in overcoming its disadvantages reflected in the jealousy of other states, a jealousy which he considered "the constant attendant of success or the prospect of it." As he explained:

> As long as the South was church-rat poor, there was nothing to be jealous of. But today there is much to arouse jealousy. We in Texas are now a sort of whipping boy for the nation. Wherever we go, people tell us stories, all unfavorable to

Texas. This attitude of criticism has reached such proportions that the *Houston Post* recently assigned a top reporter to make an investigation and write a series of articles to explain the phenomenon.[21]

Although Webb considered many of these tall tales damaging and malicious, he appreciated those that were clever and enjoyed repeating them. One such story concerned a Texan in New York making a long distance phone call. The Texan requested that the operator report charges to him, but when she told him that the bill came to $16, he immediately started spewing forth invectives and abuse on the company and the service. The operator endured the tirade as instructed until the Texan ended by declaring, "Why in Texas I could phone to hell and back for less than that." "Yes, sir," the operator patiently explained, "but there it would be a local call." Webb urged the South, like western and central Texas, to accept the challenge inherent in the future and take the path to progress.[22]

This new position signified a certain change of political posture for Webb. Whereas he had long been quietly active in state politics, this represented his first venture on the national scene. Throughout his life he had played the role of the respected elder counsellor rather than the "door-knocking participant." Recognized as a liberal, he was never as aggressive as J. Frank Dobie or even his wife Jane, or daughter Mildred; yet people deferred to his wisdom and politicians appreciated his support. He worked for University of Texas president, Homer Price Rainey, in his campaign for the governorship, even writing speeches for him. He also supported Henry Wallace, when it was not the popular thing to do. His influential essay, "How the Republican Party Lost Its Future," published in *The Southwest Review*, charged Republicans with forsaking the people long before the people gave up the party. He pointed out that Republicans after the Civil War had rejected the South, the West, labor, and the farmers, supporting only big business. Then with the depression, and the collapse of business in 1929, the party was left with nothing to stand on, and erstwhile Republicans turned coats at the polls.[23]

Webb's article provoked widespread and intelligent response. Ironically, the Republicans seemed to derive the most benefit from it: they used it to rally the Grand Old Party and show that it still had life. Democrats also took note. President Harry Truman, after reading a reprint of the essay in *Time* magazine, wrote to Webb saying that he considered it of such interest that he had asked for extra copies for distribution among Democratic leaders. Truman declared it to be "the best article on the real situation I've seen."[24] E. C. Barksdale, who was himself very much involved in Texas politics, recalled that Webb had advised him repeatedly to vote for Truman in the election of 1948, which he did.

On another occasion, Barksdale remembered distinctly a long conversation between Webb and Bill Kittrell, the former Chairman of the Democratic Executive Committee, the "Mr. Behind-the-Scenes" of Texas politics. Kittrell strongly urged Webb to declare for Lyndon Johnson for the Democratic Presidential nomination in 1960, pointing out that such a statement from Webb would have a profound effect on Texas liberals who generally did not favor Johnson. Barksdale knew that Webb greatly admired "Keetrell," as he called him, and he was afraid that he might act impulsively. As they left Kittrell's home, Barksdale said, "Dr. Webb, I hope you are not going to let Bill make a damned fool of you." Webb replied gruffly, "Hell, I'm not going to make any statement on the Democratic National Convention before the Convention." According to Barksdale, "That was that." And finally, it was through his involvement in Texas politics that Webb became acquainted with Terrell Maverick during his active support of her son Maury's "wild-goose race" for the United States Senate.[25]

The next two years were filled with sadness for Webb, for on June 28, 1960, his wife of forty-three years passed away. Jane had always led a very active life, as much involved in her own affairs as Webb had been in his. Just ten days prior to her death, she had hosted a supper and Flag Day Program for the United Daughters of the Confederacy and on the night she became ill, Mildred had helped her prepare refreshments for a gathering of Webb's poker playing friends at their home.[26]

Because Jane and Mildred were both traditionalists who disliked hospitals, doctors, and what Webb called "highly formalized and homogenized funerals," his daughter chose to have an old-fashioned home service. She met opposition on all sides, from the preacher, friends, and indirectly from her father. Through all attempts to alter her decision, she stood firm in her belief to do it "the old way." When the minister pointed out that the people

would not be able to hear, Mildred said they would just have to put
in a public address system. Despite the funeral director's astonishment and the fact that he had never done this before, with
Mildred's help, he strung the necessary wire and got the system in
operation. Joe Frantz made arrangements for someone "to sit up"
in two-hour shifts. Through all of this Webb was conscious of the
heat, the discomfort of those in attendance, and the imperfections.
He was therefore surprised when told by friends that the service
was fitting "and that the old way was not altogether a bad way."[27]

In a letter to J. Frank Dobie, he expressed his admiration and
respect for his daughter's wisdom in the matter. "Since you are
something of a champion of the old and simpler ways," he wrote,
"you may be interested in the home funeral, mainly because of
something it reveals about Mildred. I knew she had character, but
she revealed it in this case beyond my expectations." He concluded
by saying, "Maybe one reason I am telling you this is that I thought
you will [sic] appreciate knowing someone with that much iron, or
steel, in the makeup. It would be fine, if you could, at the
appropriate time let her know that you approve."[28]

The following year Webb had surgery for an aneurysm in his leg.
As he wrote to C. B. Smith, "I have received your letter and have
not been in touch with you before because I spent eighteen days in
the hospital for an operation that equipped me with a brand-new
dacron femoral artery in my right leg."[29] Despite the fact that he
felt "like a walking subsidiary of Dow Chemical," as he told one
hospital visitor, by February 6, 1961, he was back at his desk in
Garrison Hall.[30]

His graduate assistant in 1961, Neville Baird, observed that this
seemed to be a very bad year for Webb. He was depressed by his
wife's death, his own ill-health, and according to Baird, "seemed to
view life very cynically, as a sort of cosmic joke played on human
beings."[31] Soon, however, he developed a friendship with a
charming lady whose association helped to dispel his depression
and filled his remaining years with happiness.

Terrell Maverick, the widow of New Deal Congressman and
former Mayor of San Antonio, Maury Maverick, was a petite and
pretty woman who had led a fascinating life. The first time she took
note of Walter Webb had been when her husband brought home a
copy of *Divided We Stand*. Maury, she remembered, was very
excited about it and declared that he planned to steal it all for one

of his speeches on the floor of Congress, "which I am sure he did," she added. They became further acquainted through political and social affairs; then after the death of Jane Webb, as one friend would do for another, she called Mildred to extend condolences. Several months later Terrell invited them both to come over to San Antonio to attend the symphony. Their friendship ripened and soon Webb was making regular trips to San Antonio to visit the widow Maverick. The Austin scene watched with pleasure as Webb seemed to bloom like a cactus flower under the spell of the vivacious and charming Texas lady. Like an "aging Andy Hardy" he began hinting of his intentions and asking the advice of everyone from friends to waitresses at the Night Hawk. Webb, after all, was seventy-three years young and his intended not exactly a child-bride at sixty.[32]

With the sanction of friends and relatives, Walter Webb and Terrell Maverick were married December 14, 1961, at a place suggested by her son—a small rustic Episcopal church in Fredericksburg. The ceremony, performed by the Right Reverend Everett Jones, a former Webb student and Bishop of the Diocese of West Texas, was attended by only a few close friends and relatives. Terrell's dear friend, Elma Dill Spencer, was the bride's only attendant. After the ceremony, the wedding party went to the old Nimitz Hotel for a brunch, then the newlyweds returned to San Antonio to pick up Terrell's luggage. Webb became ecstatic when she suggested that they take a honeymoon trip to the Big Bend country that he loved so well. He had expected her to want to go to New York or some place similar, but instead they drove to Brownsville and Matamoros, working their way back up the Rio Grande. Terrell reflected upon their courtship and marriage as "the icing on the cake of a colorful life."[33]

On their return to Austin, they rented an apartment from Lyndon B. Johnson and took up a very busy and happy life together. Webb taught a night seminar at the university, initiated the Oral History series where he was responsible for introducing all the guest lecturers, and wrote and promoted the search for William E. Hinds. But as the new Mrs. Webb candidly admitted, "His major interest was me!"[34] In the spring of 1962, they went to New York en route to Providence, Rhode Island, where Webb gave a lecture at the Brown Library. While in New York, they conferred with editors at *Harper's* on a joint venture to be released in February

1963. The following summer they planned to travel to Fairbanks, Alaska, where Webb had agreed to teach a summer session. As it turned out, Terrell had suffered a flare-up with her heart and her doctor would not permit her to go. The forced separation was difficult for both; as Webb told Joe Frantz, he "much preferred the frontier in theory to fact." During this time apart, Webb wrote religiously. His wife termed the letters "fantastic" and hopes one day to publish them.[35]

After Webb's return from Alaska, they began editing for *Harper's* a journal that Terrell's first husband, Maury Maverick, had inherited from his aunt, Ellen Slayden. In the process of moving Terrell's valuable documents from her home on Maverick Hill in San Antonio to the University of Texas, they had discovered a remarkable manuscript written by Ellen Slayden during her years in Washington with her husband, James L. Slayden, a Congressman from San Antonio in 1897. The Slayden manuscript was composed of twenty-two chapters, one for each of her years spent in Washington. As an intelligent social commentary, it was extremely valuable, for it covered the period from the Spanish-American War through World War I when they returned to San Antonio. Mrs. Slayden, a mature woman of intelligence and social acceptance, had excellent opportunity to record vivid impressions of Washington personalities and events of the period. The Webbs had a fascinating time editing the diary, which was published as *Washington Wife: The Journal of Ellen Maury Slayden.* Webb was fond of saying that the easiest way to acquire a best seller was to marry one.[36]

By this time, he had been forced to hire a private secretary to help him with the voluminous correspondence regarding the Hinds story and the Oral History Project now in progress. In addition to his Garrison Hall office, he had set up a secret hideaway on the eighteenth floor of the Tower. It consisted of a small room lined floor to ceiling with books, a retreat that not even some of his best friends knew existed. When his secretary, Eileen Guarino, walked in the first day, she found him sitting at his desk behind ten baskets of unopened letters. It was amazing to her, she recalled, that he had functioned for so many years without help. He had previously used the departmental secretary and various assistants from among the students. He welcomed her aboard and eventually paid her the compliment of saying that "she helped clear the clutter from his mind."[37]

At the Tower office he worked in privacy and quiet, but at Garrison Hall 102, the door was generally open. His brusque and crusty manner frightened young students and intimidated the secretaries thoroughly. In his later years he did become somewhat cantankerous and testy; as one observer noted, "he was playing the part of the senior scholar and enjoying the hell out of it." Although he could be blunt to the point of rudeness, most often he was "a kind and gentle man and a little astonished at his own success."[38]

Even in later years he retained a delightfully wry sense of humor. His secretary recalled that he delighted in interjecting some slightly smutty remark in his dictation, couched in such beautiful terms that it would take a while to sink in. He would sit back with a twinkle in his eye, watching closely, while she absorbed the meaning and turned red. Then he would rear back in his swivel chair and let loose a roar of laughter. After concluding his work at the university, he would generally go home to work with Terrell on the Slayden book.[39]

In the spring of 1963, the Webbs planned autographing sessions at Scarborough's in Austin and at Rosengren's Book Store in San Antonio. On the morning of March 7, 1963, Webb kept a 9:30 appointment with Dr. W. Gordon Whaley, Dean of the Graduate School, and Dr. Audrey Nelson Slate, editor for *The Graduate Journal*. Webb was in good spirits and a jovial mood. Shortly before 10:30, he donned his Stetson, a gift from his friend, Vice-President Lyndon B. Johnson, and crossed the hall to tell Eileen Guarino good-bye prior to leaving with Terrell for the hill country to talk to Friends of the Kerrville Library about *Washington Wife*. From Kerrville, they planned to go on to San Antonio where he was to present a speech to a retired teachers' group. He left the office whistling; it was spring, and he was looking forward to seeing the peach trees and redbud in bloom. Mrs. Guarino called out, "Have fun." Webb smiled back and assured her that they would.[40]

The next morning she called him at the Purple Sage Motel in Kerrville to tell him that Ernest Gruening, Senator from Alaska, would be arriving to tape his lecture for the Oral History Project on March 15. Webb mentioned that he had been pleased with the evening in Kerrville and planned to leave for San Antonio shortly.

They hoped to be back in Austin Friday evening in time for a dinner engagement with J. Frank Dobie and Frank Wardlaw.[41]

Thoroughly exhausted after several days of autographing and speechmaking, they got in their car to return home. Terrell lay down in the front seat with her head in her husband's lap and went to sleep. The next thing she remembered was opening her eyes to pain and the glare of the overhead lights in the emergency room at Breckenridge Hospital in Austin. "I heard someone say D.O.A.," she remembered, "and I knew that meant Walter Webb." She learned that they had been involved in a one-car accident twelve miles south of Austin on Interstate Highway 35.[42]

Terrell Webb, severely injured, remained in the hospital while funeral services for Walter Webb were conducted by Dr. Edmund Heinsohn of University Methodist Church. The city of Austin was greatly shocked and grieved by the sudden loss of such a renowned and well-loved figure. The flags at the University of Texas flew at half-mast in memory of one of the institution's greatest thinkers, a man who brought to it vigor, imagination, guidance, and world-wide acclaim. Vice-President Lyndon B. Johnson wrote, "The hand of death has removed one of my closest friends."[43] He spoke for many.

The state of Texas paid tribute to the distinguished historian by granting permission for his interment in the State Cemetery in Austin.[44] Webb would have approved and appreciated this last honor, for in his final resting place near the top of the highest grassy knoll, he is surrounded by the spirit of others who played important roles in the making of history. Through the entry gates, gazing past the neat rows of the Civil War dead and further up the green hill, one can see the simple stone marker reading "Walter Prescott Webb, Historian." He rests in good company, one of few civilians to be buried in the State Cemetery. His friend J. Frank Dobie, "Storyteller of the Southwest," rests nearby with "Hound-dog Man" Fred Gipson not far away. Down the walk and to the left stands the impressive statue of Johanna Troutman, famous pioneer woman, while the figure of Stephen F. Austin on the crest of the hill watches with a father's care over his land and his people.

12

EPILOGUE: FROM THE GREAT PLAINS TO THE LIMITS OF THE WESTERN WORLD

A well-written Life is almost as rare as a well-spent one.

Thomas Carlyle, *Critical and Miscellaneous*
Essays, vol. i. *Richter*

The death of Walter Prescott Webb meant not only the loss of a personal friend to many, but also the loss of a prize-winning author, historian, and visionary whose challenging ideas reflected concerns so vital to society that there were those who resolved that investigation of these ideas and their ramifications should be continued. Meeting at Webb's funeral, C. B. Smith, Sr., civic leader and University of Texas alumnus, and J. R. Parten, Houston industrialist and former regent, agreed that something should be done to honor the great historian.[1]

The University of Texas at Arlington took the lead in implementing such a memorial. This institution, and in particular its history faculty, owed much to Walter Webb. During its early years, when best described as "a cowpasture junior college," Webb found the time to take an active interest in staffing its history department with "blue chip" young men. In 1964 when several members of the history faculty determined that a lecture series should be organized to add to the cultural offerings of the local area and enhance the prestige and stature of the university, Professor George Wolfskill suggested that the lectures be organized as a memorial to Webb. With the approbation and aid of departmental chairman, E. C. Barksdale, longtime friend of Webb, the project was launched.[2]

The lectures, in Webb's tradition, are unstructured and transdisciplinary in approach with significance to both academic and lay circles. They popularize history by illustrating that it need not

182

always be dead, dull, pedantic; that it can be living, exciting, and
interesting when presented by qualified and talented scholars. The
heuristic objective of dedicated academicians—those who are not
solely interested in impressing their peers—is thus accomplished by
exposing to public light the fallacy that all history and historians,
are in the words of J. Frank Dobie, "dry bones." A valuable fringe
benefit for the participants is the opportunity to publish the results
of their research. In Barksdale's colorful idiom, the lectures provide
"horn-tooting opportunities," a showcase for local historians "to
display their wares," and perhaps unveil some worthwhile historical find. Webb would have approved. Credit for the permanence of
the series, publication of the lectures in book form, and an annual
essay competition prize, goes to C. B. Smith, Sr., for his provision of
a permanent endowment to fund the lectures.[3]

Other efforts to continue the ideas of Walter Prescott Webb
were initiated by a meeting of interested parties at Friday
Mountain Ranch in 1966 and 1968. As a result of these meetings,
the Walter Prescott Webb Great Frontier Association was organized to bring together Webb's friends from the business world
with those from academe in an effort to perpetuate his memory in
a worthy and appropriate manner. Members of the association
selected several avenues to accomplish their objectives. Because of
the impact of his own personal benefactor on his life, Webb himself
had established a memorial fund in honor of William Ellery Hinds.
In his handwritten will, he assured its continuance by stating that
lease properties within the city of Austin, after death of his wife
and daughter, should go to the University of Texas at Austin for
perpetuation of the fund. In the interim, friends of Webb attempt
to maintain it as a permanent fund for Webb Scholarships.[4]

Although Webb's initial historical interpretation served as a
refracted image of his own regional and provincial origins, his
intellectual curiosity and ability to synthesize lured him to inquiry
on the universal scale—from Texas and the West, on to the South,
to America, and eventually to *The Great Frontier*, wherein he
projected his vision for the future of mankind. Friends of Webb
therefore attempted to develop memorials that would encompass,
not only financial help to promising and needy students, but those
that would also take into consideration the broad intellectual
concerns of this farseeing individual.[5]

In this vein, plans were initiated to conduct an international symposium bringing together a group of distinguished intellectuals to consider problems of society and their solutions. Three years in the planning stage, the International Symposium on The Great Frontier held April 3 through April 5, 1972, featured such well-known individuals as Daniel Bell, sociologist; Aaron Copland, composer; Loren Eiseley and Max Gluckman, anthropologists; Raymond Aron, French statesman and philosopher; Alfred Kazin, literary critic; Herman Kahn, Hudson Institute physicist; Sol Linowitz, Washington, D.C. attorney and diplomat; and Nathaniel Owings, architect and city planner. Following Webb's advice to devote our energies to finding solutions to problems posed by a frontierless society, these participants considered a spectrum of topics from population explosion and environmental issues to the dismantling of military bases. Underwriting for the symposium was provided by C. B. Smith, Sr., and J. R. Parten, in the amount of $50,000. Joe B. Frantz headed a faculty committee to oversee the project. Sponsors hoped that a fringe benefit of the symposium would be to produce added financial support for the humanities at the University of Texas at Austin and the University of Texas at Arlington, a concern Webb deemed crucial if man were to acquire adequate "knowledge of himself and his social order to act intelligently."[6]

Respect for Webb and his works is reflected in still other ways. Plans are being considered for the establishment of an endowed Webb Chair at the University of Texas at Austin, and the new faculty office building and center has been renamed Walter Webb Hall, commemorating his loyalty to the university and his selfless devotion to its academic community as well as to the high ideals and intellectual integrity he represented.[7] The impact and influence of Walter Webb is also exhibited in the efforts of Leon Borden Blair, Executive Director for The Texas Bureau of Economic Understanding, who has founded the Walter Prescott Webb Society to meet the need for an intermediate organization between the Junior Historians and the national history honorary society, Phi Alpha Theta. The Webb Society serves junior colleges and four year colleges which either have no Phi Alpha Theta chapter or have students interested in history but not qualified for Phi Alpha Theta membership.[8]

Walter Webb's catholic interests cast a long shadow outside academe; yet it is clear from a study of his life and works that his greatest impact lies within it—in his numerous contributions to the historical field, as teacher, faculty member, writer, and originator of thought-provoking ideas, and as inspiration to former students and associates who perpetuate his concepts and his ideals. In retrospect, what were the factors responsible for the making of this distinguished historian? A clue is to be found in the common thread that weaves its way through his major works—the frontier environment and its influence on institutions and individuals. The Great Plains and Great Frontier concepts are themselves examples of the effect of the plains environment on their originator. Though he desired escape from it, Walter Webb was close to the soil. He was receptive to Keasbey's geographic environmentalism because he knew it worked; he had seen its causative forces firsthand. He developed as a writer and historian because the world of books provided for him an escape from the drudgery of everyday existence. Though he left the farm, he never escaped its influence.

Webb's rare attributes as a historian may be placed in perspective and the rationale for the scope and impact of his works may be better understood if one considers the prevalent historiography of his time. When Webb began his career, American historians were generally steeped in Von Ranke's Germanic method of teaching history, involving a detailed study of specific segments of an era. Webb, however, believed in institutional history, interdisciplinary in approach and encompassing the whole panorama of the past. He described this generalistic view himself by saying that he looked at history through a telescope rather than a microscope.[9]

Historians, generally reporters rather than contributors, very seldom come up with new ideas. Webb's works, as exemplified by The Great Plains and The Great Frontier, if not completely original, were new in essence and in interpretation. They contained basic ideas, leading to many ramifications and paths of exploration—ideas of continuing importance to research in the fields of economics, politics, and sociology.[10] Because his works spanned such a period of time, one can see reflected in them the changing patterns of American historical thought, although his emphasis on environment as a causative factor runs throughout.

The Great Plains, written during the progressive period in American historiography, presented his interpretation of a great national experience, the idealistic saga of America's triumph over obstacles imposed by a hostile environment. The Texas Rangers also exemplified the progressive view as Webb showed the success of this force in overcoming dangers by adopting weapons and modes of operation suited to changing needs. In this work, one can discern a regression to Parkman-like romanticism as Webb actually rode with the Rangers to flavor his writing with the reality of experience. Then with *Divided We Stand*, published in 1937, the optimism of the progressive interpretation is diminished, correlating with results of the depression era and the prospect of World War II. By 1952, with publication of *The Great Frontier*, he had become counterprogressive in his views. Evidence of a cyclical theory of history is apparent as he faced the dismal reality of the future in a frontierless society.[11]

From firsthand observation of the frontier's effects on himself and his family, his view broadened until it eventually reached the limits of the western world. His ability to see the entire panorama of the past resulted in the creative synthesis of the Great Plains and the Great Frontier concepts, his additions to the inventory of human knowledge, and the basis for his acclaim as a historian of international scope. Perhaps subconsciously, he was trying to repay William Ellery Hinds.

NOTES

Introduction

1. Jerome S. Bruner, *On Knowing* (New York: Atheneum, 1967), pp. 22–23.
2. John Fischer, "An Unfashionable Kind of Historian," *The Texas Observer* 55:6.
3. W. P. Webb, "The Texan's Story," p. 1, *Walter Prescott Webb Collection* (hereafter cited as *WPWC*), Barker Texas History Center, Archives, Austin, Texas, Box 2M245.

Chapter 1

1. Walter Prescott Webb, "The Search for William E. Hinds," *Harper's Magazine* 223:62 (hereafter cited as Webb, "Search for Hinds").
2. C. B. Smith, Sr., " 'Round-Up' on Letters in Re Webb-Hinds," in *A Salute to Walter Prescott Webb and "The Search for William E. Hinds,"* ed. by C. B. Smith, Sr. (Austin: by the ed., 1961), p. vii; John Fischer, untitled tribute to Webb, in "A Man, His Land, and His Work," *The Graduate Journal* 6 (Winter 1964):35–37. Webb first revealed the moving story of his benefactor in an address to the Texas Institute of Letters where he was awarded on December 8, 1952, the Carr P. Collins Award of $1000 for publication of *The Great Frontier;* see Walter Prescott Webb, "The Confessions of a Texas Bookmaker," *Texas Libraries* 25 (Fall 1963):88–96.
3. Smith, *Salute to Webb*, p. iv; C. B. Smith, Sr., interview, Austin, Texas, February 11, 1972; [W. P. Webb], "Mr. Hinds Discovered," in *Jenkins Garrett Collection of Walter Prescott Webb Papers*, Library, University of Texas at Arlington, Division of Special Collections, Arlington, Texas, Box 21-17 (hereafter cited as *Garrett Coll.* UTA); Webb to "Dear C.B.," December 11, 1961, *Smith Personal Coll.;* permission for use generously granted by Mr. Smith.
4. Webb to C. B. Smith, September 22, 1961, in Smith, *Salute to Webb*, p. 158.
5. Smith, *Salute to Webb*, p. x; Fischer, untitled tribute to Webb, in "A Man, His Land, and His Work," p. 37. Replies were received from relatives and friends interested in passing on information about Hinds, from people whose careers had benefited from the assistance of benefactors, from those wanting to express how touched they were by the story, and from people requesting financial assistance.
6. Webb to John Fischer, March 29, 1961, *WPWC*, Box 2M250; Webb, "Mr. Hinds Discovered," *Garrett Coll.* UTA, Box 21-17.

Chapter 2

1. Frank E. Vandiver, "The Civil War as an Institutionalizing Force," in *Essays on the American Civil War, The Walter Prescott Webb Memorial Lectures:* I, ed. by William F. Holmes and Harold M. Hollingsworth with a Webb Bibliography by Margaret Francine Morris (Austin: University of Texas Press, 1968), pp. 73–74.

2. News clipping, *The Dallas Morning News,* October 22, 1939, *WPWC,* Box 2M293; commemorating the Webbs' anniversary.

3. T. R. Fehrenbach, *Lone Star: A History of Texas and Texans* (Toronto: Macmillan Company, 1968), pp. 420, 602.

4. Ibid., 602–3.

5. Webb, "Texan's Story," pp. 6–7, *WPWC,* Box 2M245. In this box there is a brief biographical sketch designated herein as "Autobiography" and a lengthy autobiography entitled "The Texan's Story," written while he was in Oxford, and covering Webb's life from birth to 1935. For brevity, the brief sketch will be designated hereafter as "Auto." and the partial autobiography as "Tx. St."

6. W. P. Webb, "Cultural Resources of Texas," p. 351, *Garrett Coll.* UTA, Box 21-10. This speech can also be found in *C. B. Smith Collection of Walter Prescott Webb Papers,* Texas State Library, Archives, Austin, Texas, Box 2-22/799 (hereafter cited as *Smith Coll.* TS).

7. Webb, "Tx. St.," p. 18.

8. Ibid., pp. 2–3; Webb, "Auto.," p. 1.

9. Webb, "Tx. St.," pp. 1, 42.

10. Ibid., p. 4; Webb, "Search for Hinds," p. 62; W. P. Webb, "History as High Adventure," *The American Historical Review* 44 (January 1959):273. This article can also be found in W. P. Webb, *History As High Adventure,* ed. with an introduction by E. C. Barksdale (Austin: Pemberton Press, 1969), where it serves as the lead article and the theme for this excellent collection of essays.

11. Webb, "Tx. St.," pp. 4–8.

12. Ima Wright, interview, Austin, Texas, January 21, 1975; August 20, 1974. Mrs. Wright has fond memories of her "big brother." She recalled that she had broken her collarbone while playing "snap the whip." To cheer her up, Walter, who was teaching at Merriman when this occurred, brought her a stuffed toy which she saved as a keepsake until moths destroyed it.

13. Webb, "Tx. St.," p. 6.

14. Ibid., pp. 20, 35; W. P. Webb and H. Bailey Carroll, eds., *Handbook of Texas,* 2 (Austin: Texas State Historical Association, 1952):677; Fehrenbach, *Lone Star,* pp. 537–51.

15. Webb, "Auto.," p. 1; W. P. Webb, *The Great Plains* (Boston: Ginn and Co., 1931), pp. 25–26.

16. Webb, "Tx. St., " pp. 11–12.

17. Webb, *The Great Plains,* p. 22.

18. Webb, "Three Geographical and Historical Concepts Essential to an Understanding of the American West," June, 1960, *Smith Coll.* TS, Box 2-22/799.

19. Webb, "Tx. St.," pp. 10–13.

20. Ibid., pp. 12–13.

21. E. C. Barksdale, interview, Arlington, Texas, June 14, 1973. The late Dr. E. C. Barksdale, formerly chairman of the department of history at the University of Texas at Arlington, was one of Dr. Webb's closest friends. As Mrs. W. P. Webb and Joe B. Frantz recall, he loved "Bert" Barksdale, who was quite an "original"—a brilliant man, a gambler, an individualistic dresser, and a successful dealer in real estate; interviews, Austin, Texas, August 20, 1974. The reference to "pop eyes" probably referred to a child's big-eyed curiosity as much as a physical characteristic.

22. Mrs. C. P. Jones, "My Unforgettable Pupil," *Smith Coll.* TS, Box 2-22/793.

23. Ibid.

24. Webb, "Tx. St.," p. 14.

25. Ibid., pp. 76–77.

26. Ibid., p. 77.

27. Ibid., pp. 41, 20; Webb, "Search for Hinds," p. 64.

28. Webb, "Tx. St.," pp. 26–31.

29. Ibid., pp. 27–28, 32; Mrs. W. P. Webb to writer, February 24, 1972. Cotton was selling for 5 cents a pound at this time, and Webb claimed that he could pick 50 pounds a day as a young boy.

30. Webb, "Tx. St.," pp. 29–30, 38.

31. Ibid., pp. 23–25.

32. Ibid., pp. 24–25.

33. Ibid., p. 25. Webb recalls the Benedict Story as being reported in *The Texas Whirligig;* however, he may have been thinking of *The Texas Merry Go-Round,* [author anonymous] (Houston: Sun Publisher, 1933), p. 78. Ronnie Dugger, in *Our Invaded Universities, Form, Reform and New Starts* (New York: W. W. Norton & Co., Inc., 1974), pp. 22–23, also tells this tale and reports that the anecdote conforms to one in *The Texas Merry Go-Round.*

34. Ima Wright, interview, Austin, Texas, January 22, 1975.

35. Webb, "Tx. St.," pp. 12–14.

36. Oscar Theodore Barck, Jr. and Nelson Manfred Black, *Since 1900,* 3d ed. (New York: Macmillan Co., 1959), pp. 140–41.

37. Fehrenbach, *Lone Star,* pp. 595, 599–601. For a vivid account of frontier religious customs, I am indebted to my grandmother, the late Mrs. L. W. Fairchild, who grew up in the German settlement of Fredericksburg, Texas, at the turn of the century. The Israelite analogy is the conception of T. R. Fehrenbach, author of the excellent and insightful Texas state history, *Lone Star.*

38. Terrell Webb, "Portraits of Two Men," speech delivered at the Western Historical Association meeting, Fort Worth, Texas, 1973.

39. Hinds to Webb, December 31, 1911, *Smith Coll.* TS, Box 2-22/788.

40. Webb, "Search for Hinds," p. 63; Webb, "Tx. St.," p. 44.

41. Webb, "Tx. St.," p. 43–46.

42. Ibid., p. 46.

43. Ibid., pp. 46–47.

44. Ibid., p. 47.

45. Ibid., p. 61.

46. Ibid., pp. 61–63.

47. Ibid., p. 63. Davenport also became a political power in the developing Rio Grande Valley and a president of the Texas State Historical Association.

48. Ibid., p. 48; Ima Wright, interview, Austin, Texas, August 20, 1974. Casner had also worked one summer selling school supplies.

49. Webb, "Search for Hinds," p. 63; Mildred Webb Bugg, interview, Austin, Texas, January 28, 1972.

50. Webb, "Search for Hinds," p. 63; Webb, "Tx. St.," pp. 48–49, 72–73.

51. Hinds to Webb, May 16, 1904, *Smith Coll.* TS, Box 2-22/788; Webb, "Search for Hinds," pp. 63–64; Webb to Lt. Col. W. H. Prescott, September 12, 1962, *WPWC,* Box 2M245, which refers to Webb being named after an uncle, Henry Prescott Webb, who was something of a writer. Thus W. P. Webb signed his letter "Prescott" thinking it sounded more literary. In reference to the subject of names, George Fuermann, columnist for the *Houston Post,* recorded in notes from a conversation with Webb, that his real name was Walton rather than Walter. There is no supporting documentation for this claim, however, either from relatives or documents. Birth records for 1888 are, of course, unavailable. Fuermann's notes are located in *Garrett Coll.* UTA, Box 21-3.

52. Hinds to "Dear Junior" [Webb], June 28, 1904, in "Search for Hinds," (draft), *Smith Coll.* TS, Box 2-22/788; Webb, "Tx. St.," p. 71; Joe B. Frantz, "He'll Do to Ride the River With," in W. P. Webb, *An Honest Preface and Other Essays* (Boston: Houghton Mifflin Co.,

1959), p. 7. Note that the draft in the Smith Collection contains many references to Webb's accomplishments, which the publishers wisely suggested editing, and placing in a "boxed" editorial introduction in the printed article.

53. Barck and Blake, *Since 1900*, p. 147.

54. Webb, "Tx. St.," pp. 40–47. Regarding the effect of the shinnery on its youth, Webb wagered; "If anyone ever cares to make a statistical study, my guess is that he will find that the Cross Timbers produced more school teachers, country lawyers, preachers, and penitentiary inmates in proportion to size and population than any region of West Texas."

55. Ibid., pp. 77–78; Barck and Blake, *Since 1900*, p. 136; Webb, "Search for Hinds," (draft dated July 8, 1961), *Smith Coll.* TS, Box 2-22/788.

56. Webb, "Recollections of Life in Ranger," 1959, *WPWC*, Box 2M293; Webb, "Tx. St.," p. 82.

57. Webb, "Tx. St.," pp. 82–83.

58. Webb, "Search for Hinds," p. 65; Webb, "Auto.," p. 5.

59. Webb, "Tx. St.," p. 89. Webb made a respectable score of 94 on his certification exam.

60. Ibid., p. 74.

61. Ibid., p. 89; Webb, "My First School," pp. 1–4, *Smith Coll.* TS, Box 2-22/788.

62. Webb, "Tx. St.," pp. 89–90; Webb, "My First School," p. 4.

63. Webb, "Tx. St.," pp. 93–95.

64. W. P. Webb, "Confessions of a Texas Bookmaker," Smith Coll. TS, Box 2-22/799.

65. Webb, "Auto.," p. 6.

66. Webb, "Tx. St.," pp. 96–99.

67. Ibid., pp. 99–105; Ima Wright, interviews, Austin, Texas, August 20, 1974 and January 21, 1975; Webb, "Search for Hinds," p. 66.

68. Susie Milam to "My dearest friend," Belton, Tx., n.d.; Susie to Walter, October 10, 1909; P. R. Crowley to Webb, March 4, 1914, *Smith Coll.* TS, Box 2-22/792. In these letters Susie asks his help on a paper she is writing saying; "I know you are gifted along these lines and want your suggestions." She also inquires when he is coming to see her, and like a good Baylor girl, urges him to go to church on Sunday. See also Susie to Walter, n.d., Box 2-22/792 wherein she indicates that Walter had evidently written her of his plans for the future. A brother-sister type relationship seemed to exist between the two. During the period 1911–13, Webb also had some interest in a girl by the name of Lena Williamson; see Annie to Walter, n.d., Box 2-22/792, in which this friend refers to Lena: "I think your Miss Williamson is a very attractive sweet appearing girl. . . . She has glorious eyes and in their sparkling depths one can read genuine admiration for 'W. P.' " "Annie" further indicated, however, that Webb had implied that he was not in love with her. See Lena Williamson to Webb, October 20, 1912, Box 2-22/792, wherein she thanks him for sending her a pennant.

69. Webb, "Search for Hinds," p. 65.

70. W. P. Webb, *The Great Frontier* (Boston: Houghton, Mifflin, 1952; reprinted, Austin: University of Texas Press, 1964, with an introduction by Arnold J. Toynbee), p. 374. Reference to Turner's agrarian perspective does not imply that he was a monocausationist, of course. See also Edward Jannes Willis, "John Steinbeck and the Frontier hypothesis of Walter Prescott Webb" (M.A. thesis, Stephen F. Austin College, 1955).

71. Webb, "Search for Hinds," p. 66; Hinds to "My dear friend," January 9, 1909; Hinds to Webb, January 31, 1909, *Smith Coll.* TS, Box 2-22/788. Hinds mistakenly referred to Webb as "J." Prescott for sometime, rather than using the correct initial "W."

72. Webb, "Search for Hinds," p. 66; Ima Wright, interview, Austin, Texas, January 21, 1975. Mrs. Wright said that the girl he had made reference to must have been Esther Bailey. See also Webb, "Tx. St.," p. 66.

Chapter 3

1. Webb, "Tx. St.," pp. 73–74; Harry H. Ransom, "Educational Resources in Texas," in *Texas Today and Tomorrow*, ed. by Herbert Gambrell (Dallas: Southern Methodist University Press, 1960), pp. 53–58.

2. Ransom, "Educational Resources," p. 106; Webb, "Auto.," pp. 6–7.

3. "Record of Mr. W. P. Webb—U. of Texas at Austin," *Smith Coll.* TS, Box 2-22/792; also in *Garrett Coll.* UTA, Box 21-6.

4. Hinds to "Dear Junior," October 5, 1909; November 7, 1909; and Postcard, April 29, 1909, *Smith Coll.* TS, Box 2-22/788. Hinds described in great detail the "Hudson-Fulton" week of celebration when the buildings were decorated with garlands of electric lights, parades were held, and the "Wright flying machine," looking "like a great bird that went like the wind," circled above the ships resting in the Hudson. Even the ships in the harbor were outlined in electric lights, "like a fairy scene," according to Hinds, and on Saturday the parks were filled with marching children. In later years, Webb retained a special place in his heart for the city of New York, and according to Joe B. Frantz, interview, Austin, Texas, January 22, 1975, he felt that he should visit the place every time he crossed the state line. He had the Texan's special disregard for distance.

5. Webb, "Auto.," p. 7; Webb, "Tx. St.," pp. 108–9; Webb, "On Choosing a Vocation," January 23, 1910, *WPWC*, Box 2M246.

6. Webb, "An Adventure," November 12, 1909, *Smith Coll.* TS, Box 2-22/789.

7. Webb, "My Object in Studying English 3," October 20, 1910, in *Smith Coll.* TS, Box 2-22/788. Webb expressed his desire for a literary career and his love of composition: "I sometimes write descriptions and narrative for my own amusement; I may say that writing is my hobby."

8. Webb, "The Old Homestead," October 29, 1909, *Smith Coll.* TS, Box 2-22/788.

9. "Record of Courses Taken in the University of Texas," *Smith Coll.* TS, Box 2-22/792; "Miscellaneous Undergraduate English Papers," *Smith Coll.* TS, Box 2-22/789. Ironically, *The Great Plains* became an optional text in freshman English at the University of Texas.

10. Webb, "The Freshman's Attitude to English 1," December 7, 1910, *Smith Coll.* TS, Box 2-22/789; Webb, "Auto.," p. 7.

11. Webb to Jane, September 11, 1915, *Smith Coll.* TS, Box 2-22/796; Webb, "Tx. St.," p. 109. As Webb indicated, the English Department evidently adhered to the strong interest in linguistics of its senior professor, Morgan Calloway, Jr. See Webb and H. B. Carroll, eds., *Handbook of Texas* 1 (Austin: Texas State Historical Association, 1952):273.

12. Webb, "My Love of Poetry," March 4, 1911, *Smith Coll.* TS, Box 2-22/789.

13. Webb, "Record of Stephens County in the University of Texas," n.d., *Smith Coll.* TS, Box 2-22/789.

14. Webb, "Tx. St.," p. 106. As Webb noted, "All my life I have had these dead periods, doldrums, and perhaps they have a psychological and spiritual value."

15. Webb, "Tx. St.," p. 116–18; Dugger, *Our Invaded Universities*, p. 20, quoting Webb; Mrs. Keasbey to Mr. Payne, December 16, 1952, *WPWC*, Box 2M254.

16. Dugger, *Our Invaded Universities*, pp. 20–21.

17. Ibid. Houston resigned shortly thereafter. He was also a friend of Wilson and Keasbey. Dugger suggests that Houston's disgust with the handling of the Keasbey affair had something to do with his departure.

18. Ibid., p. 21; Fehrenbach, *Lone Star*, pp. 642–43.

19. Dugger, *Our Invaded Universities*, p. 21.

20. Keasbey to Webb, September 14, 1931; October 10, 1931; *WPWC*, Box 2M254.

21. Webb, "Tx. St.," pp. 117–18; Webb, "History As High Adventure," p. 279.

22. W. P. Webb, "Geographical-Historical Concepts in American History," *Annals of the Association of American Geographers* 50 (June 1960):85. Although Keasbey was the teacher Webb admired the most, his annual reports register a strong *B* average in these courses in Institutional History. See "Annual Report," *Smith Coll.* TS, Box 2-22/792.

23. Webb, "Geographical-Historical Concepts," pp. 85–86.

24. Webb, "The Theory of Imagination," Exercise for Institutional History 107, *Smith Coll.* TS, Box 2-22/788.

25. Webb, "Geographic Features as a Factor in the United States of America," in ibid.

26. Ibid.

27. Webb, "The Collegiate Communal System Versus the Republican-Patriarchal System in the History of Medieval Europe," January 18, 1915, in ibid.

28. Webb, "Some Influences Determining the Political Theory of the American Revolution," July 4, 1914, in ibid. (Emphasis mine.)

29. Webb, *The Great Frontier,* pp. 415, 131. See also Mazie E. Mathews, "On the Hither Edge of Free Land: Lindley Miller Keasbey and the Frontier Thesis" (M.A. thesis, Southwest Texas State University, 1973).

30. Webb, "The Future of the American Negro," *Smith Coll.* TS, Box 2-22/788.

31. Kenneth M. Stampp, "The Tragic Legend of Reconstruction," *The American Past in Perspective Since 1865,* ed. by Trevor Colbourn and James T. Patterson (Boston: Allyn and Bacon, Inc., 1970) 2:15–17.

32. Ibid., p. 17.

33. Dugger, *Our Invaded Universities,* p. 64. Heman Sweatt, a law student at the University of Texas, was admitted in 1950 on court order, but flunked out; E. C. Barksdale to writer, September 6, 1973.

34. Joe B. Frantz, interview, Austin, Texas, August 20, 1974; E. C. Barksdale, "Introduction," *Essays on the American Civil War, The Walter Prescott Webb Memorial Lectures,* ed. by Holmes and Hollingsworth, 1:26; Joe B. Frantz, "Walter Prescott Webb," in Wilbur R. Jacobs, John W. Caughey, and Joe B. Frantz, *Turner, Bolton, and Webb* (Seattle: University of Washington Press, 1965), p. 81.

35. E. C. Barksdale to writer, September 6, 1973.

36. Webb, "Cheeko," *Smith Coll.* TS, Box 2-22/788.

37. W. P. Webb, *The Texas Rangers* with a foreword by Lyndon B. Johnson, 2d ed. (Austin: University of Texas Press, 1965), p. 14; Webb, *The Great Plains* pp. 125–26; David Weber, ed., *Foreigners in Their Native Land* (Albuquerque: University of New Mexico Press, 1973), pp. 75–76. See also Llerena Friend, "W. P. Webb's Texas Rangers," *Southwestern Historical Quarterly* 74 (January 1971):319–20.

38. Webb to Jane and Mildred, January 21, 1943, *Smith Coll.* TS, Box 2-22/798; W. Eugene Hollon to writer, January 22, 1974; Rupert N. Richardson to writer, January 24, 1974; Friend, "W. P. Webb's Texas Rangers," pp. 319–21.

Chapter 4

1. Webb, "Tx. St.," pp. 110–11, 116; Expense Account, (included with undergraduate English papers), *Smith Coll.* TS, Box 2-22/789; Webb to Jane, June 25, 1915; *Smith Coll.* TS, Box 2-22/796 explains to her his obligations to assist his youngest sister.

2. Webb, "Tx. St.," pp. 110–11, 116.

3. Ibid., pp. 111–12.

4. Ibid., p. 112; Webb, *The Great Plains,* p. 279.

5. Webb, "Tx. St.," p. 112.

6. Ibid., pp. 114–15.

7. Ibid., p. 115.

8. W. P. Webb, untitled poem written while in Thurber; copy provided courtesy of Mrs. Ima Wright, Austin, Texas, in letter to writer, February 25, 1975.

9. Webb, "Tx. St.," p. 115; Insurance form, Western Casualty and Guaranty, *Smith Coll.* TS, Box 2-22/792, revealed that on November 30, 1912, Webb, at twenty-three years of age, weighed 140 pounds and stood 5′ 10″ tall. He listed his occupation as a student in college and a waiter in a boarding house. In his autobiography he reported that this attempt at helping with expenses was unsuccessful and ended in "a violent row," whereupon he resolved to stick to jobs relating more closely to the teaching field. In a couple of years he would be forced to break his resolution.

10. Mrs. William Bradford Bugg (Mildred Webb) to writer, March 7, 1975; Webb, "Tx. St.," p. 116; Chester V. Kielman, interview, Austin, Texas, May 23, 1974. Dr. Kielman, Librarian at the Barker Texas History Center, and former Webb student, remembers Jane Webb "as a brilliant woman," who was very active in the Daughters of the Republic of Texas; Webb to Jane, August 12, 1913; November 29, 1914, *Smith Coll.* TS, Box 2-22/796.

11. Webb, "Tx. St.," p. 116.

12. Ibid. Both Krey and Duncalf were medievalists.

13. Ibid., p. 119; Webb to Jane, August 12, 1913; September 21, 1913, *Smith Coll.* TS, Box 2-22/796.

14. Webb to Jane, August 12, 1913; October 1, 1913; November 13, 1913, in ibid.

15. Webb to Jane, September 21, 1913; October 1, 1913, in ibid.

16. Webb to Jane, November 13, 1913, in ibid.; Webb, "Tx. St.," p. 120.

17. Webb, "Tx. St.," pp. 119–21; Webb to Jane, April, n.d., 1914, *Smith Coll.* TS, Box 2-22/796. The new Ku Klux Klan, founded in 1915 by Georgian Colonel William Joseph Simmons, had as its target, not only Negroes, but Catholics and Jews. By 1920, it was in full force. See also W. P. Webb, *Divided We Stand: The Crisis of a Frontierless Democracy*, rev. ed. (Austin: Acorn Press, 1940), p. 87.

18. Frederick Lewis Allen, *Only Yesterday* (New York: Harper & Row, Publishers, 1931), p. 54.

19. Webb to Jane, December 6, 1913; December 13, 1913; February 22, 1914; postcard, n.d., 1914, *Smith Coll.* TS, Box 2-22/796.

20. Webb to Jane, March 1, 1914, in ibid.

21. Webb to Jane, January 2, 1914, in ibid.

22. Webb to Jane, February 8, 1914; May 13, 1914, in ibid.; W. P. Webb, "Folklore of Texas," *Journal of American Folklore* 28 (July-September 1915):290–301.

23. Webb to Jane, April 20, 1914, *Smith Coll.* TS, Box 2-22/796.

24. Webb to Jane, November 26, 1914, in ibid.; E. C. Barksdale, interview, Arlington, Texas, 3 March 1972.

25. W. P. Webb, "Water, Soil, and Mankind," speech, *Garrett Coll.* UTA, Box 21. This was a commencement address given by Webb at Kingsville, Texas, August 27, 1954. The last sentence reads, "Because I hold this philosophy I have been called a mystic."

26. C. E. Evans to Webb, May 18, 1914; May 24, 1914, *Smith Coll.* TS, Box 2-22/792.

27. Webb to Jane, May 9, 1914, in *Smith Coll.* TS, Box 2-22/796; Webb "Tx. St.," p. 120; Joe B. Frantz, "He'll Do," p. 8.

28. Webb to Jane, May 9, 1914; Keasbey to Webb, March 22, 1914; Webb to Jane, May 7, 1914, with clipping, "Council Makes Announcement of Fellowships," *Daily Texan*, May 6, 1914, *Smith Coll.* TS, Box 2-22/796.

29. Webb to Jane, March 1, 1914; May 17, 1914; November 6, 1914, in ibid.

30. Webb, "Tx. St.," p. 122.

31. Ibid., pp. 121–22; Frantz, "He'll Do," pp. 10–11.

32. Webb, "Tx. St.," p. 121; Webb to Jane, November 26, 1914; September 28, 1914; September 29, 1914, *Smith Coll.* TS, Box 2-22/796. Webb had met Sevario the summer of 1914. Webb wrote to Jane from San Marcos, "I should write to him, [Sevario] but have not.

He seemed to be peculiarly attached to me. I never had anyone take up with me so completely. It really seemed to bother him because I went to see you in the evenings."

33. Webb to Jane, September 18, 1914; November 15, 1914, ibid. Note that many of Webb's letters are addressed to "My dearest Jean," his pet name for her; however, all citations will read Jane for consistency and brevity.

34. Webb to Jane, September 20, 1914, ibid.; Frantz, "He'll Do," p. 20.

35. Webb to Jane, November 6, 1914; November 9, 1914; November 13, 1914, *Smith Coll.* TS, Box 2-22/796. The story referred to here is "Kiowa, Kenneybrew, and Two Forty-Two."

36. Webb to Jane, October 22, 1914; November 9, 1914; November 17, 1914, ibid.

37. Webb to Jane, November 12, 1914, ibid.

38. Frantz, "He'll Do," pp. 10–11, Webb, "Tx. St.," pp. 122–23; Webb, "Search for Hinds," p. 66.

39. Webb to Jane, June 25, 1915; June 28, 1915; *Smith Coll.* TS, Box 2-22/796; Ima Wright [Webb's sister], interview, Austin, Texas, January 22, 1975.

40. Webb to Jane, September 11, 1915, *Smith Coll.* TS, Box 2-22/796; Mildred Webb Bugg, interview, Austin, Texas, August 22, 1974.

41. Webb to Jane, January 16, 1915 [1916], July 17, 1916, *Smith Coll.* TS, Box 2-22/797. (For the first two weeks in January of 1916, Webb failed to acknowledge the New Year, forgetfully dating his letters 1915.) Speaking of Jane not being able to accompany him on the Chicago trip; "It is one of the little inconveniences of being poor; you say you are glad we are poor. I'm not, and you are not either, and I think you must have been out of your head when you wrote that you were."

42. Webb to Jane, June 23, 1915; June 28, 1915; ibid., Box 2-22/796.

43. Webb to Jane, January 16, 1915 [1916], ibid., Box 2-22/797.

44. Webb to Jane, September 11, 1915; September 23, 1915; November 15, 1914, ibid., Box 2-22/796.

45. Webb to Jane, February 6, 1916, ibid., Box 2-22/797.

46. Webb to Jane, January 11, 1915 [1916], ibid.

47. Webb to Jane, June 25, 1915; January 6, 9, 11, 16, 1915 [1916], ibid.

48. Webb to Jane, January 12, 1915 [1916], ibid.

49. Webb to Jane, January 16, 1915 [1916]; January 17, 1916; March 30, 1916, ibid.

50. Webb to Jane, February 15, 27, 1916, ibid.

51. Webb, "Tx. St.," p. 124; Webb to Jane, March 31, 1916, *Smith Coll.* TS, Box 2-22/797.

52. Webb to Jane, June 28, 1916, *Smith Coll.* TS, Box 2-22/797.

53. Webb to Jane, June 30, 1916; July 3, 1916, ibid. The $1.50 seems unbelievably low; he could have meant per day, rather than per week.

54. Webb to Jane, July 9, 1916, ibid.

55. Webb to Jane, July 23, 1916, ibid.

56. Mildred Webb Bugg, interview, Austin, Texas, August 22, 1974; Webb to Jane, July 24, 1916; August 1, 1916, ibid.

57. Webb, "Tx. St.," p. 125; Harry Yandell Benedict to Webb, September 23, 1916, *WPWC*, Box 2M246. Benedict extended his "very best wishes" to the newlyweds, saying: "I thought when you were over to see me last that you looked rather flossy 'dressed up' we used to call it in ancient times, but I did not dream that so fell [swell?] a purpose lurked in your palpitating heart [word indecipherable]. I wondered why I didn't hear further from you—now I know—*non compos mentis* with joy."

58. Ida Hinds to Webb, March 2, 1916; April 26, 1916, *Smith Coll.* TS, Box 2-22/788; Webb, "Search for Hinds," p. 67; Webb, "Tx. St.," p. 125. In the Hinds Story, p. 67, Webb indicates that he received word in 1915 that Hinds had died; however, a letter from Ida Hinds to Webb, dated December 22, 1912 from New York, informed Webb of the death of his benefactor. Photograph of the Hinds gravestone in *WPWC* also shows date as 1912.

59. Mildred Webb Bugg, interview, Austin, Texas, August 22, 1974; Mittie Alma Webb died at thirty-four years of age in September of 1917.

60. Webb, "Tx. St.," pp. 125–27; "Dr. Webb's Last Writing, An Address for the San Antonio Retired Teachers' Association," in *Walter Prescott Webb: From the Great Frontier to the Threshold of Space*, ed. by C. B. Smith, Sr. (Austin: By the ed., 1969), pp. 116–19 (hereafter cited as Smith, *Walter Prescott Webb*).

61. "Dr. Webb's Last Writing," pp. 117–18; Webb, "Tx. St.," p. 129.

62. "Dr. Webb's Last Writing," p. 118.

63. Frantz, "He'll Do," pp. 13–14; Webb, "History As High Adventure," pp. 267–68; Mildred Webb Bugg, interview, Austin, Texas, January 28, 1972.

64. Mildred Webb Bugg, interview, Austin, Texas, January 28, 1972.

65. Archibald Lewis, "The Old Department Remembered," *Panorama* 7 (May 1963):2, in *Garrett Coll.* UTA, Box 21-5.

66. Webb, "Tx. St.," pp. 132–33; Webb to Jane, August 17, 1920, *Smith Coll.* TS, Box 2-22/792.

67. Webb, "Tx. St.," pp. 132–33.

68. Ibid., p. 131.

69. Webb, "History As High Adventure," pp. 268–69; Webb, "Tx. St.," pp. 131–33; Webb, *The Texas Rangers*, p. 515.

70. Webb, "Tx. St.," pp. 131–32; Webb, *The Texas Rangers*, pp. 513–16. In 1935, the Rangers merged into the state highway patrol, losing their identity as a separate force; however, the inherited folk hatred against the "Rinches" has been kept alive to this day by the instinctive phobia of the Mexicans in border areas. Edward Kennedy of Massachusetts, conducting Senate investigations of labor disputes in South Texas in 1967, could not comprehend the ethnic hatred voiced at his suggestion of having a Texas Ranger sent to the area to investigate; see Fehrenbach, *Lone Star*, p. 693.

71. Webb, "History As High Adventure," p. 269; Webb, "Tx. St.," p. 134; Llerena B. Friend in "W. P. Webb's Texas Rangers," pp. 291–323, has traced in detail the circumstances relating to Webb's writing of his book on the Rangers. Webb's thesis chapters were captioned "From Matamoros to Monterrey," "The Battle of Monterrey," "McCulloch at Buena Vista," "From Vera Cruz to Montezuma."

72. Webb, "History As High Adventure," p. 269; Webb, "Tx. St.," pp. 134–35.

73. Friend, "W. P. Webb's Texas Rangers," p. 291.

74. Webb, "History As High Adventure," p. 269; Emil Saverio to Webb, April 23, 1921, *WPWC*; quoted in ibid., p. 298.

75. Webb, "Tx. St.," pp. 135–36.

76. Webb, "History As High Adventure," pp. 270–71; Friend, "W. P. Webb's Texas Rangers," pp. 300–301.

77. Webb, "Tx. St.," p. 137; Webb, "History As High Adventure," pp. 270–71.

78. Webb, "Tx. St.," pp. 137–38; Webb, "History As High Adventure," p. 271.

79. Webb, "Tx. St.," p. 138; Webb, "History As High Adventure," p. 271.

80. Webb, "Tx. St.," p. 138.

81. For a somewhat different opinion, see Gregory Tobin, "Walter Prescott Webb and *The Great Plains:* An Historiographical Study" (Ph.D. diss., The University of Texas at Austin, 1972), pp. 207–9. Tobin's study attempts to show that the genesis of the Great Plains Concept did not occur in the "flash of intuition" Webb later recalled; rather that the "segments came together in bits and pieces." Testimony of friends and associates who heard Webb voice the basic concept during this early period would probably disagree. True, there was much proving to be done, but Webb's own recollection of the genesis of his idea is, in the opinion of this writer, equally or more valid than an attempt to retrace his thought processes half a century later.

82. Friend, "W. P. Webb's Texas Rangers," p. 302; Webb, "History As High Adventure," p. 271; Mildred Webb Bugg, interview, Austin, Texas, August 22, 1974.

83. Webb, "Increasing the Functional Value of History by the Use of the Problem Method of Presentation," *The History Teacher's Magazine* (May 1916) 7:155–63 *passim;* Webb, "How the War Has Influenced History Teaching in San Antonio High Schools," *Texas History Teacher's Bulletin* (November 1918) 7:7–13 *passim.*

Chapter 5

1. Webb, "History As High Adventure," p. 271; Avery Craven to writer, February 11, 1974.

2. Mildred Webb Bugg, interview, Austin, Texas, August 22, 1974; Webb, "Tx. St.," p. 138; Walter Prescott Webb Transcript, Office of the Recorder, University of Chicago. Permission for personal copy generously granted by Mrs. Walter Prescott Webb. At Chicago, Webb studied under professors Marcus Jernegan, Frederick Scheville, James Westfall Thompson, and supervisor William E. Dodd, among others.

3. Webb, "Tx. St.," p. 106; Webb to W. E. Dodd, January 16, 1922; Webb to A. C. McLaughlin, January 2, 1922, *WPWC*, Box 2M259; Hubert Mewhinney to writer, June 7, 1973.

4. Craven to writer, February 11, 1974.

5. Webb to Jane, July 27, 1923, *Smith Coll.* TS, Box 2-22/792; Webb, "Tx. St.," p. 140. Webb said that he took the measure of his fellow students and found few "to be supermen."

6. Walter Prescott Webb Official Transcript, Office of the Recorder, University of Chicago, shows that Webb was advanced to candidacy for the Ph.D. August 21, 1923, by recommendation of Professor C. F. Huth, Faculty Secretary. Approval by the faculty was granted July 11, 1924, nearly a year after Webb had returned to Texas. According to James Lea Cate of the University of Chicago (letter to writer, April 24, 1974); "This implied, without so stipulating that he had passed the preliminary orals." This notation is unexplainable with available data considering that he failed the exam, although it is known that Webb contemplated returning to take the exams and finish. According to Cate, the History Department kept a bound notebook (or books) which would have explained the entry and told the complete story, for it recorded the results of each oral exam—preliminaries and finals, the fields covered, personnel involved, and judgment of the examiners on the quality of the candidate. Unfortunately, however, Cate reports; "the volume (or volumes) antecedent to 1928 were lost before moving to their current position in the archives in the Regenstein Library."

7. Webb, "Tx. St.," p. 141; Cate to writer, April 24, 1974; Cate had applied for a fellowship from medievalist James Westfall Thompson, while a student at the University of Texas. When Cate, who was Webb's graduate assistant, told him, Webb replied, "Jimmy, don't go up there, those damn Yankees will work you to death." Cate admitted that he wasn't sure whether or not he was kidding, as they were on familiar terms.

8. Webb, "Tx. St.," p. 141; Craven to writer, February 11, 1974; William T. Hutchinson to writer, April 6, 1974; Rupert N. Richardson to writer, January 25, 1974; Walter Johnson to writer, March 5, 1974. William T. Hutchinson attended the University of Chicago the summer quarter of 1922, prior to Webb's arrival and the autumn quarter of 1924. He returned to teach there, a position he still holds, and became good friends with Avery Craven, a contemporary of Webb's at the university; Walter Johnson, former chairman of the department, and knew others with whom Webb had associated. Rupert N. Richardson's association with Webb was both as friend and fellow graduate student at the University of Texas at Austin.

9. Jim B. Pearson to writer, January 29, 1974; Mildred Webb Bugg, interview, Austin,

Texas, August 22, 1974. Jim B. Pearson, a former student and protégé of Webb's, is Dean of the College of Arts and Sciences at North Texas State University in Denton.

10. Webb to Charles Ramsdell, July 22, 1923, *WPWC*, Box 2M259.

11. Webb, "Tx. St.," p. 141.

12. Ibid., p. 142.

13. Ibid., E. C. Barksdale to writer, January 18, 1974.

14. Webb, "Tx. St.," p. 142; Charles Ramsdell to Webb, July 6, 1923 (personal copy from *Ramsdell Papers* provided by Mike Gillette, L.B.J. Library, August 24, 1974.) Mildred Webb Bugg, interview, Austin, Texas, August 22, 1974; Eileen Guarino, interview, Austin, Texas, August 22, 1974. Mrs. Guarino, Webb's personal secretary during the latter period of his life, was also acquainted with his daughter, Mildred, and Mrs. Terrell Maverick Webb.

15. Mildred Webb Bugg, interview, Austin, Texas, August 22, 1974; Webb, "Tx. St.," p. 142.

16. Webb, "Tx. St.," p. 143.

17. Ibid., p. 146.

18. Ibid., pp. 139–43; Webb to Jane, July 27, 1923, *Smith Coll.* TS, Box 2-22/792.

19. Webb to Jane, ibid.

20. Ibid.

21. Ibid.; Webb, "Tx. St.," pp. 146–48.

22. Webb, "History As High Adventure," p. 272; Webb, "Tx. St.," pp. 146–48.

23. Webb, "Tx. St.," p. 176.

24. Ibid., pp. 176–77; Webb, "History As High Adventure," p. 274.

25. Ibid., pp. 274–75.

26. Program, "The Two Hundred Seventy-Eighth Convocation," University of Chicago, p. 45, personal copy.

27. Walter Johnson to writer, March 5, 1974; William T. Hutchinson to writer, April 6, 1974.

28. Walter Johnson to writer, March 5, 1974; Lawrence A. Kimpton to Webb, November 19, 1958; Webb to Kimpton, November 24, 1958, *Garrett Coll.* UTA, Box 21-6.

29. James Lea Cate to writer, April 24, 1974.

30. Ibid.; Avery Craven to writer, February 11, 1974; Webb, "Tx. St.," p. 139.

31. Webb to J. Frank Dobie, February 26, 1923, *Dobie Collection*, Humanities Research Center, University of Texas, Austin; quoted in Friend, "W. P. Webb's Texas Rangers," p. 303.

32. W. P. Webb, "Notebook," *WPWC*, Box 2M246. The only dated pages in this notebook written while in Chicago and shortly thereafter include the following; pp. 4, 5—July 26, 1923; p. 10—August 12, 1923; p. 17—January 1, 1924; p. 28—January 1, 1924. This brief notebook lacks pagination, therefore pages are mentally numbered.

Chapter 6

1. Allen, *Only Yesterday*, pp. 63–79; W. H. Hutchinson, *A Bar Cross Man: The Life and Personal Writings of Eugene Manlove Rhodes* (Norman: University of Oklahoma Press, 1956), p. 173.

2. Henry Steele Commager, *The American Mind* (New Haven: Yale University Press, 1950), pp. 261–63.

3. Ibid., p. 267.

4. Allen, *Only Yesterday*, pp. 78–79; Fehrenbach, *Lone Star*, pp. 644–48.

5. Mildred Webb, interview, Austin, Texas, August 24, 1974; Webb, "Tx. St.," p. 179.

6. Webb, "Tx. St.," pp. 146–49, 179. Regarding his absorption in the developing plains

idea, Webb stated: "While I was working on the Rangers my concept of the Great Plains was expanding around the nucleus of the six shooter. I could not get away from it. I did not try."

7. Ibid., p. 146; Friend, "W. P. Webb's Texas Rangers," pp. 303–10.

8. Friend, ibid.

9. Walter Prescott Webb, *Talks on Texas Books: A Collection of Book Reviews,* ed. by Llerena Friend (Austin: Texas State Historical Association, 1970), pp. 1–94.

10. Ibid.

11. Ibid., p. 45; Webb, *The Great Plains,* p. 462.

12. Webb, *Talks on Texas Books,* p. 51.

13. Webb, *The Great Plains,* pp. 463–65.

14. Ibid., pp. 481–82.

15. Clipping quoting Webb, "Emerson Hough Center of Critical Fight," *The Chicago Evening Post Literary Review,* April 18, 1924, *WPWC,* Box 2M254; see also *Literary Digest Book Review* 1 (November 1923):34–35; for additional information on the Emerson Hough Controversy, see Hutchinson, *A Bar Cross Man,* pp. 190–93, which prints in full Stuart Henry's review, "Faults of Our Wild West Stories"; and E. M. Rhodes' response, "The Men Who Made the West," pp. 194–97. The Tobin dissertation, "Walter Prescott Webb" gives good coverage to the Hough controversy; see pages 175–93.

16. Adams to Webb, February 21, 1925, *WPWC,* Box 2M253; Webb, *The Great Plains,* pp. 462–63; Rhodes to Webb, March 24, 1930, *WPWC,* Box 2M253; and Webb to H. A. McComas, April 11, 1930; Adams to Webb, March 14, 1924, *WPWC,* Box 2M259.

17. Rhodes to Webb, January 15, 1924, *WPWC,* Box 2F457; see *Pioneer Magazine of Texas* 5 (April-May 1924):4.

18. Stuart Henry's replies can be found in *Literary Digest International Book Review* 3 (January 1925):182–84; and *Conquering Our Great American Plains* (New York: E. P. Dutton, 1930). See also W. P. Webb's review in *Mississippi Valley Historical Review* 17 (March 1931):644–45; W. P. Webb, "Commencement Address," New Mexico State College of Agricultural and Mechanical Arts, May 19, 1941, *WPWC,* Box 2M293.

19. Rhodes to Webb, March 21, [1924], *WPWC,* Box 2F457; Adams to Webb, March 14, 1924, *WPWC,* Box 2M253; Rhodes to Webb, February 27, 1924, reprinted in Hutchinson, *A Bar Cross Man,* pp. 207–8.

20. Rhodes to Webb, January 15, and February 1, 1924, *WPWC,* Box 2F457.

21. Webb, "Auto.," p. 4.

22. Rhodes to Booth, n.d., and excerpts from "The West That Was" (Rhodes' rebuttal to Stuart Henry), reprinted in Hutchinson, *A Bar Cross Man,* pp. 173–75. Speaking of "the young intellectuals," Rhodes said, "This group has decreed that a good American story must be about a Hungarian with adenoids." See also Fehrenbach, *Lone Star,* pp. 643, 653–54, wherein he traces the historic consistency of what he terms "the dominant mind" of Texans, noting that the record of their participation in both world wars, as well as the Mexican-American war, testified to their effectiveness and their belligerency. In the Spanish-American War 10,000 Texans enlisted rapidly, and they composed a large segment of the Rough Riders. The native empiricism of the state was exhibited again in the flag-waving chauvinism of World War I and repeated during World War II. At this time Texans made up five percent of the United States population, but provided seven percent of the total armed forces. A Texas farmboy named Audie Murphy became the most decorated man in the U.S. Army; and another Texan, Sam Dealey, earned the greatest number of awards bestowed by the Navy. Chester Nimitz of Fredericksburg commanded the Pacific Fleet and Eisenhower, Texas-born although reared in Kansas, headed the Supreme Allied Command in Europe. Gerald P. Nash, "Commentary," speech, Texas State Historical Association, Austin, Texas, April 1973, noted the increased interest in regional history.

23. Trombly to Webb, October 28, 1924, *WPWC,* Box 2M257. Trombly generally agreed

with Henry's views on Hough's book and failed to understand the vehemence of Webb's defense. See also Trombly to Webb, November 3, 1924; January 8, 1926, *WPWC*, Box 2M257.

24. Adams to Webb, February 21, 1925, *WPWC*, Box 2M253.

25. Webb, "History As High Adventure," pp. 271–72; Webb to Rhodes enclosed in Rhodes to Webb, March 11, 1924, *WPWC*, Box 2F457; Adams to Webb, February 21, 1925, *WPWC*, Box 2M253. For a somewhat different interpretation, see James Sutton Payne, "Texas Historiography in the 20th Century: A Study of E. C. Barker, Charles W. Ramsdell, and Walter Prescott Webb" (Ph.D. diss., University of Denver, 1972), p. 195, wherein the writer implies that Webb was motivated by personal desires "to disclose his western historical interest to a national audience."

Chapter 7

1. W. P. Webb, "Hypothesis and History," *History As High Adventure*, ed. by Barksdale, p. 177.

2. Ibid., p. 178; Webb, "History As High Adventure," p. 272.

3. Rupert N. Richardson, "Three Friends," *The Texas Observer* 55 (July 1963):14.

4. Webb, "Tx. St.," pp. 146–49, 152.

5. C. H. Thurber to Webb, May 4, 1927, *WPWC*, Box 2M254.

6. Webb, "Tx. St.," p. 165. See Tobin, "Walter Prescott Webb," for a more detailed analysis of the genesis of *The Great Plains*.

7. Webb, "Tx. St.," p. 175; Margaret Francine Morris, "A Webb Bibliography," *Essays on the American Civil War, The Walter Prescott Webb Memorial Lectures*, ed. by Holmes and Hollingsworth 1:91–92.

8. Ibid., 167–68; Webb, *The Great Plains*, p. vii.

9. Webb, "Tx. St.," pp. 167–68.

10. Ibid., p. 168.

11. Ibid., p. 169.

12. Llerena Friend, "Introduction," in Webb, *Talks on Texas Books*, p. 28.

13. Leo C. Haynes to Webb, February 25, 1933, *Smith Coll*. TS, Box 2-22/793, informs Webb of his appointment to the graduate faculty.

14. W. P. Webb, "The Historical Seminar: Its Outer Shell and Inner Spirit," *History As High Adventure*, ed. by Barksdale, p. 103.

15. W. P. Webb, "Increasing the Functional Value of History by the Use of the Problem Method of Presentation," *Smith Coll*. TS, Box 2-22/788, published in *The Texas History Teacher's Bulletin* 4 (February 1916):16–40; reprinted in *The History Teacher's Magazine* 7 (May 1916):155–63. This paper, written while Webb was teaching in Cuero, was presented at a teacher's meeting in Corpus Christi on November 26, 1915.

16. Webb, "The Historical Seminar," pp.83–85.

17. Ibid., pp. 90–91, 101.

18. Ibid., p. 104.

19. Jim B. Pearson to writer, January 29, 1974.

20. "Dr. Webb As Humorist," newspaper review of *An Honest Preface* by Walter Prescott Webb, copy, *C. B. Smith Personal Collection*, Austin, Texas (hereafter cited as *Smith Personal Coll.*). Interviews with Webb's students testify to his impact as a great teacher; Robert Amsler, Arlington, Texas, March 27, 1972; Chester V. Kielman, Austin, Texas, May 23, 1974; Robert Williamson, Arlington, Texas, March 3, 1972; George Wolfskill, Arlington, Texas, January 23, 1972; Wilbert Timmons, El Paso, Texas, April 26, 1974; Joe B. Frantz, Austin, Texas, August 20, 1974; Millicent Huff, June 18, 1973.

21. Rex Strickland to writer, February 27, 1975.

22. Joe B. Frantz to writer, March 24, 1974; Frantz, interview, Austin, Texas, August 20, 1974.

23. John Haller, "I had a Seminar with Walter Prescott Webb," *WPWC*, Box 2M245. Former instructor W. E. Dodd paid his former student an expansive compliment when he wrote to Webb while he was in London as Harkness Lecturer: "You have been one of the most successful teachers and writers we have had during the last fifteen or twenty years"; see W. E. Dodd to Webb, June 30, 1937, in *WPWC*, Box 2M245.

24. Edith Parker to Webb, July 4, 1954, *WPWC*, Box 2M245.

25. Mildred Webb Bugg, interview, Austin, Texas, August 22, 1974.

26. Webb, "Tx. St.," p. 175; also in W. P Webb, "Art of Writing," *Smith Coll.* TS, Box 2-22/799; "University Prof Wins Honor on Book," *The Austin American*, April 11, 1933, *WPWC*, Box 2M300. The Loubat Prize instituted in 1893 by a grant of Joseph Florimond Duc de Loubat is conferred every five years for the best book in the Social Sciences in North America. A first prize of $1000 and a second prize of $400 are awarded.

27. Mildred Webb Bugg, interview, Austin, Texas, August 22, 1974; Webb, "Tx. St.," pp. 171–72.

28. Review excerpts in "Biographical Data," *WPWC*, Box 2M254; Richard Thornton to Webb, June 1, 1950, *WPWC*, Box 2M245.

29. Webb to R. D. Mason, August 11, 1939, *WPWC*, Box 2M254.

30. Fred A. Shannon, *An Appraisal of Walter Prescott Webb's The Great Plains: A Study in Institutions and Environment* (New York: Social Science Research Council, 1940).

31. John W. Caughey, "A Criticism of the Critique of Webb's *The Great Plains*," *Mississippi Valley Historical Review*, 27 (December 1940):442–48; see also Walter Rundell, Jr., "Walter Prescott Webb: Product of Environment," *Arizona and the West* 5 (Spring 1963):8–10; Sister Anne Marie Young, V.H.M., "Walter Prescott Webb," *The Texas Quarterly* 11 (Spring 1968):70–79.

32. George Fuermann to Webb, n.d., *Garrett Coll.* UTA, Box 21.

33. Webb, *The Great Plains*, p. 85; "Introduction," *Journal of the West* 3 (January 1969):1–6.

34. Herbert Eugene Bolton, "Epic of Greater America," *Wider Horizons of American History* (New York: D. Appleton-Century Co., 1939) pp. 2, 49–52; John Francis Bannon, *Bolton and the Spanish Borderlands* (Norman: University of Oklahoma Press, 1968), pp. 3–4.

35. Rupert N. Richardson to writer, January 25, 1974.

36. J. Francis Bannon to writer, February 20, 1974.

37. Odie B. Faulk to writer, February 4, 1974. Vigness studied under Hackett who had been a Bolton student.

38. W. Eugene Hollon to writer, January 22, 1974.

39. Webb to E. C. Barker, July 2, 1938, *WPWC*, Box 2M254; W. P. Webb to Calhoun, June 8, 1938, *WPWC*, Box 2M258.

40. Webb, "Tx. St.," pp. 184–85.

41. Ibid.; W. P. Webb, "The Quality of Courage," *True West*, April, 1955, pp. 3–4, *Smith Coll.* TS, Box 2-22/799; Webb, *The Texas Rangers* p. 549.

42. Ibid., p. 551; Webb's Ranger Certificate shows that Webb enlisted July 30, 1924, at 36 years of age, *Smith Coll.* TS, Box 2-22/794; W. Eugene Hollon to writer, January 22, 1974.

43. E. C. B. [Eugene C. Barker] to Webb, February 2, 1930, with explanatory typed note on same letter by Webb, dated February 25, 1930, *WPWC*, Box 2M254.

44. Webb, "Tx. St.," p. 188; Lonnie Rees to Webb, November 14, 1933, June 12, 1934, *Smith Coll.* TS, Box 2-22/793.

45. Webb, "Tx. St.," pp. 189–90; Webb to Dale Warren, April 11, 1960, *Webb Papers*, University of Texas Archives, Library, Arlington, Texas, Box 20-9.

46. Webb, "Tx. St.," pp. 188, 192–93.

47. Ibid., p. 195.

48. Ibid., pp. 195–97.
49. "R.N.L." to Webb, May 19, 1963, *WPWC*, Box 2M255.
50. E. C. Barksdale to writer, January 18, 1974; W. Eugene Hollon to writer, January 22, 1974; "Biographical Data," *WPWC*, Box 2M254.
51. W. P. Webb, "The Art of History Writing," in *History As High Adventure*, ed. by Barksdale, p. 138; Webb, "Art of Writing," *Smith Coll.* TS, Box 2-22/799. This is a speech draft and pages are numbered intermittently. Webb dates this February 1935. It is likely that he meant 1936 when the AAA was declared unconstitutional by the Supreme Court in the case *U.S.* vs. *Butler.*
52. Webb, *Divided We Stand,* pp. 3–151; Webb, "Art of Writing," *Smith Coll.* TS, Box 2-22/799.
53. Webb, "Art of Writing," *Smith Coll.* TS, Box 2-22/799. Webb noted that he had intended to dedicate this book to his wife, Jane, but when the title "Divided We Stand" was selected, she declined the honor.
54. Ibid.; Review in "Biographical Data," *WPWC*, Box 2M245; Roy Bedichek, "Important Fresh Material in New Edition of Webb Book," *The Times Herald,* March 19, 1944.
55. Carl Sandburg to Webb, December 8, 1937, *WPWC*, Box 2M260; Webb, "Art of Writing," *Smith Coll.* TS, Box 2-22/799; "Biographical Data," *WPWC*, Box 2M254.
56. Webb, *The Great Frontier,* pp. 407–10. Webb, "History As High Adventure," pp. 277–78.
57. W. P. Webb, "The Great Frontier, An Interpretation," in *History As High Adventure,* ed. by Barksdale, pp. 183, 196–98; Joe B. Frantz, "Walter Prescott Webb," in Jacobs, Caughey, and Frantz, *Turner, Bolton, and Webb,* pp. 90–91.
58. Reviews in *WPWC*, Box 2M300.
59. Webb, "History As High Adventure," p. 278–80.
60. Ray Allen Billington, *The Genesis of the Great Frontier Thesis* (San Marino: The Huntington Library, 1971), pp. 134–37, 155–56.
61. Ray Allen Billington, *Frederick Jackson Turner, Historian, Scholar, Teacher* (New York: Oxford University Press, 1973), pp. 337–43.
62. Turner notes in *WPWC*, Box 2M249; Ray Allen Billington to writer, May 15, 1975.
63. W. P. Webb, "The American West: Perpetual Mirage," *Harper's* 214 (May 1957): 25–31.
64. Webb to George Fuermann, October 17, 1956, January 27, 1957, in *Garrett Coll.* UTA, Box 21; Webb, "Three Geographical and Historical Concepts" 82, *Smith Coll.* TS, Box 2-22/799.
65. Webb, "The American West, Perpetual Mirage," pp. 25, 29, 31; J. B. Frantz, "He'll Do," pp. 37–38.
66. John Fischer to Webb, February 1, 1957, *Garrett Coll.* UTA, Box 21. This was to be the thesis for the proposed book, *The West, 1860–1950,* for Harper's New American Nation Series, which never materialized. Regarding his resignation from the New American Nation series, Webb wrote that he had discovered that his "books did not fit into niches" and got out. See Webb to Edith Parker, December 7, 1960, *WPWC*, Box 2M245.
67. "Bedi" to Webb, May 30, 1957, *WPWC*, Box 2M253.
68. W. P. Webb, "The West and the Desert," in *An Honest Preface,* pp. 179–85; "The Desert Country," *Congressional Record,* Appendix, May 13, 1957, p. A3610 in *Webb Papers,* University of Texas Archives, Library, Arlington, Texas, Box 20-10.
69. Bert [E. C.] Barksdale to Webb, July 16, 1955; March 21, 1955, *WPWC*, Box 2M253. Many of these letters pertain to travel plans for the trip across the desert states in 1955. Barksdale accompanied him on this jaunt. Webb, "The West and the Desert," in *An Honest Preface* (originally printed in *Montana, The Magazine of Western History,* 8:192–93); Webb, "Three Geographical and Historical Concepts," p. 82.

70. Webb, "History As High Adventure," p. 278; "Webb Views His Mistakes," *The Austin American,* December 30, 1958, *Smith Coll.* TS, Box 2-22/799.

Chapter 8

1. Mildred Webb Bugg, interview, Austin, Texas, August 22, 1974; Webb to Crane Brinton, November 20, 1934, *Smith Coll.* TS, Box 2-22/793.
2. Eugene N. Anderson to Webb, February 24, 1937, *WPWC,* Box 2M257; see also Eugene N. Anderson to Webb, March 14, 1937, *Smith Coll.* TS, Box 2-22/793.
3. Dobie to Webb, October 30, 1923, November 30, 1923, January 26, 1925, *WPWC,* Box 2M254; see also Mody Boatright, "A Mustang in the Groves of Academe," in *Three Men in Texas,* ed. by Ronnie Dugger (Austin: University of Texas Press, 1967), p. 191.
4. Harry Ransom to Joe [B. Frantz], June 29, 1958, *WPWC,* Box 2M245. For a good analysis of Webb's character traits see Frantz, "He'll Do," pp. 3–60.
5. Joe B. Frantz, interview, Austin, Texas, August 20, 1974.
6. Ransom to Frantz, June 29, 1958, *WPWC,* Box 2M245.
7. Jim B. Pearson to writer, January 29, 1974.
8. Fehrenbach, *Lone Star,* p. 650.
9. W. P. Webb, "The Regents v. Diogenes," *Smith Coll.* TS, Box 2-22/794.
10. Ibid.; Herbert Gambrell to Webb, October 6, 1937, in ibid. Webb's choice for the presidency in 1937 was W. E. Wrather.
11. W. P. Webb, "An Interesting Play," May 7, 1943, *Smith Coll.* TS, Box 2-22/798. This is, in reality, not a play at all, but a letter to Webb's wife written while at Queen's College in Oxford, England. It is a review of their marital life, couched in the third person, with particular emphasis on the causes for a gradual estrangement that occurred and divergent interests that drew them apart. Considering the speculation in some quarters regarding their relationship, this is a valuable document, although it presents only Webb's view of the story. The object of the letter/play is apparently reconciliation.
12. Mildred Webb Bugg, interview, Austin, Texas, August 22, 1974.
13. Webb, "Tx. St.," pp. 219–21.
14. Webb, "Biographical Data," p. 4, *WPWC,* Box 2M254.
15. W. Eugene Hollon, "Adventures of a Western Historian," *Western Historical Quarterly* 2 (July 1971):249.
16. Mildred Webb Bugg, interview, Austin, Texas, August 22, 1974.
17. Webb, "An Interesting Play."
18. Mildred Webb Bugg, interview, Austin, Texas, August 22, 1974.
19. Webb, "An Interesting Play."
20. Jane to "My dearest Walter," August 27, 1938, *Smith Coll.* TS, Box 2-22/793.
21. Webb to R. D. Mason, May 15, 1939, *WPWC,* Box 2M254.
22. Dorman H. Winfrey, "Seventy-Five Years of Texas History: The Texas State Historical Association," *Texas Libraries* 34 (Summer 1972):96, 102–4, published in book form by Jenkins Publishing Co., 1975. Roberts was a former Texas governor.
23. Winfrey citing in ibid., p. 112, from C. Stanley Banks, Sr., "Address . . . on the occasion of the 50th Anniversary Dinner of the Texas State Historical Association held March 25, 1947, at Stephen F. Austin Hotel in Austin, Texas," Archives Collection, University of Texas Library, Austin, Texas. See also William C. Pool, *Eugene C. Barker Historian* (Austin: Texas State Historical Association, 1971), pp. 60–65.
24. In 1913 Webb joined the Folklore Society. Webb to R. D. Mason, May 15, 1939, *WPWC,* Box 2M254.
25. Ima Wright, interview, Austin, Texas, January 22, 1975; Lucille [Hewlett] to Lee, October 27, 1924, *Smith Coll.* TS, Box 2-22/792; and Dad to Walter, March 16, 1939, *Smith Coll.* TS, Box 2-22/793.

26. Ibid.; Webb's father died June 30, 1940; his mother June 14, 1949. See also Ima to Webb, January 10, 1939, *WPWC*, Box 2M260.

27. W. P. Webb, "Texas Collection," *The Southwestern Historical Quarterly* 51 (January 1948):259.

28. Ibid., pp. 259–60.

29. Ibid., p. 260.

30. Frantz, "He'll Do," pp. 22–23.

31. A. Q. Schimmel to Webb, June 11, 1942, *WPWC*, Box 2M256.

32. Frantz, "He'll Do," pp. 23–24.

33. Friend, "Introduction" in Webb, *Talks on Texas Books*, pp. 18–23; W. P. Webb, "Caldwell Prize in Local History," *The Texas History Teacher's Bulletin* 12 (October 1924):5–16.

34. Winfrey, "Seventy-Five Years of Texas History," pp. 4–5; Frantz, "He'll Do," p. 22; W. P Webb, "Salute to Youth," *The Junior Historian, Garrett Coll.* UTA, Box 21-9.

35. Winfrey, "Seventy-Five Years of Texas History," p. 13. In 1970, *The Junior Historian* was renamed the *Texas Historian* in deference to the new voting status of 18 year olds.

36. In an address, "The Confessions of a Texas Bookmaker," Webb describes his love of books as "an obsession fully as absorbing to me as horse racing is to a compulsory horse player. This obsession goes back to the time when I could extract meaning from a printed page." See Webb, "The Confessions of a Texas Bookmaker," p. 109; Wilbert H. Timmons, interview, Austin, Texas, April 26, 1974; Dorman Winfrey to writer, February 2, 1972.

37. Joe B. Frantz, interview, Austin, Texas, January 20, 1975; Wilbert Timmons, interview, El Paso, Texas, April 26, 1974; Coral H. Tullis, "Address to Members of the Executive Council of the Texas State Historical Association," *WPWC*, Box 3L18; Dorman Winfrey, interview, Tulsa, Oklahoma, October 9, 1975.

38. Joe B. Frantz, interview, Austin, Texas, January 20, 1975; W. P. Webb, "On Personal Privilege," *Smith Coll.* TS, Box 2-22/799. This was the address Webb presented to the Council in response to Bailey Carroll's letter to Fred Cotten and in defense of the latter.

39. Webb, "On Personal Privilege," p. 2.

40. Ibid., pp. 3–4.

41. Ibid., pp. 4–5.

42. The presidency of the Association usually follows a pattern from "civilian historian to professional to civilian, etc. Cotten was a civilian." Joe B. Frantz, interview, Austin, Texas, January 20, 1975; Dorman Winfrey, interview, Tulsa, Oklahoma, October 9, 1975.

43. J. F. Dobie [speaking on Junior Historian Movement], Conference on the Great Plains Area, *Proceedings*, April 17–18, 1942 (New York, 1942), pp. 49–50.

Chapter 9

1. Webb to T. W. Riker, n.d., *Garrett Coll.* UTA, Box 21-16; W. P. Webb, "Biographical Data," *WPWC*, Box 2M254.

2. Ibid.; Mildred Webb Bugg, interview, Austin, Texas, August 22, 1974.

3. W. P. Webb, "An Interesting Play."

4. W. P. Webb, "To England in War Time," for release December 6, 1942 in *Dallas News, Garrett Coll.* UTA, Box 21.

5. W. P. Webb, "Report on the Harmsworth Professorship in American History Oxford University, 1942–1943," *WPWC*, Box 2M246.

6. Webb to Jane and Mildred, January 21, 1943, *Smith Coll.* TS, Box 2-22/798.

7. Ibid.; Webb to Mildred, January 30, 1943; and Webb to Jane, January 11, 1943, *Smith Coll.* TS, Box 2-22/798.

8. Webb, "An Interesting Play," May 7, 1943, *Smith Coll.* TS, Box 2-22/798.

9. J. Frank Dobie, "For Years We Three Sat Together," *The Texas Observer*, 55 (July 1963):2.

10. C. B. Smith, Sr., interview, Austin, Texas, August 25, 1974.

11. Webb to Hollon, November 8, 1944, *WPWC*, Box 3L18.

12. Dugger, *Our Invaded Universities*, p. 36; Joe B. Frantz, interview, Austin, Texas, August 20, 1974.

13. Joe B. Frantz, interview, Austin, Texas, August 20, 1974.

14. Homer Price Rainey, *The Tower and the Dome: A Free University versus Political Control* (Boulder: Pruett Publishing Co., 1971), p. 30.

15. W. Eugene Hollon to Webb, October 25, 1944, *WPWC*, Box 3L18.

16. Rainey, *The Tower and the Dome*, pp. 6–7; *Investigation of University of Texas by Senate Investigating Committee*, hearings held in the Texas Senate Chamber, Austin, November 16–28, 1944, 4 vols.; hereafter cited as "Sen. Inv."; see 4:577–78.

17. "Sen. Inv.," 1:449–59; 2:961–67; 3:1–38.

18. Rainey, *The Tower and the Dome*, pp. 8–9; see also Dugger, *Our Invaded Universities*, pp. 41–48, 420 n. 8. William C. Pool concentrates on E. C. Barker's position in the controversy in *Eugene C. Barker, Historian*, pp. 187–210.

19. W. Eugene Hollon to Webb, October 25, 1944, *WPWC*, Box 3L18.

20. Dugger, *Our Invaded Universities*, pp. 45–46; Rainey, *The Tower and the Dome*, pp. 14, 100; see also "Sen. Inv.," 1:31–32, 55; 2:571; 3:333–35; 4:574. At a subsequent meeting with the Regents, Rainey refused to retract and was threatened with ruin. Bullington later denied this.

21. Hollon to Webb, October 25, 1944, *WPWC*, Box 3L18; Dugger, *Our Invaded Universities*, p. 46.

22. Dugger, *Our Invaded Universities*, p. 46.

23. Rainey, *The Tower and the Dome*, pp. 55–58, 120–21, quoting Bernard de Voto, editor of *Harper's* and author of "The Easy Chair" commentary, who editorialized on the controversy in the August 1945 issue.

24. Clarence Ayres, untitled tribute to Webb in "A Man, His Land, and His Work," in *The Graduate Journal* 6:53–55.

25. Ibid., p. 55.

26. C. O. Pollard to Webb, telegram, November 1944, *WPWC*, Box 3L18; Webb to Hon. Charles S. McCombs, November 8, 1944, *WPWC*, Box 3L18.

27. Dugger, *Our Invaded Universities*, pp. 49–52; Joe B. Frantz, interview, Austin, Texas, August 20, 1974.

28. Quoted in Dugger, *Our Invaded Universities*, pp. 50–51; William A. Owens, *Three Friends: Bedichek, Dobie, Webb* (New York: Doubleday, 1969), pp. 75–78.

29. Rupert N. Richardson to writer, January 25, 1974; ECB [Eugene C. Barker] to Webb, January 28, 1945, *Smith Coll.* TS, Box 2-22/795.

30. Dugger, *Our Invaded Universities*, p. 51. Dugger records the vote as 160 to 186.

31. Webb to Jane and Mildred, November 20, 1944, *Smith Coll.* TS, Box 2-22/798.

32. Rainey, *The Tower and the Dome*, 135–36.

33. Joe B. Frantz, interview, Austin, Texas, August 20, 1974; James P. Hart to writer, February 18, 1972. Judge Hart recalls that his association with Webb was principally at meetings of the Town and Gown, which generally meets every two weeks from October through May. Webb supported Hart in his unsuccessful race for the United States Senate in 1957.

34. James P. Hart to Barker, June 3, 1952; Webb to Hart, June 9, 1952; and Hart to Webb, June 12, 1952, *WPWC*, Box 2M258.

35. Lynn W. Landrum, "Dobie is Needed," *The Dallas Morning News*, September 29, 1947, *WPWC*, Box 2M254.

36. W. P. Webb, "Concerning Mr. Dobie and the University of Texas," September 30, 1947, *Smith Coll.* TS, Box 2-22/799.

37. R. G. Patterson to Webb, October 8, 1947, *WPWC*, Box 2M254.

38. Z. Starr Armstrong to Webb, April 19, 1947, in ibid.

39. J. Evetts Haley to Webb, October 2, 1947, in ibid.

40. E. C. Barker to Webb, October 1, 1947, in ibid.

41. Webb to Evetts [Haley], October 6, 1947, in ibid. See also Boatright, "A Mustang in the Groves of Academe," pp. 198–99, for more concerning "The Dobie Rule."

42. "Argument on UT Press May Quit Strict Circles," *The Austin Statesman*, April 13, 1948, *WPWC*, Box 2M257.

43. Ibid.; Stuart McGregor to Dudley K. Woodward, May 7, 1948.

44. Chester Kerr to R. H. Griffin, August 9, 1949; Frank Wardlaw to writer, April 13, 1972; see also Frank H. Wardlaw, "Idea Man—Organizer—Expediter," in Smith, *Walter Prescott Webb*, pp. 28–31.

45. James P. Hart to writer, February 18, 1972; C. D. Richards, interview, Arlington, Texas, June 14, 1973.

46. C. B. Smith, Sr., interview, Austin, Texas, February 11, 1972.

47. Rodney Kidd, interview, Austin, Texas, January 29, 1972.

48. Webb, "Tx. St.," p. 200–217.

49. C. B. Smith to Webb, October 7, 1949, *Smith Coll.*, Box 2-22/798; C. B. Smith, Sr., interview, Austin, Texas, August 24, 1974; Webb to "C. B.," May 25, 1950 and March 4, 1963, *Smith Personal Coll.*

50. Webb to C. B., February 20, 1961, January 8, 1958, *Smith Personal Coll.*

Chapter 10

1. W. P. Webb, "The Big Bend of Texas," April 25, 1937, *Smith Coll.* TS, Box 2-22/799; Webb, "Tx. St.," p. 179.

2. Webb, "Tx. St.," p. 179; Webb, "The Big Bend of Texas," *Smith Coll.* TS, Box 2-22/799.

3. Bill Hogan to Branch Spaulding, January 18, 1937. Personal copy generously provided by W. Eugene Hollon in letter to writer, March 29, 1972.

4. Herbert Maier to Dr. Webb, April 26, 1937, *Smith Coll.* TS, Box 2-22/799.

5. Webb, "The Big Bend of Texas," April 25, 1937, ibid.

6. Thomas Skaggs to Webb, April 3, 1937; May 2, 1937, ibid.

7. "Press Release for Big Bend Trip," May 15, 1937, ibid.

8. Jane to "My dearest Walter," May 12, 1937, ibid. Jane urged Webb to "Please be careful in going through the canyons. I'll certainly be glad when you get home. I have a whole book of over 300 pages to read to Woozie [Mildred] before Friday." See also Biographical Clipping regarding the trip, *The Houston Post*, March 26, 1939, *WPWC*, Box 2M246.

9. Webb to Jane, May 15, 1937, *Smith Coll.* TS, Box 2-22/794.

10. Pete Crawford to Webb, April 6, 1937, ibid.; Western Union Telegram, Coast Guard to Mrs. W. P. Webb, May 8, 1937, ibid; Telegram, W. P. Webb to Mrs. Webb, May 18, 1937, ibid. Jane wired in return, May 19, 1937; "Thankful trip over much worried by it come home soon—Jane," ibid.

11. Mildred Webb Bugg, interview, Austin, Texas, August 22, 1974; Joe B. Frantz, interview, Austin, Texas, August 20, 1974.

12. Webb to J. T. Long, January 10, 1941, *WPWC*, Box 2M257.

13. Ibid.; Jack Wise to "Lupe" G. Hernandez, January 5, 1941, *WPWC*, Box 2M257; Jack

Wise to Webb, January 25, 1941, *WPWC*, Box 2M257. "Lupe" was the owner of the property.

14. Webb to J. T. Long, May 15, 1941, *WPWC*, Box 2M257.

15. John W. Meaney to Webb, January 15, 1959, *WPWC*, Box 2M254; W. P. Webb, *More Water For Texas: The Problem and the Plan* (Austin: University of Texas Press, 1954), preface.

16. Webb, *More Water For Texas*, preface; Lyndon B. Johnson, "Your Senator Reports," newsletter, February 11, 1954; personal copy provided courtesy Mike Gillette, L.B.J. Library, Austin, Texas. See also "Webb Cites Need of Law Revision," clipping, *Webb Papers*, University of Texas Archives, Library, Arlington, Texas, Box 20.

17. W. P. Webb, "Social and Economic Factors Influencing the Grazing Industry of Texas and the Southwest," January 23, 1962; *Webb Papers*, University of Texas Archives, Library, Arlington, Texas, Box 20. This was a speech presented to the American Society of Range Management.

18. "UT Representative Wins Literary Honors," *The Dallas Moring News*, November 8, 1951, clipping, *WPWC*, Box 2M246. This deals with Webb's selection as a fellow of the Texas Institute of Letters in 1951.

19. W. P. Webb, *Flat-Top: A Story of Modern Ranching* (El Paso: Carl Hertzog, 1960).

20. W. P. Webb, "Texas Is Our Garden," November 1, 1961, *Garrett Coll.* UTA, Box 21. This was a speech presented to a Houston garden club.

21. Webb to Jane and Mildred, October 23, 1942, *Smith Coll.* TS, Box 2-22/798.

22. Ibid., Mildred Webb Bugg, interview, Austin, Texas, August 24, 1974; Rupert N. Richardson to writer, January 25, 1974. Rupert N. Richardson is distinguished professor of history and president emeritus of Hardin-Simmons University at Abilene, Texas.

23. Webb to Jane and Mildred, October 23, 1942, *Smith Coll.* TS, Box 2-22/798; Dobie, "For Years We Three Sat Together," pp. 2–5.

24. Webb to Jane and Mildred, October 23, 1942, *Smith Coll.* TS, Box 2-22/798; Ima Wright, interview, Austin, Texas, 20 August 1974; W. P. Webb, "Transcript of Colloquy Program," June 31, 1961, *WPWC*, Box 2M254.

25. W. P. Webb to W. Eugene Hollon, June 18, 1945, *Webb Papers*, University of Texas Archives, Library, Arlington, Texas, Box 20. Permission granted for use of Webb-Hollon Restricted File by letter March 16, 1972.

26. H. Stanley Marcus to Webb, October 27, 1945; Webb to Marcus, October 30, 1945; Webb to Harry C. Wiess, January 29, 1946; all in *WPWC*, Box 2M253.

27. H. Bailey Carroll to Webb, Friday 17th, *Smith Coll.* TS, Box 2-22/793.

28. "Bedi" to "Dear Old Scout," July 31, 1945, ibid.

29. Rodney J. Kidd, interview, Austin, Texas, January 29, 1972; see also Rodney J. Kidd, "Walter Prescott Webb at Friday Mountain," commemorative pamphlet presented as a memento for guests at Friday Mountain during the Walter Prescott Webb International Symposium. Copy provided courtesy of C. B. Smith, Sr.

30. Ibid., p. 2; see also Rodney J. Kidd, "Going to Places in the Pasture," *The Texas Observer* 55 (July 1963):7.

31. Ibid.

32. Ibid.

33. Rodney J. Kidd, interview, Austin, Texas, January 29, 1972; Webb to "C. B." [Smith], February 20, 1961, *Smith Personal Coll.*

34. Rodney Kidd to George Fuermann, October 10, 1960, *Smith Personal Coll.*

35. Dorman Winfrey to writer, February 2, 1972.

36. Mildred Webb Bugg, interview, Austin, Texas, August 22, 1972; Woozie [Mildred] to Charlotte, July 11, 1934, *Smith Coll.* TS, Box 2-22/793.

37. Robert Amsler, interview, Arlington, Texas, June 14, 1973.

38. Dobie, "For Years We Three Sat Together," p. 2.

39. Rodney Kidd, interview, Austin, Texas, January 29, 1972; Kidd, "Walter Prescott Webb at Friday Mountain," p. 4.

40. Ibid., pp. 2–3.

Chapter 11

1. Webb to John Fischer, May 1, 1961, *WPWC*, Box 2M250; "Dr. Webb Gets Award of Learned Societies," *Dallas Morning News*, January 25, 1958, *WPWC*, Box 2M246.

2. W. P. Webb, "The Teachers and Writers of History," n.d., *Smith Coll.* TS, Box 2-22/799; W. P. Webb, "The University Historians and History Teachers," in *History As High Adventure*, ed. by Barksdale, pp. 106–13.

3. Webb, "The University Historians and History Teachers," pp. 107–13

4. Webb, "The Teachers and Writers of History," in *History As High Adventure*, ed. by Barksdale, pp. 149–50; ibid, pp. 109–11.

5. Webb, "The Teachers and Writers of History," pp. 156–58; Jim B. Pearson to writer, January 29, 1974.

6. Pearson to writer, January 29, 1974.

7. Webb, "The University Professor and the Social Studies," in *History As High Adventure*, ed. by Barksdale, p. 130.

8. W. P. Webb, "For Whom the Historian Tolls," in *An Honest Preface*, pp. 131–35.

9. Arnold Gutfeld, speech given at the University of New Mexico, Albuquerque, April 9, 1974.

10. Webb, "The Teachers and Writers of History," n.d., *Smith Coll.* TS, Box 2-22/799.

11. W. P. Webb to Robert L. Williamson, February 9, 1961, *Williamson Personal Papers*, Arlington, Texas.

12. Ibid.

13. Webb to Miss [Edith] Parker, March 19, 1953, *WPWC*, Box 2M245.

14. W. P. Webb, "Down to the Texas Sea," *Garrett Coll.* UTA, Box 21. This story is also told as W. P. Webb, "The Writing of History in Texas," in *History As High Adventure*, ed. by Barksdale, pp. 122–24.

15. Ibid.

16. Press release, "University of Texas News and Information Service," December 12, 1962, University of Texas, Library, Division of Special Collections, Arlington, Texas, Box 20-17; Joe B. Frantz to writer, February 25, 1972.

17. Robert E. Baskin, "Texas Foremost Historian Forging Out to New Areas," *Dallas Morning News*, April 20, 1959, *Smith Personal Coll.*, Austin, Texas.

18. Webb to Edith Parker, February 10, 1959, *WPWC*, Box 2M245.

19. "Brilliant Future Ahead for South, Says Dr. Webb," *The Waco News-Tribune*, *WPWC*, Box 3M300; W. P. Webb, "Economic Progress of the South, 1930–1950," November 7, 1957, *Smith Coll.* TS, Box 2-22/799.

20. W. P. Webb, "A Corner of the Old South," *Houston Post*, June 14, 1959; *Smith Coll.* TS, Box 2-22/799, a speech delivered at the inauguration of Dr. Ralph Steen as president of Stephen F. Austin College, Nacogdoches, February 7, 1959, and reprinted in the *Houston Post*.

21. Webb, "A Corner of the Old South."

22. Webb, "Economic Progress of the South, 1930–1950," November 7, 1957, in *Smith Coll.* TS, Box 2-22/799; a speech presented to the Southern Historical Association in Houston, Texas. Other speeches on the same subject include "The South's Future Prospects," n.d., and "The South's Call to Greatness: Challenge to All Southerners," January 29, 1959, *Smith Coll.* TS, Box 2-22/799.

23. E. C. Barksdale to writer, January 18, 1974; Joe B. Frantz, interview, August 20, 1974;

W. P. Webb, "How the Republican Party Lost Its Future," *Southwest Review* 34 (Autumn 1949):329–37.

24. Harry Truman to Webb, January 31, 1950, *Garrett Coll.* UTA, Box 21-16; see also W. P. Webb, "The Art of Historical Writing," in *History As High Adventure*, ed. by Barksdale, pp. 141–42.

25. E. C. Barksdale to writer, January 18, 1974; Terrell Webb, interview, Austin, Texas, August 22, 1974.

26. Mildred Webb Bugg, interview, Austin, Texas, January 28, 1972. Webb's poker gang included E. C. Barksdale, chairman of the department of history at Arlington; Captain Frank Hamer of the Texas Rangers; Jimmy Taylor, chairman of the department of history at Southwest Texas State Teachers College; Captain Ernest Best, Texas Ranger; Judge Bruce Bryant of Austin; Claude Voyles of the board of regents; C. D. Richards, professor at the University of Texas at Arlington; Harry Akin, owner of the Night Hawk; newspaperman Joe Small; realtor M. L. Crockett; Ronnie Dugger, journalist, and George Watt, professor of history.

27. Webb to J. Frank Dobie, July 8, 1960, *WPWC*, Box 2M254.

28. Ibid.

29. Webb to C. B. Smith, February 6, 1961, *Smith Personal Coll.* Austin, Texas.

30. Ibid.; Chester V. Kielman, interview, Austin, Texas, May 23, 1974.

31. Neville Baird, interview, Albuquerque, New Mexico, February 12, 1975.

32. Joe B. Frantz, interview, Austin, Texas, August 20, 1974.

33. Terrell Webb, interview, Austin, Texas, August 22, 1974.

34. Ibid.

35. Ibid.; Webb to Joan Walker Wenning, January 14, 1963, *WPWC*, Box 2M258, Joe B. Frantz, interview, August 20, 1974.

36. Terrell Webb, interview, Austin, Texas, August 22, 1974; W. P. Webb, "Confessions of a Texas Bookmaker."

37. Eileen Guarino, interview, Austin, Texas, August 22, 1974.

38. Ibid.; Odie B. Faulk to writer, February 4, 1974.

39. Eileen Guarino, interview, Austin, Texas, August 22, 1974.

40. Ibid.; Webb to C. B. Smith, March 4, 1963, *Smith Personal Coll.*, Austin, Texas; Helen Yenne, "Dr. W. P. Webb Dies in Crash," *The Daily Texan*, March 10, 1963, *Garrett Coll.* UTA, Box 21-14.

41. Helen Yenne, "Dr. W. P. Webb Dies in Crash," *The Daily Texan*, March 10, 1963, *Garrett Coll.* UTA, Box 21-14.

42. Terrell Webb, interview, Austin, Texas, August 22, 1974.

43. Helen Yenne, "Dr. W. P. Webb Dies in Crash," *The Daily Texan*, March 10, 1963, *Garrett Coll.* UTA, Box 21-14.

44. My gratitude to Mrs. Eileen Guarino for driving the writer to view the gravesite. "Official Memorandum," John Connally, Governor of Texas, March 11, 1963, Austin, Texas, granting permission for Webb's interment, copy in C. B. Smith, ed., *Walter Prescott Webb*, p. 124.

Chapter 12

1. C. B. Smith, Sr., interview, Austin, Texas, August 23, 1974.

2. E. C. Barksdale, "Introduction," *Essays on the American Civil War, Walter Prescott Webb; Walter Prescott Webb Memorial Lectures*, ed. by Holmes and Hollingsworth 1:21.

3. Ibid.; E. C. Barksdale, interview, Arlington, Texas, October 21, 1971.

4. C. B. Smith, interview, Austin, Texas, January 29, 1972; "Webb Estate Goes to Wife," clipping, *Smith Personal Coll.*, Austin, Texas.

5. [Larry Goodwin], Report on "Origin of Symposium, Background: 1963–1968," *Smith Personal Coll.*, Austin, Texas.

6. "International Forum Planned, UT to Host 'Great Thinkers,'" March 21, 1972, *The Daily Texan, Smith Personal Papers;* Larry Goodwin, "Status Report on Walter Webb International Symposium, March 7, 1971," *Smith Personal Coll.*, Austin, Texas.

7. Harry Ransom [Chancellor Emeritus], "Supporting Statement to Faculty," January 4, 1975, *Smith Personal Coll.*, Austin, Texas.

8. Leon Borden Blair to writer, April 15, 1972; Blair to Kenneth Ragsdale, August 15, 1973; August 27, 1973; personal copies courtesy of Leon Borden Blair.

9. E. C. Barksdale, interview, Arlington, Texas, October 21, 1971.

10. Ibid.

11. For an excellent analysis of transitions in American historiography, see Gene Wise, *American Historical Explanations* (Homewood, Illinois: The Dorsey Press, 1973), passim.

BIBLIOGRAPHY

Manuscripts

The University of Texas Archives, Arlington
  The Walter Prescott Webb Collection
  The Jenkins Garrett Collection of Walter Prescott Webb Papers
The University of Texas Archives, Barker Texas History Center, Austin
  The Walter Prescott Webb Papers
Texas State Library, Archives Division, Austin
  The C. B. Smith, Sr., Collection of Walter Prescott Webb Papers

Personal Collections

Leon Bordon Blair, Personal Correspondence, Arlington
W. Eugene Hollon, Personal Webb Collection, Toledo, Ohio
C. B. Smith, Sr., Personal Papers, Austin
Robert L. Williamson, Personal Correspondence, Arlington

Interviews

Robert W. Amsler, Arlington, Tx., March 27, 1972.
Neville Baird, Albuquerque, N.M., February 12, 1975.
E. C. Barksdale, Arlington, Tx., October 21, 1971; March 3, 1972; June 14, 1973.
Leon B. Blair, Arlington, Tx., March 6, 1972.
Mildred Webb Bugg, Austin, Tx., January 28, 1972; August 22, 1974.
Joe B. Frantz, Austin, Tx., August 20, 1974; January 20, 1975.
Llerena B. Friend, Austin, Tx., August 22, 1974.
Eileen Guarino, Austin, Tx., August 22, 1974.
Millicent Huff, Austin, Tx., June 18, 1973.
Rodney J. Kidd, Austin, Tx., January 29, 1972.
Chester V. Kielman, Austin, Tx., May 23, 1974.
C. D. Richards, Arlington, Tx., June 14, 1973.
C. B. Smith, Sr., Austin, Tx., January 29, 1972; February 11, 1972; August 23, 1974.
Wilbert H. Timmons, El Paso, Tx., May 7, 1974.
Frank Wardlaw, Arlington, Tx., by telephone, March 24, 1972.
Terrell Webb, Austin, Tx., August 22, 1974; Arlington, Tx., April 13, 1972.
Blaine T. Williams, Arlington, Tx., March 14, 1972.
Robert L. Williamson, Arlington, Tx., March 3, 1973.
Dorman Winfrey, Tulsa, Okla., October 9, 1975.
George Wolfskill, Arlington, Tx., January 23, 1972.
Ima Wright, Austin, Tx., August 20, 1974; January 21, 22, 1975.

Letters to Author

J. Francis Bannon, February 20, 1974.
E. C. Barksdale, September 6, 1973; January 18, 1975.
Ray Allen Billington, January 24, 1972; May 15, 1975.
Leon Borden Blair, April 15, 1972.
Mildred Webb Bugg, March 7, 1975.
James Lea Cate, April 24, 1974.
Avery Craven, February 11, 1974.
Odie B. Faulk, February 4, 1974.
Joe B. Frantz, February 25, 1972.
James P. Hart, February 18, 1972.
W. Eugene Hollon, March 16, 1972; January 22, 1974.
William T. Hutchinson, April 6, 1974.
Walter Johnson, March 5, 1974.
Hubert Mewhinney, June 7, 1973.
Jim. B. Pearson, January 29, 1974.
Rupert N. Richardson, January 25, 1974.
Rex W. Strickland, February 27, 1975.
Wilbert H. Timmons, April 5, 1974.
Terrell Webb, February 24, 1972; March 3, 1972.
Dorman Winfrey, February 2, 1972.
Ima Wright, February 25, 1975.

Dissertations

Mathews, Mazie E. *On the Hither Edge of Free Land: Lindley Miller Keasbey and the Evolution of the Frontier Thesis.* M.A. thesis, Southwest Texas State University, 1973.
Payne, James Sutton. *Texas Historiography in the Twentieth Century: A Study of Eugene C. Barker, Charles W. Ramsdell, and Walter Prescott Webb.* Ph.D. diss., University of Denver, 1972.
Tobin, Gregory. *Walter Prescott Webb and The Great Plains: An Historiographical Study.* Ph.D. diss., University of Texas, 1972.
Willis, Jannes Edward. *John Steinbeck and the Frontier Hypothesis of Walter Prescott Webb.* M.A. thesis, Stephen F. Austin State College, 1955.

Speeches

Nash, Gerald. "Commentary." Texas State Historical Association. Fort Worth, Texas. April, 1975.
Webb, Terrell. "Portraits of Two Men." Western Historical Association. Fort Worth, Texas. October, 1973.
Winfrey, Dorman. "A Bridge Between Generations: The Junior Historians of the Texas State Historical Association." Texas State Historical Association and Harrison County Historical Survey Committee Joint Meeting. Jefferson, Texas. November, 1971.

Magazines, Journals, Newspapers

Untitled tributes by different authors. "A Man, His Land, and His Work." *The Graduate Journal.* 6 (Winter 1964):19–61.

Caughey, John W. "A Criticism of the Critique of Webb's *The Great Plains.*" *Mississippi Valley Historical Review.* 27:442–48.

Dobie, J. Frank. "For Years We Three Sat Together." *The Texas Observer.* 55:2–5.

Dugger, Ronnie. "The Great Plains." *The Texas Observer.* 55:11–12.

Evans, Glen. "Free of Hate and Fear." *The Texas Observer.* 55:15.

Fischer, John. "An Unfashionable Kind of Historian." *The Texas Observer.* 55:6.

Frantz, Joe B. "Walter Prescott Webb." *The American West.* 1:42.

———. "Webb's Politics." *The Texas Observer.* 55:10.

Friend, Llerena. "Walter P. Webb and Book Reviewing." *The Western Historical Quarterly.* 4:281–401.

———. "W. P. Webb's Texas Rangers." *Southwestern Historical Quarterly.* 74:293–322.

Hollon, W. Eugene. "Adventures of a Western Historian." *Western Historical Quarterly.* 2:249.

Johnson, Lyndon B. "Your Senator Reports." February 11, 1954.

Jones, Oakah, Jr. "Introduction." *Journal of the West.* 3:1–6.

Kidd, Rodney. "Going to Places in the Pasture." *The Texas Observer.* 55:7.

Rundell, Walter, Jr. "Walter Prescott Webb: Product of Environment." *Arizona and the West.* 5:4–28.

Webb, Walter Prescott. "Caldwell Prize in Local History." *The Texas History Teacher's Bulletin.* 12:5–16.

———. "Dynamics of Property in the Modern World." *Southwest Review.* 37:298–309.

———. "Folklore of Texas." *Journal of American Folklore.* 28:290–301.

———. "Geographical Historical Concepts in American History." *Annals of the Association of American Geographers.* 50:85–97.

———. "History As High Adventure." *The American Historical Review.* 64:265–81.

———. "How the Republican Party Lost Its Future." *Southwest Review.* 34:392–37.

———. "Increasing the Functional Value of History by the Problem Method of Presentation." *Texas History Teacher's Bulletin.* 4:16–40.

———. "Official Transcript." Office of the Recorder. University of Chicago. Chicago, Illinois. Copy.

———. "Review of *Conquering Our Great Plains.*" *Mississippi Valley Historical Review.* 17:644–45.

———. "Texas Collection." *The Southwestern Historical Quarterly.* 51:259–61.

———. "Texas: Eternal Triangle of the Southwest." *The Saturday Review of Literature.* 25:16–17.

———. "The American West: Perpetual Mirage." *Harper's Magazine.* 214:25–31.

———. "The American Revolver and the West." *Scribner's Magazine.* 81:171–78.

———. "The Big Bend of Texas." *The Panhandle Plains Historical Review.* 10:7–20.

———. "The Confessions of a Texas Bookmaker." *Texas Libraries.* 25:88–96.

———. "The Desert Is Its Heart." *Saturday Review.* 40:8–9.

———. "The Historical Seminar: Its Outer Shell and Its Inner Spirit." *Mississippi Valley Historical Review.* 42:3–23.

———. "The Search for William E. Hinds." *Harper's Magazine.* 223:62–68.

Winfrey, Dorman H. "Seventy-Five Years of Texas History: The Texas State Historical Association." *Texas Libraries.* 34:96–112.

Wolfskill, George. "Program Insert, Webb Memorial Lecture Series." Arlington, Texas.

Young, Sister Anne Marie, V.H.M. "Walter Prescott Webb." *The Texas Quarterly.* 11:70–79.

Books

Allen, Frederick Lewis. *Only Yesterday.* New York: Harper & Row, Publishers, 1931.

Bannon, John Francis. *Bolton and the Spanish Borderlands.* Norman: University of Oklahoma Press, 1968.

Barck, Oscar Theodore, Jr., and Blake, Nelson Manfred. *Since 1900.* 3d ed. New York: Macmillan Company, 1959.

Billington, Ray Allen. *The Genesis of the Frontier Thesis.* San Marino, California: Kingsport Press, Inc., 1971.

Bolton, Herbert Eugene. *Wider Horizons of American History.* New York: D. Appleton-Century Company, 1939.

Bruner, Jerome S. *On Knowing.* New York: Atheneum, 1967.

Colbourn, Trevor and Patterson, James T. *The American Past in Perspective Since 1865.* 2 vols. Boston: Allyn and Bacon, Inc., 1970.

Commager, Henry Steele. *The American Mind.* New Haven: Yale University Press, 1950.

Dugger, Ronnie. *Our Invaded Universities: Form, Reform, and New Starts.* New York: W. W. Norton & Company, Inc. 1974.

————, ed. *Three Men in Texas.* Austin: University of Texas Press, 1967.

Fehrenbach, Theodore R. *Lone Star: A History of Texas and the Texans.* Toronto: Macmillan Co., 1968.

Gambrell, Herbert, ed. *Texas Today and Tomorrow.* Dallas: Southern Methodist University Press, 1960.

Henry, Stuart. *Conquering Our Great American Plains.* New York: E. P. Dutton, 1930.

Holmes, William F. and Hollingsworth, Harold, eds. *Essays on the Civil War: The Walter Prescott Webb Memorial Lectures: I.* Austin: University of Texas Press, 1968.

Hutchinson, W. H. *A Bar Cross Man: The Life and Personal Writings of Eugene Manlove Rhodes.* Norman: University of Oklahoma Press, 1956.

Investigation of University of Texas by Senate Investigating Committee. Hearings Held in the Texas Senate Chamber. 4 vols. Austin: 1944.

Jacobs, Wilbur R., Caughey, John W., and Frantz, Joe B. *Turner, Bolton, and Webb.* Seattle: University of Washington Press, 1965.

Literary Digest International Book Review. 3. January 1925.

Owens, William A. *Three Friends: Bedichek, Dobie, Webb.* New York: Doubleday, 1969.

Pool, William C. *Eugene C. Barker Historian.* Austin: Texas State Historical Association, 1971.

Powell, John Wesley. *Report on the Lands of the Arid Region of the United States.* 2d ed. Washington: U.S. Government Printing Office, 1879.

Rainey, Homer Price. *The Tower and the Dome: A Free University versus Political Control.* Boulder: Pruett Publishing Company, 1971.

Smith, C. B., Sr. *A Salute to Walter Prescott Webb and "The Search for William E. Hinds."* Austin: By the editor, 1961.

————. *Walter Prescott Webb: From the Great Frontier to the Threshold of Space.* Austin: By the editor, 1969.

Webb, Walter Prescott. *An Honest Preface and Other Essays.* Ed. with an Introduction by Joe B. Frantz. Boston: Houghton Mifflin, 1959.

————. *Divided We Stand: The Crisis of a Frontierless Democracy.* Rev. ed. Austin, Texas: Acorn Press, 1944.

————. *Flat Top: A Story of Modern Ranching.* El Paso: Carl Hertzog, 1960.

———— and Carroll, H. Bailey, eds. *Handbook of Texas.* 2 vols. Austin: Texas State Historical Association, 1952.

————. *History As High Adventure.* Ed. with an introduction by E. C. Barksdale. Austin: Pemberton Press, 1969.

————. *More Water for Texas: The Problem and the Plan.* Austin: University of Texas Press, 1954.

————. *Talks on Texas Books: A Collection of Book Reviews.* Ed. by Llerena B. Friend. Austin: Texas State Historical Association, 1970.

————. *The Great Frontier.* Boston: Houghton Mifflin Co., 1952; Rev. ed. with an introduction by Arnold J. Toynbee. Austin: University of Texas Press, 1965.

————. *The Great Plains.* Boston: Ginn and Company, 1931.

————. *The Texas Rangers: A Century of Frontier Defense.* Rev. ed. Foreword by Lyndon B. Johnson. Austin: University of Texas Press, 1965.

Weber, David, ed. *Foreigners in Their Native Land.* Albuquerque: University of New Mexico Press, 1973.

Willard, James F. and Goodykoontz, Colin B., eds. *The Trans-Mississippi West.* Boulder: University of Colorado, 1930.

Wise, Gene. *American Historical Explanations.* Homewood, Illinois: The Dorsey Press, 1937.

INDEX

217

02

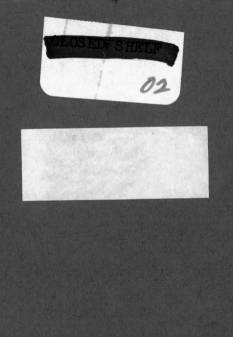